The Gallant Edith Bratt:
J.R.R. Tolkien's Inspiration

Edith Bratt, age seventeen
(© Tolkien Estate)

The Gallant Edith Bratt: J.R.R. Tolkien's Inspiration

by Nancy Bunting
and Seamus Hamill-Keays

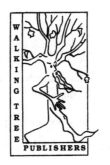

2021

Cormarë Series No. 46

Series Editors:
Peter Buchs • Thomas Honegger • Andrew Moglestue • Johanna Schön • Doreen Triebel

Series Editors responsible for this volume:
Peter Buchs & Thomas Honegger & Doreen Triebel

Library of Congress Cataloguing-in-Publication Data

Nancy Bunting and Seamus Hamill-Keays:
The Gallant Edith Bratt: J.R.R. Tolkien's Inspiration
ISBN 978-3-905703-46-7

Subject headings:
Tolkien, Edith Mary (née Bratt), 1889-1971
Tolkien, J.R.R. (John Ronald Reuel), 1892-1973
Middle-earth
Biography
The Lord of the Rings
The Hobbit

Cormarë Series No. 46

First published 2021

© Walking Tree Publishers, Zurich and Jena, 2021

Set in Adobe Garamond Pro and Shannon by Walking Tree Publishers

Cover: Edith Bratt, age seventeen (Courtesy of the Tolkien Estate)

It can be seen as a sign of maturation that Tolkien studies are now branching out into the exploration of topics and persons beyond his immediate academic environment. People like his mother Mabel Tolkien, his guardian Father Francis Morgan, or his wife Edith Tolkien have often been generally acknowledged as being of importance for J.R.R. Tolkien's overall development yet have not been the subjects of independent studies. José Manuel Ferrández Bru's biography of Tolkien's guardian and surrogate father figure, Father Francis Xavier Morgan (*Uncle Curro. J.R.R. Tolkien's Spanish Connection.* Spanish original 2013, English translation 2020) was spearheading the development of investigating these lesser-known persons. The selection of Father Francis as a subject to receive full biographical treatment may have been motivated mainly by the author's 'Spanish connection', yet it is also indicative of the general neglect women have suffered from in most biographical accounts of Tolkien's life. This original study on Edith Tolkien aims at correcting this sorry state of affair at least partially. Nancy Bunting and Seamus Hamill-Keays's book provides the first full biographical treatment of her life up to 1917 and explores the crucial role she played in the formation of Tolkien's artistic vision. We hope that this volume will stimulate further research into Edith's life and contribution to Tolkien's work, and inspire other researchers to look into the biographies of other 'neglected' women such as Mabel Tolkien or Jane Suffield.

The research that went into *The Gallant Edith Bratt* was both aided and hampered by the availability of many of the documents and data on the internet. On the one hand, the digitalization of documents has given us access to sources otherwise very difficult to consult. Yet on the other, the quality of the scans and pictures provided are often not very good. Furthermore, the restrictions due to the pandemic situation in Britain made it impossible to procure better quality pictures, so we had to make do with the material freely available and have to ask our readers to 'turn a blind eye' to the (sometimes) less-than-perfect quality of the illustrations and to concentrate on their documentary function.

Lastly, we would like to thank all those who worked on this project: our peer-reviewers who read and commented on the original manuscript, Larissa Zoller, who layouted the text, Peter Buchs who proofread the text with a 'critical historian's eye', Andrew Moglestue who smoothed the wrinkles of the layout and touched up the illustrations as far as possible and, of course, the authors themselves, Nancy Bunting and Seamus Hamill-Keays, who invested so much time and energy into rescuing Edith from scholarly neglect.

April 2021

Walking Tree Publishers

Table of Contents

The authors would like to thank the many people who have generously offered their time and help. Without their taking the trouble to respond, this paper would have been lacking in significant ways.

The authors are very appreciative of Walking Tree Publishers' vote of confidence in accepting our manuscript. We can only express our gratitude to Dr. Honegger, the editor, and his staff whose meticulous attention to detail and numerous productive suggestions have magically transformed our manuscript into this book.

In Chapter 3, many thanks to the very helpful Mr. Richard F. Ball at The Vale of Evesham Historical Society, and many thanks for the Society's permission to publish the photograph of the Dresden House School. Mr. Lukasz Rusiecki of Gallery Properties, Evesham kindly allowed the use of the photographs of the façade and interior of Dresden House. Mr. David Gregory of Postcards of the Past allowed the use of the photograph of the Avon in Evesham. Also, Ms. Lucy Rose at the Jerwood Library of the Performing Arts, Faculty of Music, Trinity Laban Conservatoire of Music and Dance helped with information on the music evaluations.

In Chapter 4, we extend our appreciation to Mr. Steve Ponty for his photograph of the Suffield family funeral plaque of 1706/1713 in the Evesham church.

In Chapter 5, Ruth Lacon's background material on King Edward's Horse contributed substantially to the discussion of that unit.

In Chapter 6, I would like to thank Dale Heath for her insightful comments on Tolkien's art. An image appears courtesy of Michael Zeiler, GreatAmericanEclipse.com.

In Chapter 8, Mr. Scott Whitehouse and Mr. David Robbie, local historians of Staffordshire, provided invaluable background and corrections on information on Great Haywood and Cannock Chase.

In Chapters 8 and 9, we are indebted to Mr. Michael Flowers for his photographs of 1 Bank Terrace, 76 Queen's Street, the lawns of Brooklands Officers' Hospital, and a nightingale.

In Chapter 10, Mr. Bill Teale's knowledge and help with nightingales was priceless. We are very appreciative that Mr. Willis Ainley and *The Rooster, the Roos Village Newsletter* allowed publication of their picture of the approximately 1920 Roos Post Office. Mr. Ainley, a previous editor of *The Rooster*, provided resources on the local history of Roos.

Finally, we are grateful to Mark Hooker for his help with Elvish.

                                        Nancy Bunting & Seamus Hamill-Keays

This project explores the life of Edith Bratt Tolkien, the wife of J.R.R. Tolkien, who wrote that she was his Lúthien, the peerless Elvish princess of *The Silmarillion*, though he never called her by that name (*Letters* 420). A review of previously published and new materials reveals the reasons for Tolkien's acclamation of Edith in such a powerful role. This new perspective on the life of Edith Bratt should appeal not only to readers of biographies, but also to a range of Tolkien admirers, from the casual to the most serious.

Information from Humphrey Carpenter's official biography, *J.R.R. Tolkien. A Biography* has dominated biographical studies and references to Tolkien's life. Although later Carpenter became known for "revealing" biographies (Unwin 250), in his first biography, he concentrates largely on Tolkien's academic background and colleagues. Carpenter's biography has only one scene to suggest why Tolkien would say his wife was Lúthien (*Bio* 97, *Letters* 420). This is because Tolkien's literary executor and editor, his son Christopher Tolkien, required Carpenter to rewrite his original draft of the official biography. Carpenter's first draft of the biography was "unacceptable," and Carpenter then "cut out everything which was likely to be contentious" ("Learning" 270). Rayner Unwin confirms this report writing Christopher Tolkien "tore Humphrey's draft to pieces" and Humphrey "re-wrote the whole book, which in its revised form, Christopher approved" (Unwin 249).[1]

Carpenter stated that asking someone to write a biography is "a bit like inviting a private detective to investigate your family secrets" ("Learning" 270, 271).

---

1 In Douglas Anderson's "Obituary: Humphrey Carpenter (1946-2005)," Anderson quotes from "Learning about Ourselves: Biography as Autobiography," but he runs together two of Carpenter's paragraphs (219-20). The altered context leads the reader to believe Carpenter's first draft was the same as the draft in which Carpenter treated Tolkien as a "rather comic Oxford academic – the stereotype of the absent-minded professor" in a "slightly slapstick" way (219-20). This conflation suggests the initial draft was rejected because of a disrespectful presentation of Tolkien (Bunting, "Checking" 54). Carpenter denied he was "censored" (Ross qtd. in Anderson 220) because to fulfill one's contract is not technically censorship, though the result may be as misleading and inaccurate.

Carpenter could neither explicitly confirm nor deny that writing Tolkien's biography led to unearthing family secrets, as he was almost certainly bound by a Nondisclosure Agreement like everyone who has access to the Tolkien archives (Testi 97). While Carpenter repeatedly tried to advertise the limitations and unreliability of the official biography ("Review", *Bio* 260), the book does contain a great deal of information which must be used as the starting point for any biographical investigation of Tolkien and consequently of his wife, Edith.

Dimitra Fimi, in *Tolkien, Race and Cultural History*, argues Tolkien's statement that he held "the key" to the study of his works, especially his invented languages, mandates the setting of Tolkien's fiction in the context of his biography (7). Citing Tomaševskij, she cautions that authors often create a "biographical legend," a romanticized, distorted image of their biography, controlled by the author and used as the basis of literary criticism (7). This appears to be the case with the official Tolkien biography.

Nicole duPlessis' "On the Shoulders of Humphrey Carpenter: Reconsidering Biographical Representation and Scholarly Perception of Edith Tolkien" challenges the "biographical legend" found in the Carpenter biography. Her paper is part of the growing body of women's studies on Tolkien, which include such works as *Perilous and Fair* by Janet Brennan Croft and Leslie A. Donovan. DuPlessis shows that Tolkien scholarship, with or without explicit citations, has assumed Carpenter's interpretations as facts which are treated as "common knowledge," especially in discussions of Edith Tolkien. DuPlessis highlights how Carpenter abbreviated J.R.R. Tolkien's quotations "usually without giving references" and omitted "the customary row of dots to indicate a passage omitted in the middle of a quotation" (44-45, *Bio* 276), thereby alerting the scholar to opportunities for misinterpretation. Christopher Tolkien's control and approval of the manuscript would include Carpenter's style of documentation (Unwin 249). She identifies a false dichotomy between Tolkien's academic interests, tied to male colleagues and often his writings, and his marriage and domestic life, which are seen as leading to failures in the marital relationship (46). She concludes that Carpenter's perspectives and methods lead to a negative and misleading presentation of Edith, creating a picture of dysfunction or sentimentalism.

This book also challenges the official "biographical legend" by presenting a fuller picture of Edith Bratt Tolkien. This project combines new primary sources with sources that have previously been unused or overlooked. It elaborates and clarifies information about Edith found in Tolkien's letters, in Carpenter's authorized biography of her husband, and in secondary sources which are independent of the Tolkien Estate such as Bru, Priestman, Morton and Hayes, etc. A little used primary source, John and Priscilla Tolkien's 1992 memoir of their family, *Tolkien Family Album* was also utilized. This was published when John Tolkien was 75- and Priscilla 63-years old. It was used because it provided information not available elsewhere, even though retrospective accounts are well known to be vulnerable to errors.[2] The reports by John and Priscilla Tolkien, like the claims of the official biography, are reexamined when there is independent information available. Various public records, including census forms, property records, legal documents, trade directories, newspapers, archives, maps, and military records, uncovered by Seamus Hamill-Keays, open up new vistas on Edith's past.

Because Edith's life can only be understood in the context of the Victorian and Edwardian England in which she was raised, a number of historical sources were consulted. A close reading of Tolkien's works, which refer to and are inspired by Edith, supplement this historiographic approach which endeavors to place Edith's life in a wider context. While the information from primary and new secondary sources creates a fuller picture, gaps and omissions are always present in the available documents. Logical projections, based on the available data, are presented for the reader's consideration.

Edith, like most wives of famous men, has been overshadowed by her husband. It is standard practice to refer to J.R.R. Tolkien, a world-famous author, by his last name. However, in order to establish Edith and her husband on an equal footing, we have chosen to refer to both of them by first name when discussing their lives and relationship. When discussing Tolkien's writings and artwork, we have used his last name.

---

2 This project may have been started much earlier, in the 1970s, according to Rayner Unwin (249).

The historical context of Victorian England dictated that Edith's illegitimate birth limited her options and choices. Tolkien's phrase, "the shadow of the past," fell heavily on Edith throughout most of her life. Due to editorial decisions made by Christopher Tolkien, only a ghost of Tolkien's "gallant" Edith Bratt is left in the official Tolkien biography. Edith Bratt Tolkien triumphed over her background to snatch love and happiness from the iron jaws of social strictures and rigid class consciousness in a life with Ronald Tolkien. She created the security and stability which Ronald Tolkien needed to write. Hers is a very Victorian story of luck and pluck. Because Edith's influence on Tolkien's writing and art has been previously minimized, Tolkien's work has been understood and admired without the key context of much of his biography, namely Edith Bratt. Readers have, therefore, missed the rich interconnections between the man's personal life and his works. Edith's vitality and her co-creation with Ronald Tolkien have been kept so secret that Tolkien's transformation of his wife into the brave and gay Lúthien seems puzzling and without justification. Edith's story, as presented here, hopes to remedy this omission.

Edith's life is presented chronologically. The first chapter covers the drama of Edith's parents' relationship and how this set the stage for Edith's life. The second chapter considers Edith's childhood and the effects of Edith's illegitimacy. The third chapter reveals new information about Edith's education and experiences at Dresden House in Evesham from the age of fourteen to approximately eighteen. The fourth chapter finds the nineteen-year-old Edith at the Faulkners' boarding house in Birmingham where she meets the sixteen-year-old Ronald Tolkien and his brother Hilary, who are also boarders there.

The fifth chapter covers Edith's residence in Charlton Kings at the home of C.H. Jessop after her separation from Ronald, until shortly after their reunion and engagement. This chapter also assesses the impact of Ronald Tolkien's loss of Edith during their separation of 1910 to 1913 with its effects on his mythology and artwork. The sixth chapter covers Edith's life in Warwick from 1913 to 1915, while she waited for Ronald to finish his studies at Oxford. Chapter Seven continues Edith's story with the critical transitions of 1915, which includes Ronald's graduation from Oxford and his induction into the British Army to fight in World War I, followed by their marriage in 1916. Chapters Eight and Nine deal with Edith as an anxious and faithful war bride, standing by her husband throughout his active service, his extended convalescence from trench fever, and the creation of a new family with the birth of their first son, John, in November, 1917. The final chapter analyzes the crucial 1917 scene in Garth's Dent, the unexpected origins of the Lúthien story, and the centrality of Tolkien's early relationship with Edith as evidenced in his drawing, *i glin grandin a Dol Erethrin Airi* or *The Fair (walled) Towns of (the) Holy/Sacred Tol Eressëa (the Lonely Isle)*.

All artwork by J.R.R. Tolkien is under copyright. The Tolkien Estate declined the authors' request for permission to reproduce. Images of the artworks, which are discussed in this book, are available online at the Tolkien Estate website and elsewhere.

In the Beginning

To understand the course of Edith Bratt Tolkien's life requires an initial exploration of the rigid and complex mores of Victorian England and her parents' place in that society. She was born in Gloucester, England to Frances (Fannie) Bratt of Wolverhampton and Alfred Frederick Warrillow of Handsworth on January 21, 1889 (*C&G* 1.1).[1] Edith Mary Bratt was baptized on February 13 in the Wesleyan Methodist chapel in Gloucester to Fanny Bratt and Frederick [with no last name given] (*C&G* 1.2). Edith was illegitimate. Because her birth certificate records no name for her father, she was given her mother's surname of Bratt.[2]

A brief introduction of the *dramatis personae* and their social and financial standing in the class conscious society of Victorian England is necessary. Edith's father, Alfred Warrillow (1842-1891) was seventeen years older than Fannie Bratt (1859-1903). His father, Alfred Warrillow (Sr.) was a stationer and so was his namesake and son, Alfred (Jr.), who was born in London (1861 census).[3] On January 13, 1866, the twenty-four-year-old Alfred Warrillow married the twenty-two-year-old Charlotte Harrison O'Brien at the Anglican church of St. Bartholomew. Following an 1869 bankruptcy, the Warrillow couple was living by themselves in Birmingham with a servant, and the 1871 census

---

1 Arthur Tolkien, J.R.R. Tolkien's father, was born in Handsworth in 1857 (*C&G* 1.1).
2 The birth certificate, a legal document, has a slash drawn through the empty box where the father's name should go. The Carpenter biography correctly states the certificate was unsigned. The entry in the *Chronology*, which states "Frederick" is written, seems to refer to a signature in the Methodist church's baptismal registry (*C&G* 1.2). A "registry" is both the book in which events are registered and a semi-private room in a church where the principals, witnesses and the officiating clergyman, sign any documents relating to the service just performed.
3 Stationers ran stationery stores, an important institution in Victorian England, with its enthusiasm for letter-writing and fancy penmanship. For more see https://hobancards.com/stationery-of-the-victorian-era, last viewed on 9/23/2020 and https://www.raabcollection.com/blog/authentication-check-paper-pen-and-ink, viewed on 9/23/2020.

Edith Bratt's 1889 Birth Certificate

lists Alfred as a stationer.[4] In 1878, the family moved to 41 Heathfield Road, Handsworth, a town just northwest of the center of Birmingham. By 1881, the thirty-seven-year-old Charlotte and thirty-nine-year-old Alfred Warrillow, now a paper dealer, had engaged the twenty-two-year-old Fannie Bratt as a governess for the Warrillows' only child, five-year-old Nellie Elizabeth (born November 5, 1865). A nurse and a cook completed this prosperous middle-class household. In 1883, Alfred Warrillow was running a retail stationery business,

4 An "Alfred Warrillow" had a record of bankruptcy on September 13, 1844 and in 1857. These legal actions must have been for Alfred Warrillow (Sr.), not Alfred Warrillow (Jr.), Edith Bratt's father, as Alfred (Jr.) would have been only two and fifteen years of age respectively in 1844 and 1857. Public records did not indicate a "Senior" or "Junior" when fathers and sons carried the same name, as was frequent in the nineteenth century. The 1869 bankruptcy of Alfred (Jr.), Edith Bratt's father, was probably due to the massive disruption in the Birmingham area caused by the Union Army's blockading the cotton of the Confederacy in 1864-1865. The Birmingham textile industry was heavily dependent on American cotton. As a result, businesses failed, and there was an exodus of workers seeking employment in other areas of Britain. John Benjamin Tolkien, J.R.R. Tolkien's paternal grandfather, also filed for bankruptcy in 1869 as he too probably endured the downstream effects of the Civil War on the economy of Birmingham.

but by 1890 he was a stationery wholesaler, a more lucrative enterprise (Kelly's Directory 1883, 1890).[5]

Governesses of the Victorian era were single, often older, women who were not highly educated, though they were of genteel background (Rose 165). Lionel Rose portrays the typical life of well-to-do, Victorian and Edwardian girls, like Nellie Warrillow, as being sequestered in the attic nursery suite: a day nursery, a bedroom, the nanny's room and maybe a schoolroom, and the governess ruled this realm (223). The educational curriculum was standardized and emphasized practicing handwriting and the rote memory of tables, dates

41 Heathfield Road (Google Earth)

5 Wikipedia provides the following explanation: "Kelly's Directory (or more formally, the Kelly's Post Office and Harrod & Co Directory) was a trade directory in England that listed all businesses and tradespeople in a particular city or town, as well as a general directory of postal addresses of local gentry, landowners, charities, and other facilities. In effect, it was a Victorian version of today's Yellow Pages." (https://en.wikipedia.org/wiki/Kelly%27s_Directory)

and passages from literature and the Bible (165). A range of subjects, including arithmetic, history, needlework, drawing, French, and botany were taught to girls, but not Latin, algebra, chemistry, and physics as these were "masculine" (165). Nannies and governesses were expected to teach "etiquette." A governess provided the constant prodding to be proper and polite, a monotonously formal routine of being "ladylike," i.e. demure and modest, never admitting to needing to use the toilet which could only be used in secret after making sure no males were present (229, 227), never using colloquial speech, such as "awfully," "jolly," and "Great Scott," and sitting and standing straight with the aid of a backboard (165). The Victorians regarded children as smaller adults and consequently dressed them like adults. Victorian parents expected their children to act like adults as quickly as possible (Rose 230, 215).

Although Fannie Bratt would have been considered working-class because of her father's occupation as a shoemaker, a small tradesman (1861 and 1871 census), she could claim the label of "genteel" because her mother (née Grove) had a possible, distant family relationship with the esteemed Sir George Grove (*Bio* 39), who published the first two volumes of his celebrated *A Dictionary of Music and Musicians* in 1879 and 1880 (Kennedy 355). There is no record that Fannie did invoke the Grove name, but embellishing one's resume is not a twentieth-century invention.

In 1861, when the Bratt family had five children, they lived in a prosperous neighborhood with an inspector of police, an alderman/justice of the peace, and a baker as neighbors. Their address from the 1861 census, as seen in a 1901 map of Wolverhampton, shows the neighborhood around Mitre Fold and North Street near the town's administrative and business centers of Market Place and Market Hall. By 1871, when the Bratts had nine children, they had moved to an Aston address in an area with a number of factories, including a rolling mill, soap and asphalt works, and a tool factory, next to canals and railroads (1886 OS map). The working-class terraced houses all had backyards. The neighbors' occupations seem indicative of a more modest level of working-class, including a factor's clerk, edge tool worker, gun lock forger, a dressmaker, and a Roman Catholic (R.C.) teacher.[6] The official biography's report that Frances' family

---

6 No 1881 census could be found for Fannie Bratt's family.

1889 OS Map Showing the location of Mrs. Bratt's School
(National Library of Scotland, with annotation by SH-K)

"owned a boot and shoe manufacturing business" leaves room for an interpretation of a possibly more middle-class enterprise (*Bio* 38).

The most likely source of Fannie Bratt's qualification to become a governess
is her remarkable mother, Jane Bratt (1831-1905). In 1861, the thirty-year-old
Jane Bratt was married to William Bratt, a thirty-seven-year-old shoemaker in
Wolverhampton in Staffordshire, part of the West Midlands. They had nine
surviving children. By 1878, as indicated in a Birmingham directory listing,
Mrs. Bratt was running a day school in the Summer Lane area in one of the
rooms in the space previously occupied by the Methodist Mission on Porchester

Street, Birmingham. Mrs. Bratt's school was remarkable as married women were not hired to teach, so Mrs. Bratt must have created her own independent school. Further, in the 1870s, social convention ruled that only single women ran schools, like Misses Eliza Cooper and Harriette Codrington Watts of Dresden House School in Evesham, where Edith Bratt would later receive her education.[7] Mrs. Bratt's employment suggests not only the need for more income to feed her large family, but also some educational background.[8] Mrs. Bratt probably recruited her daughters, including Fannie, as monitors or pupil-teachers to help manage classes, which could be as large as 80 students in the 1880s.[9] Until 1880 pupil-teachers could be as young as age thirteen and were paid (Rose 209). Monitors and pupil-teachers lit fires, filled inkwells, coached small groups or tutored students who were lagging, supervised needlework, marked books, heard spellings, etc. (Rose 209, 121-22). Fannie's likely experience in teaching would have provided some of the credentials she needed to be hired as a governess by the Warrillows.

However, less than two weeks before Christmas, on December 12, 1888, Mrs. Warrillow felt compelled to invoke what was then an irrevocable social calamity and filed for a judicial (or, as we say now, legal) separation. She did not file for divorce with its stigma and likelihood that, under the 1857 law which allowed remarriage, she might have the further humiliation and intolerable injury of having her former employee, Fannie Bratt, with a working-class background, become the new Mrs. Alfred Warrillow.

The Divorce Act of 1857 transferred the handling of the legal proceedings for divorce from the ecclesiastical courts to a newly established civil court, the Court for Divorce and Matrimonial Causes.[10] All divorce suits took place in

---

7   "The Story of Dresden House, Evesham" by E.A.B. Barnard, F.S.A. (1914). Vale of Evesham Historical Society, last viewed on 5/31/2020. http://www.valeofeveshamhistory.org/articles/dresden-house/.

8   Mrs. Bratt's later success shows she could well prepare Fannie to work as a governess. By 1892, Mrs. Bratt had opened a private school for a young ladies next door to her residence at 13 Wheeler Street (Kelly's Directory 1892). This school was successful enough it was taken over in 1900 by Kate Buttery (Kelly's Directory 1900).

9   Fannie's younger sister, Eva, is listed as an assistant school mistress at a Board School in the 1891 census.

10 "A short history of divorce in England and Wales since 1858." UK National Archives, last viewed on 5/31/2020. https://www.nationalarchives.gov.uk/help-with-your-research/research-guides/divorce/#2-a-short-history-of-divorce-in-england-and-wales-since-1858.

London, thus restricting divorce to wealthier couples until after the 1920s. The court handled petitions for restitution of conjugal rights, judicial separation, dissolution of marriage (i.e. divorce), and nullity of marriage. Under the 1857 Divorce Act, only following the dissolution of a civil, or religious, marriage, could either party be free to marry again.

The precipitating event for filing could have been Mrs. Warrillow's knowledge that Fannie Bratt was leaving the Warrillows' employment to go to

1888 Warrillow vs. Warrillow Petition for the
Dissolution of Marriage, i.e. Separation

Gloucester, possibly accompanied by Mr. Warrillow. Fannie would probably be going into confinement for the last trimester of her pregnancy with Alfred Warrillow's child.

By the time of the December 1888 filing, Mrs. Warrillow had already moved out of the house she had shared with Mr. Warrillow to Bosall [Super] Heath in Worcester, while Mr. Warrillow continued to reside at 41 Heathfield Road in Handsworth. Mrs. Warrillow did not ask the court to have Mr. Warrillow pay court costs or damages, so she may have gotten financial support from family to file for the separation or have expected Mr. Warrillow to pay her barrister's fees if she won, as was established in English case law.[11] According to the preliminary legal papers, Mrs. Warrillow obtained custody of Nellie, and Mr. Warrillow was ordered to pay £156 per year to maintain his wife and child. In terms of 2018 goods and services, this would translate into £19,918 or $24,473 in 2019.[12] This fee was called "alimony," and it included what would now be called "child support". The award of custody to Mrs. Warrillow was typical because even though the father legally had custody of his children, the "innocent party" in a separation usually obtained custody. This uncontested arrangement suggests either Mr. Warrillow was agreeable to the judgment and/or the court would consider his conduct egregious enough to warrant this action.

In the 1800s for a man, the grounds for divorce were proof of adultery by the woman, but the woman had to prove her husband's adultery as well as his cruelty, incest, or rape. The grounds for legal separation would be similar, though theoretically adultery or cruelty was sufficient. This Court required the name of the person, with whom adultery had been committed, to appear as a co-respondent in the petition. Fannie Bratt was named as the accessory and various dates in August 1888 were given for when she and Mr. Warrillow stayed in Weston Super Mare, presumably without Nellie, during an adults-

11 The court document states the alimony for the child is "without prejudice to any question of permanent alimony" for Mrs. Warrillow. However, no other court papers are known regarding these divorce proceedings. *The Digest of English Case Law Containing the Reported Decisions of the Superior Courts*, Volume 7, London: Sweet and Maxwell, 1898.

12 "Inflation calculator." Bank of England. https://www.bankofengland.co.uk/monetary-policy/inflation/inflation-calculator, last viewed on 5/31/2020. A slightly different estimate can be obtained from the United Kingdom Office of National Statistics at https://www.ons.gov.uk/, last viewed on 5/31/2020. XE Currency Converter, last viewed on 5/31/2020. https://www.xe.com/currencyconverter/convert/?Amount=727%2C262&From=GBP&To=USD.

only outing. Other alleged acts occurred in September, October, and November 1888, in Gloucester. In the eyes of the court, this blatant and repeated flouting of propriety and decorum may have counted as cruelty because these actions exposed Mrs. Warrillow and her family to humiliating gossip and derision. However, the Warrillow/Bratt couple must have had previous assignations beginning in May 1888, for Edith to be born in January 1889.

While Queen Victoria (1837-1901) and her exemplary consort, Albert, may have set the standard for decorum, immortalized in the name "Victorian Era," the rich and privileged could do what they wanted. In 1834, King William IV was on the throne and "had his nine illegitimate children all living happily *en famille* with him and the Queen at Windsor" (Pinchbeck and Hewitt 590). The Victorian public remembered The Duchess, the fabulous Georgiana Cavendish, Duchess of Devonshire (1757-1806) of the noble Spencer family, an English socialite, political activist and organizer, style icon, and author, married to the very wealthy William Cavendish, fifth Duke of Devonshire, who maintained a ménage à trois with the Duchess' best friend, Lady Elizabeth Foster, a situation unusual even for that period. The Duchess later became pregnant from an affair with Charles Grey (later Earl Grey) in 1791 and had to give up this illegitimate child. However, Duchess Street in Birmingham was named in her honor (Foreman 285-86).

In contrast, Victorian literature pointedly portrayed the fate of the unmarried mother and child as the workhouse, emigration, or death. Mrs. Gaskell (1810-1865), the widely read English Victorian novelist, biographer, and short story writer, began publishing in 1848, offering a detailed portrait of the lives of many strata of Victorian society, including the very poor. Her 1853 novel, *Ruth*, which blamed society as the "criminal" for an unwed pregnancy, met hostile criticism. Tellingly, Mrs. Gaskell would not let her own daughter read this novel (Pinchbeck and Hewitt 591).

Fannie Bratt had been in the Warrillow household since at least 1881 and did not become pregnant until 1888. Her position as "the other woman" would have been likely to result in social ostracism and destitution. In the 1800s, if a young single woman became pregnant and "was in domestic service she would almost certainly be dismissed at once," and if she worked elsewhere her "continued employment depended on her reliability before and after the birth of the child and her employer's attitude" (Pinchbeck and Hewitt 591). Given the prevailing Victorian social constraints and the probable consequences of a sexual liaison, Fannie, who had no independent financial security or social standing, seems to have placed her trust in Alfred Warrillow's promises and assurances. After knowing Fannie must be pregnant by the summer of 1888, Fannie Bratt and Alfred Warrillow's repeated trysts in Weston Super Mare and Gloucester suggest he was courting a divorce or separation as opposed to merely carrying on a discreet, furtive seduction and liaison. Further, after the Warrillows' separation, Fannie Bratt and Alfred Warrillow lived together at Hudson House, 100 Frederick Road, Stechford, east of the center of Birmingham. Alfred Warrillow died on March 12, 1891 in Hudson House at the age of forty-nine. In Warrillow's 1891 will, Fannie, described as "Spinster" and Alfred's "friend and Housekeeper," was named sole executrix and bequeathed the bulk of the estate "including my trade or business of a Paper Dealer." His estate's net worth was £5,827 4s 8d or £727,262 worth of goods and services in 2018, which is roughly equivalent to $893,583 in 2019.[13] In the 1891 census, which was taken in April following Alfred's death, Fannie Bratt was listed as a "stationer." Her rapid assumption of managing the business supports the idea she would have been helping with the business prior to Alfred Warrillow's death in March 1891.

The Warrillow petition for judicial separation was dismissed at the end of April 1889, with the consent of and to the benefit of both parties. Having the case dismissed was in the interest of both of the Warrillows because then the Birmingham newspapers could not publish a report of the separation. Newspapers used divorce cases to titillate their readers. Jury trials for divorce and separation were such a popular form of entertainment that people had a hard time getting a seat in the courtroom to witness the proof concerning the affairs and defense of the accused (Horstman 89). Charlotte Warrillow kept her marital standing, her social status, and presumably some financial support, though no longer the £156 per year as ordered by the court, without having to tolerate the presence of Alfred's infidelity. Charlotte also avoided possible

---

13 "Inflation calculator." Bank of England, last viewed on 5/31/2020. https://www.bankofengland.co.uk/monetary-policy/inflation/inflation-calculator. "XE Currency Calculator," last viewed on 5/31/2020. https://www.xe.com/currencyconverter/convert/?Amount=727%2C262&From=GBP&To=USD.

religious censure of a divorce because of the divine injunction "What God has joined together, let no man put asunder" (Matthew 19:6). She may also have hoped to protect her daughter Nellie's inheritance as any illegitimate child of Alfred must be specifically named in the father's will to inherit. Given that Alfred Warrillow wrote Nellie out of his will by August 1889, Nellie presumably stayed with her mother.

Alfred kept his reputation, which was almost a tangible asset in Victorian business, and no longer had Charlotte in his life. He probably paid Charlotte's solicitor's fees as part of the legal maneuverings. The dismissal of the petition for judicial separation led to Alfred Warrillow writing a will, dated August 19, 1889. Victorian law gave ownership of all assets and property to the husband. Alfred Warrillow left some money for his brother, John, a fellow stationer; some moneys for his two work assistants; and the rest to Fannie Bratt; but nothing for his wife, Charlotte, or their daughter, Nellie.[14] As the Victorians would have said, Alfred could not make an honest woman of Fannie Bratt, but he ensured her financial security.[15]

The Bratt family appears to have benefited from Fannie's association with Alfred Warrillow, and their attitude may have been less harsh toward Fannie given this situation. The 1891 census lists Fannie's twenty-one-year-old brother, Ernest William, as a "stationery traveller," [sic] something like a manufacturer's representative, a salesman who visits (potential) business clients.[16] Warrillow's wholesale business appears to have given Ernest a start in a career which he continued to follow as seen in his occupation as a manager of a stationery business in 1901. He had a four-year-old daughter, Frances, in 1901. Whether or not this child was named for his sister, Ernest's giving of his sister's name

---

14 Charlotte Warrillow died on October 14, 1898, seven years after Alfred's death. The value of her estate was £102.7s.7d. The executors were John Warrillow, Alfred's brother and a paper dealer, and George Frederick Smith, a bank clerk. Nellie E. Warrillow is found in the 1891 census as a boarder at a small school. While there is a "Teacher of Dancing" with the name, Nellie Warrillow, recorded in 1901 in Liverpool, she was born in 1875, not 1865 like the daughter of Alfred Warrillow.

15 Even if Edith's parents had married, she would not have been considered legitimate under the law at that time, though the law did change in 1926. "People and Parliament transforming society – private lives." UK parliament, last viewed on 6/3/2020. https://www.parliament.uk/about/living-heritage/transformingsociety/private-lives/relationships/overview/legitimacyadoption, last viewed on 6/3/2020.

16 Warrillow died on March 12, 1891. It is not known when Ernest was hired. It is possible Ernest was hired prior to Warrillow's death on the recommendation of his older sister, Fannie, or it is possible Fannie hired him after Warrillow's death and prior to the April census. The same possibilities exist for Mrs. Bratt's school.

to his daughter in 1897 suggests Ernest had some positive feelings about his sister Fannie. Fannie named Ernest as one of the executors of her 1904 estate, from which he would have typically received a substantial fee for this role. Also, Fannie's mother, the now-widowed Mrs. Jane Bratt, appears to have benefited. Mrs. Bratt now had the funds to move to a better neighborhood by 1891 and had the capital to furnish and open a more profitable and less onerous school for young ladies next door at 13 Wheeler Street in 1892 (Kelly's Directory 1892). Given the school's designation, social graces, deportment, and etiquette, were taught, with academic subjects secondary.

Further tolerance by the Bratt family was indicated by the fact that, shortly after Alfred Warrillow's death in 1891, Fannie's sister, twenty-six-year-old Alice Maud, an assistant school mistress, was living with the thirty-two-year-old Fannie, and a thirty-one-year-old domestic servant (1891 census). Fannie's Stechford location must have been sufficiently distant that no gossip would taint Alice Maud and endanger her employment. The family must also have thought well enough of Fannie to allow Alice Maud to live with Fannie. Finally, Fannie named her mother, Mrs. Jane Bratt, as Edith's guardian, ensuring her mother received a substantial sum for assuming those legal responsibilities.

There would have been limits to this tolerance. Mrs. Bratt and the rest of the Bratt family, whatever their feelings about Fannie, must have gone to enormous lengths to keep Fannie's part in the Warrillow affair and her out-of-wedlock pregnancy hidden from anyone and everyone, as any hint of impropriety would compromise Mrs. Bratt's ability to attract pupils to her school, teach, and earn a living. Mrs. Bratt's clientele of aspiring middle-class families placed a high value on a Christian orientation (Pinchbeck and Hewitt 163, 166-67). Just as Alfred Warrillow's reputation was a business asset, so was Mrs. Bratt's. Most Victorians would believe Fannie's affair with a married man and the resulting pregnancy meant she was ruined or fallen. Her entire family would have been disgraced, as Victorians believed moral failure was inherited, i.e. "children begotten in sin would naturally inherit their parents' weakness" (Pinchbeck and Hewitt 584).

Edith was the result of a Victorian middle-class drama. Her mother, Fannie, a governess, grasped for a fragile opportunity to better her life, leading to a violation of class boundaries and an entanglement with the nineteenth-century legal system. By August 19, 1889, the date of Alfred Warrillow's will, Fannie would have known Warrilow had stood by his promises and her future was secure. Fannie would escape the poverty and abandonment which was the fate of most unwed mothers. Edith's father, Alfred Warrillow, left Fannie and their child well provided for financially, but still at risk of social ostracism in the rigid Victorian class system. Edith's illegitimacy would be the deciding factor in her childhood.

Chapter Two

Childhood

While the official biography acknowledges that Edith was illegitimate (*Bio* 38), Carpenter's statement about Edith's happiness in childhood (*Bio* 39) is, however, contradicted by the historical evidence of the treatment typical for illegitimate children in Victorian England. As an illegitimate child, Edith's treatment at her foster parents' home, from birth until an unknown older age, would have typically been one of hunger, neglect, and ostracism. Further, Edith's mother was unlikely to welcome a child she had not seen for years, if only from the fear the child might reveal a past Fannie Bratt would wish to conceal.

Edith Bratt's birth certificate states she was born on January 21, 1889 at 25 Arthur Street, Gloucester. This is most likely the address where her mother stayed during her confinement. Confinement or lying-in, prior to the birth of the baby, was not only a Victorian custom, but endorsed by medical professionals due to the high rate of death during childbirth.[1] Given the rising rate of death in childbirth during the 1880s as documented in the graph below, the risk of childbirth was a serious subject. The length of confinement varied with a woman's financial and social standing, but confinement for at least the last few weeks of pregnancy was recommended. As women, who were no longer seen in public, the soon-to-be mothers could then take off their corsets.

During earlier visits of Fannie Bratt and Alfred Warrillow to Gloucester in 1888, they had probably already selected a midwife, who would have come to the house for a home delivery. Hospital births were not the norm at that time. We do not know when Fannie Bratt left the Warrillow household to go to Gloucester, but a wish to hide her increasingly obvious pregnancy and fear of death in childbirth, would have been likely factors in the timing of

---

1 Six weeks of confinement before childbirth is seen as needed to prevent miscarriage (Bulletin of the Bureau of Labor. No. 75 March, 1908. Washington D. C., 532).

Annual Death Rate per 1000 Total Births from Maternal Mortality
in England and Wales (1850-1970)
("British maternal mortality in the 19th and early 20th century."
Journal of the Royal Society of Medicine. https://www.ncbi.nlm.nih.
gov/pmc/articles/PMC1633559/, last viewed on 5/31/2020)

her departure. Being pregnant for the first time, the almost thirty-year-old Fannie Bratt was at some risk in childbirth. For Victorians, a subsequent post-partum confinement, which lasted between four and six weeks, typically followed the baby's delivery.[2] Consistent with Alfred Warrillow's providing for Fannie's financial security in his 1889 will, he almost certainly would have been the one to pay for what was seen as optimal care during pregnancy and the dangerous onset of childbirth.

The proposed 1888 Warrillow separation decree named "Arthur House" as the residence where Alfred Warrillow and Fannie Bratt stayed in Gloucester in September, October, and November 1888. It was located at 25 Arthur Street,

---

2 Slemons, chapter 9.

one in a row of terraced houses.[3] The property was centrally located within easy walking distance of the city, cathedral and parks. The census of 1888 shows Wallace Bloomfield, a bookseller and a stationer, living there. Bloomfield's large house had extra rooms to let as it had four stories and a basement. Wallace Bloomfield appeared in the 1879 business directory as a stationer in Eastgate Street, Gloucester. Wallace Bloomfield died in 1891, so in 1888 and 1889 he was alive and could have had contact with Alfred Warrillow through the stationery business. In the 1891 census, his widow, Mary Ann Bloomfield, was the landlady of this dwelling, listed as a "boarding house."

Edith Mary Bratt was baptized on February 13, 1889 in the Wesleyan Methodist chapel in Gloucester. In the church's baptismal registery, the child's last name was listed as Bratt; her mother's name was given as Fannie, and the father's name as Frederick, Alfred Warrillow's middle name. Fannie Bratt may have used Warrillow's middle name in an attempt to both comply with the church's expectation and to protect him. There is no evidence Alfred Warrillow was present. He understandably would have been eager to shield his identity and reputation, a vital asset to a businessman in Victorian England.

Probably after the baptism, Fannie Bratt delivered the infant Edith Mary Bratt to a "baby-farmer." Baby farming was the custom of paying a family to take custody of an infant or child. This child-care arrangement had a long history in both England and on the Continent. It was pervasive and widely accepted. The author, Jane Austen (born 1775), and all her siblings were fostered in this manner until they were toddlers. In 1871, the parents of Rudyard Kipling (born 1865) placed the five-year-old Rudyard and his younger sister, Trixie, with a couple, who advertised in the newspaper, and the parents returned to India. The children were retrieved in 1877. Both of these families were definitely middle-class with legitimate children, but placement with a baby-farmer was one of

---

3 "Arthur House" is now Number 12 Arthur St. as evidenced by the number on the wall in the photograph. Originally there were 27 properties on Arthur Street. Built about 1852, the houses were numbered consecutively starting at the Wellington Street end. There were nineteen built in the same style until Kings Barton Street was reached. This terrace contained Numbers 1 to 19. Examining the census sheets shows the enumerator collected the completed sheets from the occupant(s) on the north side of the street, then crossed over and worked back up the street eventually reaching Number 23 at the corner of Belgrave Road. He then collected sheets on Belgrave Road. Consequently, Arthur House, Number 25, was the middle house of the block of five on the south side of the street. Sometime later the Gloucester City Council decreed all houses on the left side of the street from its start should be odd-numbered. That remains the situation today.

25 Arthur Street, Gloucester, where Edith Bratt was born and
where her parents stayed in the fall of 1888 (Google Earth)

the most common fates of an illegitimate child (Pinchbeck and Hewitt 597).
This practice was so familiar in Victorian England that Gilbert and Sullivan's
1878 *HMS Pinafore* featured the sympathetic Buttercup warbling:

> *A many years ago*
> *When I was young and charming*
> *As some of you may know*
> *I practised baby-farming.*

Pinchbeck and Hewitt review the terrible conditions for unwanted children in
late Victorian England. In 1870, the number of dead babies found on the streets
of London was 276 with the majority being under one week of age (613). This
desertion of infants and the notorious 1870 case of Margaret Waters, who had
advertised in the newspapers offering to adopt babies for a fee – to "A good
home, with a mother's love and care, is offered to any respectable person," –
galvanized Parliament in 1872 to pass the first legislation to counter this abuse.

"The Infant Life Protection Bill" required "baby-farmers" to be registered and deaths reported, though this law was widely evaded and little enforced (619). For most baby-farmers, the cost paid by the mother was known to be inadequate for the child's long term maintenance. Consequently, the child soon died through neglect and starvation (619). Also, the law only applied to persons "receiving for reward two or more children under one year of age." The famous 1896 case of Mrs. Dyer of Reading, who was found guilty of strangling babies and throwing them in the Thames, showed this business continued to flourish (597). She was even memorialized in song.

The 1889 Methodist Chapel Building is now owned by Barton and
Tredworth Community Trust, at the corner of Faulkner and Conduit Street,
Gloucester. (Google Earth)

The research of Pinchbeck and Hewitt presents the status of the illegitimate child in England. An illegitimate child in Victorian England could not inherit from its father because under the law it was the child of nobody, a *filius nullius*, unless the father's will specifically mentioned the child. The child could inherit from its mother even without a will (584). Further, for the Victorians, the stigma attached to the moral failing, which led to a child being a bastard, was so great that orphanages would not accept such children. Pinchbeck and Hewitt note the largest single class of destitute children was defined as "children begotten in sin [who] would naturally inherit their parents' weakness."[4] Illegitimacy was an offense against Christian morality and the institution of marriage (583). The existence and prevalence of incest and sexual assault in all its forms were simply not considered. The death rate for illegitimate children was higher than that for legitimate children throughout the nineteenth century, and causes included desertion and infanticide (589). For many single mothers, without any other support, the only practicable solution was to put the child in the workhouse (589). The largest single category of children in the workhouse in the nineteenth century was illegitimate (595).

Fannie Bratt and Alfred Warrillow created a new home and a new life in Stechford, four miles east of central Birmingham, where they could hope no one would know them from Handsworth. On an 1886 Ordnance survey map, Stechford is mainly a cluster of buildings around the railway station, and, until 1900, most of the area was still farmland. Fannie could pass as Warrillow's housekeeper, and no baby needed to be explained. Edith was the "Scarlet Letter" who could reveal the secret of Fannie Bratt and Alfred Warrillow's illicit relationship and expose Fannie to social censure. While Fannie Bratt was probably present for Edith's baptism, few, or more likely, no other visits to see Edith in Gloucester were likely if only to deflect any suspicion away from Alfred Warrillow.

Given the high infant mortality rates in England and Wales, Fannie and Alfred may not have expected Edith to survive. Infant deaths, i.e. deaths of children under the age of one year, in England and Wales eventually rose to approximately

---

4 Part of the popularity of Freud and others' talking therapy at the end of the nineteenth century was that it created an alternative explanation for mental and psychological disorders and held hope for the patient's improvement without the stigma of heritability as primary (Sulloway 92-3). This fear of hereditary "'taint" is an entirely different cultural and historical context than the one of the twenty-first century.

150 deaths per 1000 births by the 1890s.[5] Further, the childhood diseases of scarlet fever, "respiratory diseases" including tuberculosis, measles, as well as diarrhea, killed many young children (Corsini 68). Being both illegitimate and being placed in foster care would increase Edith's risk of illness and death. In the 1891 census, Edith, age two, is listed as a "boarder" in the house of George and Emma Clifford, #2 Matson in Barton St. Mary, Gloucester. No Clifford child of Edith's age is listed in the census so it was likely Edith was not breast-fed but was raised on "dry nursing," meaning animal milk mixed with other nutrients. Although an increase in medical problems and infant mortality was identified as associated with dry nursing as early as 1846, an adequate infant formula was not developed until the early twentieth century (Apple 18).

#2 Matson, home of the Cliffords, Edith's foster family (Google Earth)

---

5 "Infection and immunity" "2.2 Infant death in 19th century England." The Open University, last viewed on 5/31/2020. https://www.open.edu/openlearn/ocw/mod/oucontent/view. php?id=28151&section=2.2. For an estimate of childhood mortality rates see "Child and Infant Mortality" by Max Roser, Hannah Ritchie, and Bernadeta Dadonaite of University of Oxford's Oxford Martin Programme on Global Development in conjunction with Global Change Data Lab, last viewed on 6/2/2020. Their graph for all children under five years of age in 1890 appears to show one in four children died before the age of five. This would include infant mortality.

The forty-five-year-old George Clifford was a "Deal Porter," which meant he carried planks of softwood or "deal," such as pine, stacked on his shoulders and walked up and down gangplanks to load and unload the ships at the nearby busy inland harbor of Gloucester. This stevedore job demanded good balance and skills and was very physically demanding.[6] He lived quite close to both the docks and a successful manufacturing plant for ladders, the "Step Works," which would have been a prime consumer of wood (1901 Ordnance Survey map).[7] His forty-six-year-old wife took care of their seven-year-old William who was in school, their four-year-old Florence, and two-year-old Edith Bratt (1891 census). The Cliffords were a working-class family who could use some extra money.

The 1891 census lists Edith as "a boarder" so Alfred Warrillow must have been paying the Cliffords something for Edith's room and board. At best, Alfred Warrillow, whose name was not on the birth certificate, was likely to have had mixed feelings about Edith. He wrote his only other known child, Nellie, out of his will in 1889. It is possible the Cliffords' contact was limited solely to Fannie Bratt or perhaps a solicitor in an effort to mask Warrillow's identity.

The implications of the commercial nature of baby farming in the Victorian period meant that the children "in care" would often be shorted on food so that the "carers" could pocket part of the money they received for the child's keep for their own purposes. It is unknown if this was actually the case with the Cliffords and Edith, but it would not have been uncommon had they done so. The Cliffords' temptation to cut Edith's food ration would have been an easy choice if Edith's parents paid no visits, as the possibility of

---

6 "Docked and Parked" by Jo Stockham. Royal College of Art, last viewed on 6/2/2020. https://researchonline.rca.ac.uk/2083/1/JS.%20Pages%20from%20160509_WCL_Editors_Check_RB_.pdf, and "Topic: What was a deal porter." RootsChat, a nonprofit organization, the largest free family history forum site in the UK, last viewed on 6/2/2020 https://www.rootschat.com/forum/index.php?topic=165721.0.

7 The factory opened in 1885. "The Former Norville Factory Site, Tarrington Road, Tredworth. Archaeological Evaluation (OASIS ID: borderar1-272557)." Archaeology Data Service, University of York, last viewed on 6/2/2020. https://archaeologydataservice.ac.uk/archives/view/borderar1-272557/index.cfm.

someone discovering the diversion of the funds was unlikely.[8] If the Cliffords did yield to temptation, the resulting malnutrition could have contributed to Edith's health problems in the 1940s and 1950s. Though the historical context indicates this possibility, there is no specific, direct documentation to support this hypothesis.[9]

In Victorian England, children may have been family assets in the long run, but the need to have them work as soon as possible had much to do with the cost of feeding them. The underfeeding of children in working-class England was rampant in the late 1800s and early 1900s, leading to decreased height (Pinchbeck and Hewitt 632-33). The pervasiveness and acceptability of this custom of shorting children's food can be seen in the policy of orphanages, which underfed orphans to such an extent it led to stunted growth and malnutrition (Simpson 143, 145).[10] In working-class families, "girls were given smaller portions, as it was commonly believed that they needed less than boys" (Rose 216). This scrimping should be placed in the context that in 1904, due to malnutrition, working-class children were on average 3 inches shorter than their peers at a more middle-class elementary school (Rose 155, also 153). Whatever other abuse and neglect Edith may have suffered as a foster child, she very likely suffered from hunger. She was called "little one" by J.R.R. Tolkien (*Bio* 67) at least partly because she was shorter than he. Ronald Tolkien was 5 feet 8 ½ inches tall (*Letters* 373). Their relative heights can be seen in pictures from 1917 (*TFA* 41, 65).

Even if the Cliffords had not been told Edith was illegitimate, they could have drawn that conclusion. If the Cliffords had been approached by a third party, like Wallace Bloomfield, the stationer and owner of Arthur House, or a

---

8 The modern reader has difficulty appreciating the relative cost of food at the turn of the twentieth century. "At the start of the First World War, food purchases consumed half the average paycheck; today the figure is six percent. According to the federal statistics, an American in 1919 had to work for two and a half hours to earn enough money to buy a chicken; these days it would take less than fifteen minutes of labour" ("Freedom from Fries." Michael Spector. *The New Yorker*. October 26, 2015, 58). These costs are for Americans, but the figures should be comparable in England. The Federal Reserve Bank of Dallas published a table on the high cost of living in 1897 as compared to 1997 based on Sears Catalog prices. (https://www.dallasfed.org/~/media/documents/fed/annual/1999/ar97.pdf), last viewed on 5/31/2020. There is also a table on food prices.

9 See Stratton et al. 24.

10 The connection between poor diet and height continues to receive support. See https://www.bbc.com/news/health-54828544, last viewed on 11/7/2020.

solicitor, they would have assumed Edith was illegitimate. If their contact was only with Fannie Bratt, they would have immediately noticed if this young woman had not taken the precaution of wearing a wedding ring, though the absence of the father alone would likely lead to the same assumption. The secrecy about who Edith's parent(s) were and a lack of visits would reinforce their conclusion.

Being illegitimate would have meant Edith was even lower in status than the working-class Cliffords. As a result, it is likely Edith would have been treated differently from Cliffords' children because she was illegitimate. The illegitimate daughter of a Kent farm worker before the First World War recalled how her being a bastard was a barrier and a stigma at the local school: only some girls at school played with her, but even those girls never invited her to their homes, and a mother refused to have this illegitimate child walk with her daughter to school as she was "born in disgrace" (Rose 173). As one historian noted, "Britain was in 1914 arguably the most class-conscious nation in Europe if not the world," and this statement was also certainly true in the 1890s.[11]

The 1891 census shows that, after Alfred Warrillow's death in March 1891, Fannie Bratt did not bring her daughter to live with her. Fannie had to run Warrillow's business after he died and would have had difficulty not only explaining who this two-year-old child was, but also taking care of her without a nurse and while working. The lengthy separation due to foster care, the possible expectation of no reunion with the child due to the probability of an early death, and the knowledge this child was the evidence of the shame Fannie Bratt had brought on herself and her family strongly suggest the relationship between mother and daughter was not very close.

However, in a 1901 census, Fannie Bratt was living at 22 Linwood Road in Handsworth with the twelve-year-old Edith who is listed as Fannie's niece. The household was completed by Fannie's mother's first cousin, thirty-seven-year-old Jennie Grove, who was working there as a servant. The Rate Book of 1901, which determined taxes, shows Fannie Bratt is both the occupant and the owner of 22 Linwood Road. Real estate was a good investment, and

---

11 The website of the Royal Army Pay Corps Association reports, last viewed on 5/31/2020. https://rapc-association.org.uk/pay-services-history/ww1/pen-and-ink.html.

Fannie either sold the previous house in Stechford to finance the Linwood house or invested Warrillow's money in it. This residence may have eventually become one of the rental houses Carpenter reported as providing income for Edith (*Bio* 39).

While Fannie probably had moved before having Edith come to live with her partly in order to avoid explaining the child to her neighbors, Fannie's reasons for moving back to Handsworth where people would be familiar with her history are uncertain. While Mrs. Warrillow had moved by the time she filed for a separation in December 1888, Alfred Warrillow's affair and separation would have been gossiped about for months and even years. Fannie Bratt may have needed to return to Handsworth because of the wholesale business, which was still under Alfred Frederick Warrillow's name at 101 and 102 Great Hampton Street. Alfred's brother, John Warrillow had a wholesale stationer's shop nearby, occupying 23 Great Hampton Street (Kelly's Directory 1895). From Fannie Bratt's Linwood residence, a tram line could quickly take her to Great Hampton Street.

We do not know when Edith came to live with Fannie Bratt, but no affectionate family ties would have speeded this reunion given the long years of separation between the two and the risk Edith presented to Fannie's reputation in the community. Fannie had to be sure the child would never slip and reveal their true relationship, so Fannie may have maintained the fiction Edith was her niece, even with Edith. There is no evidence that the Cliffords knew Fannie Bratt was Edith's mother or of what the Cliffords might have told Edith. The Cliffords would not have had access to the baptismal records to check on Edith's parentage. It is possible Fannie introduced herself to Edith as her aunt.

However, if Edith knew Fannie Bratt was her mother, then it could have been as late as a possible age of seven, i.e. around 1896, before Edith joined Fannie's household. At the age of seven, most children have an understanding one can act and speak more freely among family members as compared with non-family. Fannie needed a child who could be counted on not to volunteer family information and to maintain the pretense of an aunt and niece relationship. The age of seven could still agree with the memories of the Tolkien children that their mother "spent most of her early life in the Handsworth area" (*TFA* 27).

How and when Edith learned the name of her father, and possibly who her mother was, is unknown, although the Bratt family knew Alfred Warrillow was her father (*Bio* 38). If Fannie Bratt kept her relationship with Edith secret, it was likely to have increased the distance between the two. The silence surrounding her parentage would have caused Edith to wonder, and this too would have precluded a close mother-daughter relationship.

Fannie Bratt's life may have centered on teaching Edith and supervising the business. Jennie Grove, a distant family member, may have been glad to find employment with Fannie, perhaps in a way similar to Fannie's brother and mother appreciating Fannie's help. Jennie worked as Fannie's servant who could run errands and deal with the local shopkeepers, who, like many Victorians, were likely to regard Fannie as a brazen hussy, if not a scarlet woman. Attempting to avoid ostracism and public censure may have led Fannie to attend a church in the city, where she was not likely to be recognized. She may have had some discreet contact with her mother and siblings who were now closer. It seems unlikely Edith had contact with her grandmother, aunts, uncles, and cousins because of the shame of her birth. Edith's visits would have put Fannie's subterfuge in jeopardy should Edith innocently address Fannie's relatives as "grandmother" or "aunt" in front of others.

The thirty-seven-year-old Jennie Grove would have had her hands full doing the time-consuming tasks of cooking, cleaning, laundry, and shopping and could not be spared to do child care. That could suggest Edith might have been at least five before she came to live with Fannie as Edith would have been able to dress, feed, and care for herself by that age, i.e. 1894. That is, she would not create any additional burden to management of the household. This age would agree with the Tolkien children's report of how long their mother lived in Handsworth.

While Edith led an isolated life due to her illegitimacy, she now had someone she could talk to as they shared similar backgrounds: Jennie Grove. Mary Jane Grove (1864-1938) – or Jennie – lived with Edith until 1903 when Fannie Bratt died and Edith was sent to school at Dresden House. They resumed visiting when Edith lived in Birmingham at the Faulkners' from 1908 to 1911 (*Bio* 41). According to John and Priscilla Tolkien, Jennie "became a substitute mother to Edith." The label of "substitute mother" could indicate that, not only when the Tolkien children knew Jennie, but during Fannie Bratt's lifetime, Edith's closest relationship was with Jennie rather than with her biological mother (*TFA* 36). If Fannie Bratt, to protect her reputation by posing as Edith's aunt, required Edith not to know Fannie was her mother, then the close relationship with Jennie would be all the more likely.

Artist's reconstruction of 22 Linwood Road, Handsworth, during the Edwardian Era

Jennie Grove was only four feet eight inches in height, reportedly "due to an accident in her youth" (*TFA* 36). Some of Jennie's diminished stature was also probably due to poor nutrition, as was common for working-class girls (Rose 216, 155). Victorians were not kind to people with handicaps or physical deformity, exhibiting many as "freaks" like "The Elephant Man" with his neurofibromatosis or P.T. Barnum displaying "Tom Thumb." Jennie could understand the kind of humiliating social ostracism which Edith endured, as she probably had experienced something similar due to her smaller size, and the pain of losing family as a child.

John and Priscilla Tolkien's memoir of their family gives some of the few snapshots we have of Edith Bratt Tolkien's early life. While *Tolkien Family Album* was published in 1992 when John Tolkien was seventy-five years old and Priscilla was sixty-three years old, the information about Jennie Grove should be reliable as they were not just recalling what they had been told. Both John and Priscilla knew Jennie or "Auntie Ie" and could recall interacting with her because she died when they were twenty-one and nine years old, respectively (*TFA* 36). Jennie joined the twenty-four-year old Edith's household in 1913 in Warwick and continued to live with Edith and help her until April, 1921 (*C&G* 1.124). Jennie usually spent Christmases with the Tolkien family as one would expect for a cherished family member (*C&G* 1.152). Jennie's importance to the Tolkien family can be seen in Ronald Tolkien's sending her a copy of *The Hobbit* in September 1937 as he did to other close friends and family (*C&G* 1.215).

Jennie's father, Frederick Grove, the brother of Jane Bratt, Fannie Bratt's mother and Edith's grandmother, was listed as a thirty-five-year-old clerk and widower in the 1871 census. He married Margaret Mounsey Richardson in 1861 (1849-69) and by 1864 they were living in Liverpool. Jennie, born in 1864, could recall watching big ships sail up Liverpool's Mersey River (*C&G* 2.474). Jennie's twenty-five-year-old mother died when Jennie was five, and Jennie, like Edith, would have been placed either with relatives, who were likely to have seen her as a burden, or in foster care. Before the twentieth century and psychoanalysis's validation of the importance of childhood memories and experiences, orphans went where they were told to go "with the admonition that they should be grateful to be fed, clothed, and sheltered" (Simpson 148). If sympathy was expressed at the death of a parent, it was not offered to the children, but "offered to the surviving relatives who would be burdened with raising someone else's child" (Simpson, 148).

Edith would have been schooled at home as her mother had been a governess. Like J.R.R. Tolkien, whose mother was also a governess, Edith would have been "very well brought up" to have impeccable manners (Lee 139). Edith's mother, from a working-class family with nine children, was very unlikely to have known how to play the piano, the status symbol of the middle class in the 1800s. However, given that Fannie now had a middle-class income, she would have bought a piano and arranged for Edith to have lessons like a proper middle-class child (*Bio* 39). Edith probably had no friends her own age as her mother's social and occupational standing required the secret of Edith's birth to be sealed. Typically, little girls were Victorian symbols of purity, and Edith, with her parentage, did not match this standard. The lesson of secrecy was drilled into Edith's soul: she did not tell Ronald Tolkien the truth about her father until after their wedding and only when forced to do so by the requirements of the marriage certificate (*Bio* 79).[12] She never told her own children the name of her father, their grandfather (*Bio* 39). Edith's mother had a photograph of Alfred Warrillow (*Bio* 38) which presumably Edith would have seen and inherited.

On April 14, 1903, Frances "Fannie" Bratt died at the age of forty-four. In her will, she named as executors her younger brother, Ernest William Bratt, who was also a stationer, and Stephen Gateley, Alfred Warrillow's solicitor. She designated her mother, Mrs. Jane Bratt, to educate and bring "up my child Edith Bratt by Alfred Frederick Warrillow until she marries" and whose monies are "for her sole and separate use and free from marital control" (*C&G* 1.9).

When J.R.R. Tolkien wrote of the "dreadful sufferings of our childhoods" which "records do not record" (*Letters* 421), he was likely, in the case of Edith, to have had in mind Edith's upbringing in a foster family who let her go hungry and treated her as inferior because she was illegitimate. Edith's arrival at her mother's house certainly improved her life materially. Fannie Bratt, the governess, was likely to have strict expectations of Edith's deportment and education.

---

12 Edith would have been required by the Catholic Church to provide a copy of her baptismal certificate before her wedding to Ronald Tolkien. This document had only the name "Frederick" in the box for the name of her father.

A close relationship between the mother and child was unlikely, given the years of separation and the stigma of an out-of-wedlock pregnancy. Edith did gain a close relationship with Jennie Grove, a "substitute mother." Edith reconnected with Jennie when Edith returned to Birmingham during the time she lived at the Faulkners from 1908 to 1911. When Edith established her own household in Warwick in 1913, Jennie joined her. But with the death of Fannie Bratt and the assumption of Edith's guardianship by Mrs. Jane Bratt, Edith's grandmother, a new opportunity and a new life came to Edith in the form of being sent away to be educated at Dresden House in Evesham.

Chapter Three

Dresden House, 1903-1907

Neither the Carpenter biography nor the family tales reported in the *Tolkien Family Album* give scarcely any information about Edith's years at Dresden House. However, the move to Dresden House was a dramatic change for Edith when compared to her isolated life in Handsworth. It presented new opportunities for relationships with friends and teachers, as well as for learning. What can be gleaned from primary sources is that this setting allowed Edith to begin to have a life made possible by the inheritance her mother received from Alfred Warrillow. The 1903 probate notice of Frances Bratt shows an estate of £5269, 14 shillings and 9 pence or £645,569.65 in terms of 2019 goods and services. This is equivalent to $807,845.95 in 2019 dollars.[1]

Edith was "sent away" in 1903 at the age of fourteen by Mrs. Jane Bratt, her grandmother, to be a boarder at Dresden House in Evesham, Warwickshire (*TFA* 27). While the Tolkien children do not say why Edith was "sent away" by her grandmother, the most likely reasons were she and the rest of the Bratt family did not want the responsibility of raising Edith (Simpson 148) nor any contact with an illegitimate child, who might raise questions in other people's minds about the family's respectability. Edith's being an heiress did not remove these compelling considerations. By sending Edith to a boarding school, Mrs. Jane Bratt would both further Edith's education and remove her from the Birmingham area, sparing the family any further shame. The thirty-mile trip from Birmingham to Evesham would have required approximately two hours

1 "Find a Will." Government.UK, last viewed on 5/31/2020. https://probatesearch.service.gov.uk/Calendar#calendar. A figure of £3,797 2s 11d is given as the net value of Frances' estate (*C&G* 1.9). This figure is about £1,500 less than the £5,269 the estate was valued at after being "Resworn" from the original listing of £4,394. The figure of £3,797 2s 11d may be the result of the 3% death duties, funeral and burial expenses, debts, and/or legal costs. Scull and Hammond give no documentation about or explanation of the source of this lesser amount. ("Inflation Calculator." Bank of England, last viewed on 5/31/2020. https://www.bankofengland.co.uk/monetary-policy/inflation/inflation-calculator).

Dresden House, Evesham
(Courtesy of Lukasz Rusiecki, Gallery Properties, Evesham)

on an Edwardian train, given train speed and the time needed to stop at other local stations.[2]

When Edith's grandmother died in 1905, Stephen Gateley, previously both Alfred Warrillow's and Fannie Bratt's solicitor, became Edith's legal guardian and continued Edith's placement at Dresden House until she was probably too old to stay there anymore, i.e. around 1907 when she would have turned eighteen.[3] The advantage for Edith in attending Dresden House was that she, too, could keep her background a secret and probably could have friends for the first time in her life. Any reticence by the orphan, Edith, to talk about her deceased parents would not be a surprise to others.

Edith's attendance at Dresden House was from 1903 to approximately 1907 during the Edwardian period (1901-1910). Dresden House is a historic landmark in Evesham, an important market town on the River Avon, both then and today. Located on High Street, the name of this 1692 townhouse comes

---

2 "At the beginning of the twentieth-century railroads had an average speed of 40 mph."
   "The development of the railway network in Britain 1825-1911." Dan Bogart, Leigh Shaw-Taylor and Xuesheng You, last viewed on 6/4/2020. https://pdfs.semanticscholar.org/beca/ae2e1cf76dca3ecc5a252d529e583806ecec.pdf.

3 A legal guardianship would have come with a substantial fee for the guardian. Grandmother Bratt's choice of Stephen Gateley as Edith's guardian suggests either her unwillingness or the unwillingness of any other member of the Bratt family to claim this opportunity due to its association with Edith's illegitimacy and its "filthy lucre." This attitude would be consistent with the family's shunning of Edith in order to avoid having their own reputations tarnished. Alternately, Grandmother Bratt may have thought access to Edith's money too tempting for other members of the Bratt family, creating a need for a professional like Stephen Gateley. The ability to access a copy of Frances Bratt's will was impeded in 2020 by the disruption of services to the archives by the pandemic. We were unable to locate a copy of Mrs. Jane Bratt's probate.

View of Avon River at the Evesham Bridge
(Courtesy David Gregory, Postcards of the Past)

from Dr. Baylies, who married Elizabeth Cookes, the daughter of the builder of "the Mansion," thereby becoming its owner. After his wife's death, he settled as a physician at Dresden, where his skill led Frederick the Great to send for him in 1774.

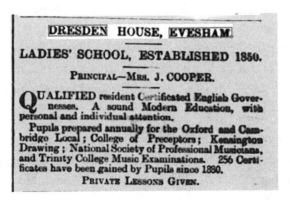

Advertisement in *Evesham Journal* (March 16, 1889)[4]

---

4 The advertisement gives a date of 1850 for when the school started. This date does not agree with
  Mr. Barnard's date of 1860. Given that all the local residents would have known when the school was
  established, it is likely the newspaper date of 1850 is correct.

> **DRESDEN HOUSE EVESHAM**
>
> *LADIES' SCHOOL, ESTABLISHED 1860.*
>
> PRINCIPAL—MRS. J. COOPER.
>
> QUALIFIED resident English Governesses. A Sound Modern Education, with personal and individual attention.
>
> Pupils prepared annually for the Cambridge Local College of Preceptors, Kensington Drawing, and Trinity College Examinations. 111 Certificates have been gained by the Pupils since 1880.
>
> *Private Lessons given.*

Advertisement in *Evesham Standard and West Midland Observer*
(Saturday, July 7, 1894)

Mrs. Cooper, then Miss Harriette Codrington Watts, together with Miss Eliza Cooper bought Dresden House in October, 1876, taking over a Ladies' School previously established there in 1860. Mrs. Cooper was the first to give the name "Dresden House" to "the Mansion" because of its connection with Dr. Baylies.[5] According to the 1881 census, the school's four teachers offered English, Latin, music, and drawing. In 1887, the forty-five-year-old Miss Watt (1881 census) married the fifty-four-year-old Joseph Cooper, who then became the owner of Dresden House. They used part of the house as their residence while reserving part for the school. In the 1891 census, five resident teachers, including Alice and Kate Watts, two of Harriette's nieces, teaching English, music, and art, lived at Dresden House plus a guest, a theological student, who may have taught Latin.

No information on the fees for tuition plus room and board at Dresden House is available, but given the school's reputation and setting, it is likely to have been substantial. In both the 1891 and 1901 census, Dresden House had thirteen

---

5 "The Story of Dresden House, Evesham" by E.A.B. Barnard. (1914). Vale of Evesham Historical Society, last viewed on 5/31/2020. http://www.valeofeveshamhistory.org/articles/dresden-house. Dr. Baylies was a memorable character. In an early interview with Dr. Baylies, "the Emperor remarked to him that to have acquired such skill he must have killed a great many people, and that the doctor replied, 'Not as many as your Majesty'." A smooth bon mot did contribute to Dr. Baylies' job security. From a reading of the *TFA*, it could be construed that the school was named for Dresden because Dresden was where the Watts sisters trained in music. This may have, in fact, been either Edith's or the Tolkien children's understanding.

Dresden House School with the Garden House or "Temple" in the background, showing the influence of eighteenth-century chinoiserie
(Courtesy of the Vale of Evesham Historical Society)

boarders, and in the 1901 census, the girls who boarded ranged in age from
nine to sixteen. The school also had day-students. The commemorative group
photograph above, probably taken either for the festivities of Queen Victoria's
Diamond Jubilee of 1897 or at the turn of the century in 1900, shows 64
students with five staff members, though some of the students may be alum-
nae. The students, who were boarders, probably resided on the top floor of
Dresden House, which had a fine view of the surrounding countryside. Edith
Bratt recalled "high-spirited games and midnight feasts" which probably took
place in the dormitory (*TFA* 27). The neighbors, peering from behind their
lace curtains, carefully monitored the girls' shenanigans and felt compelled to
report these to the police (*TFA* 27).

Mrs. Cooper's two nieces, the two single Watts sisters, ages 31 and 28 (census
1901), who ran the school in 1903 when Edith attended, received their musical education in Dresden (*TFA* 27).[6] Dresden had a well-known reputation for
music education, and Felix Mendelssohn (1809-1847) had been a principal at
a music school there. The Dresden House School of Music, Evesham was listed
by the Trinity College of Music as a "Local Centre for Examinations" in both

---

6 From the 1881 census, the Watts sisters appear to be the daughters of Harriette Watts Cooper's older
   brother, John.

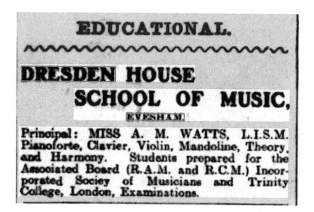

Music Preparation in *Evesham Standard and West Midland Observer*
(Saturday, September 26, 1908)

the 1903 Calendar and the 1908 Calendar.[7] A musical certificate from the Trinity College of Music was a sought after testimony to musical competence for aspiring teachers and performers of music. The school advertised it prepared students for such evaluations.[8]

Edith appears to have thrived at Dresden House. At the end of her first year there, she won a prize in sewing and Sunday lessons and performed in the drill display (*Evesham Standard and West Midland Observer* Saturday, July 30, 1904). "Drill display" meant Swedish drill which was the standard for physical education. The 1820 education code had allowed for "drill" in imitation of the well-drilled Prussian Army, a series of movements performed as "healthy exercise." Swedish drill involved the use of staves or clubs, and the girls marched to music (Rose 140).

The *Evesham Standard and West Midland Observer* Saturday, July 30, 1904 announced:

PRIZE DAY AT DRESDEN HOUSE SCHOOL, EVESHAM. There was an interesting programme [...]. It opened with the performance of a

---

7 Personal email to Seamus Hamill-Keays from Lucy Rose at Jerwood Library of the Performing Arts, Faculty of Music, Trinity Laban Conservatoire of Music and Dance (jlpa@trinitylaban.ac.uk).
8 While there is an announcement in the *Evesham Standard and West Midland Observer* of Saturday, December 16, 1905 for two of Dresden House's students passing the Trinity College exam for a certificate, we found no notice for Edith Bratt.

very pretty cantata "The Silver Lily" (W. H. Maxfield) [...]. There was a chorus of peasant maidens. The cantata was very prettily given and much enjoyed. [...] The other items of the programme were [...] all creditably given: Introduction. instrumental, L. Haines; chorus "Awake Arouse!"; recitative. "Yes! Wake! Arouse!" D. Byrd air. "Hark The Songsters!" D. Byrd choral recit. "The woodland spreads;" duet "'neath the branches," duet, C. Weeks and D. Beardsley; choral recit., "Alas! Alas !"; intermezzo, "Ripples on the stream," L. Haines: Choral recit. chorus, "Away! Away!" recitative, "'Tis here! 'Tis here!" C. Weeks air, "Ah! Lucky, dear Florette!" D. Beardsley choral recit. "Our jaunt is o'er"; finale, trio and chorus "Hand in hand" [...] pianoforte duet. "Bolero" (by M. Bergson), [...] recitation. "Bruce and the Spider." [...] violin duet. "Unter den Linden" (by Basil Althaus), [...] kindergarten song, small singing class: suite for two pianos (1) Le Savant, (2) La Coquette, (3) La Danseuse (by A. Arensky), the Misses Watts; (composed especially for the occasion). E. Marcham, D. Byrd, **E. Bratt**, W. Pepper, D. Morey, Z. Beach, M. Ashley, E. Marshall, C. Weeks, D. Beardsley; drill display.[9]

Besides piano, Edith's education included "scripture and English" for which she merited "distinction" (*Evesham Standard and West Midland Observer* Saturday,

COLLEGE OF PRECEPTORS.—The following pupils of Mrs. Cooper and the Misses Watts have gained certificates at the local examinations, in connection with the above College, held at Dresden House. Evesham on December 6th 7th, and 8th. 1904 :—Class III., Honours: Edith Bratt, Birmingham, distinction in scripture and English language.   Pass: Dorothy Clarke Bengeworth, distinction in scripture; Winifred Pepper, Evesham, distinction in English language; Emily Horseman. Salford Priors; Edith Byrd. Bengeworth; Ada L. Collins, Leigh. Manchester; Mabel E. Wealsby. Beckford; Dorothy Byrd. Evesham: Elsie Fisher, Evesham; Eunice Beach. Teddington.

Evesham Standard and West Midland Observer
(Saturday, February 4, 1905)

---

9 In the newspaper article, Miss Watts addressed the audience, "I would like to say a word to the parents who are present, and ask that they would send their children regularly to school. I know girls are very useful at home, and perhaps there are more temptations to stay away in the summer. At any rate the attendance last term has not been as good as we could wish." The usefulness of girls in maintaining the labor-intensive household routine was a serious obstacle to their obtaining an education all through the nineteenth century and into the twentieth (Rose 192).

February 4, 1905). While we do not know if Edith was taught any Latin, it would have helped Edith to perform with "distinction" in the English language. Dresden House had a tradition of offering Latin as the 1881 census documents a resident Latin teacher, and the 1891 census documents a theological student, who could have continued the school's tradition of offering Latin. Latin was part of a quality education but rarely offered to girls. Quality was what Dresden House presented. While a knowledge of Latin was not required for Catholics, a familiarity with Latin would have eased Edith's later conversion to Catholicism as the mass and all other liturgies were in Latin. Experience with Latin would also have created a basis for Edith to empathize with Ronald Tolkien's fascination with languages.

Edith's education would also include learning to dance. A capable Edwardian young lady would know waltz, polka, schottische, and quadrille, but not the foxtrot as it became fashionable later. In the Edwardian era (1901-1910), everyone danced.

> Every public space had a dance floor and regular live music; most restaurants had dancing; every hotel hosted regular dances; and you couldn't have a celebration or large social gathering without dancing […] You went down into the town hall on a Saturday night, and you all knew how to waltz and polka, and do a quad drill. Some people even knew how to do another 10, […] but the point was that the average person knew six or eight different kinds of dances, and that didn't change for a long time.[10]

A dance instructor probably came to the school. With all those pianists and violinists, providing music for dancing would not have been a problem.

While some students at Dresden House might have had a musical career in mind, Dresden House also appears to have been a finishing school for daughters of the well-to-do with a particular emphasis on music, piano, violin, and singing. Society expected an adept Edwardian young lady, when invited out, to contribute to and participate in the evening's entertainment with such accomplishments. Dresden House offered a rather posh and cultured setting, as it had a representative eighteenth-century townhouse garden including such

---

10 "When (And Why) Did We All Stop Learning How to Dance?" Andrew Fiouzi, last viewed on 6/1/2020. https://www.dollarshaveclub.com/content/story/when-and-why-did-we-all-stop-learning-how-to-dance.

features as a sundial from about 1720, a summerhouse, and a three-story garden house or "temple" dated about 1750 seen in the school photograph.

Nothing of the previously published information about Edith would suggest the distinction of the Dresden School. When Dresden House was recently offered for sale, the interior was described as having well-preserved contemporary features comprising a staircase (not shown) with twisted balusters, pine and oak paneling, door casings and doors in ground floor rooms and an angled fireplace in the room to the left of the entrance with a carved pine over-mantel. In his 1914 report, E.A.B. Barnard reports the first floor [American second floor] was originally one large drawing room, "now divided into two rooms, one of which has never been papered or painted since 1856, and yet the colours have scarcely faded at all, and the whole is in excellent condition." Edith would have seen this wallpaper in 1903-7. These large, first floor "reception rooms" would have been the place for the number of pianos which the girls needed for their music studies complete with metronomes and copies of Carl Czerny's (a pupil of Beethoven) exercise books or possibly the more modern C. L. Hanon's *The Virtuoso Pianist* (1900), as a serious piano student would know. Edith Bratt recalled a routine of getting up at 6 am to practice for two hours in unheated

One of Dresden House's first floor reception rooms
(Courtesy of Lukasz Rusiecki, Gallery Properties, Evesham)

rooms before breakfast (*TFA* 27). Even if the fires in the fireplaces had just been lit for the day, these would have supplied inefficient and inadequate heat from a modern point of view.

The 1901 census gives a likely picture of what the school was like when Edith arrived in 1903. Mrs. Cooper's nieces, Misses Alice and Kate Watt, listed as governesses, were running the school along with two other governesses and a housekeeper. Other resident staff included two housemaids, a laundry maid, and a kitchen maid. Servants did the menial work which was inappropriate for the middle-class students. The staff probably occupied the second or attic floor of the large two-story eighteenth-century wing, projecting to the rear at the south side, with its molded plaster ceilings. E.A.B. Barnard reports this wing was originally a one-story "Banquet Hall," later divided into two stories. "The doors of these rooms are massive, and they open on pivots in lieu of hinges. The mantelpieces here, and elsewhere in the house, are in imitation of the Adam's style, and are of plaster molded upon oak. Nearly all the rooms are paneled."[11]

Edith could enjoy the fine garden tucked behind Dresden House (as seen in the map below) with its tunnel leading down to a sunken expanse below the level of Dresden House.[12] The garden map shows the tunnel, clearly marked, which goes under Brick Kiln Street and emerges in the garden by means of steps. To the right (north) of the steps is the garden wall, marked in red, which cuts off the larger area that had previously been part of the garden. The dotted line represents a path. The semicircle by the steps may be the summerhouse. Part of the original garden boundary wall of local blue limestone is still found by Littleworth Street on the west, and the red boundary may also have been of this stone or alternately a hedge or fence. The "temple," which forms the background of the school group photograph, is likely to have been the round structure at the south base of the oval lawn bordered by trees. Placed at the

---

11 "The Story of Dresden House" by E.A.B Barnard (1914). Vale of Evesham Historical Society, last viewed on 5/31/2020.http://www.valeofeveshamhistory.org/articles/dresden-house.

12 Dresden House's address is on High Street. The designation of High Street indicated not only the main road with the main shops, but also that it was located on higher ground. Consequently, it is not surprising the rear garden occupied a much lower piece of ground. A number of the main "highways" in England follow ancient roads, e.g. the Roman Fosse Way and Watling Street, which were on top of the chalk downs so that one had a clear view of the surrounding countryside. These roads were literally the "high" ways.

other end of the oval, the sundial was likely to have anchored and created a much-prized view of the "temple."

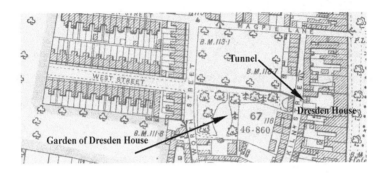

An annotated 1904 Ordnance Survey Map of Dresden House and its garden
(SH-K, National Library of Scotland)

An important part of Edith's life at Dresden House was the friends she made there. Both of the two friends, who are known, were younger than Edith. This may be because the older girls already had their cliques and/or Edith, being shorter and young-looking, fit in better with the younger girls. Molly Field was one of the friends we know about (*TFA* 30). Molly was a popular nickname in the 1800s and early 1900s, and Molly would have been how Mary Emily (census 1911) or Emily Mary (1891, 1901 census) Field was known to Edith Bratt. Molly lived at The Elm in Evesham, and she would have been a day student and not a boarder. She was born in 1892 making her three years younger than Edith Bratt. Her father was a market gardener, and Molly was the sixth of eight children. She had an older brother, George, who was born in 1890, making him one year younger than Edith Bratt. Edith would later become engaged to George Field (*Bio* 61).

Edith's "oldest" friend (*TFA* 67) was Mabel Moore (after her marriage, Mabel Sheaf) who was also three years younger than Edith (Haines-Bellamy).[13] Mabel can be positively identified because the recent photograph, seen below, of The Manor, where Mabel lived, matches Edith's photograph (*TFA* 67). The Manor

---

13 Recalling years later what they remember their mother saying, the Tolkien children report Edith and
  Mabel were both fourteen in 1903 (*TFA* 67).

An annotated 1903 Ordnance Survey Map of Evesham showing the relation
of Dresden House to Molly Field's home, The Elm
(SH-K, National Library of Scotland)

An Annotated 1903 Ordnance Survey Map of Hinton-on-the-Green with
Manor Farm (SH-K; National Library of Scotland)

is the remaining wing of an early seventeenth-century house burnt by Royalist
troops in the Civil War. Mabel was an only child and helped on the family
farm which they leased from the local church in nearby Hinton-on-the-Green
(Haines-Bellamy). She too was probably a day student at Dresden House as
Hinton-on-the-Green is only three miles from the school. Mabel Sheaf, née
Moore, and her husband, Frank, after living at The Manor for years, emigrated
to New Zealand in 1948 (Haines-Bellamy).

Edith "stayed in close contact" (*TFA* 67) with Mabel and would have known
her family. In the 1891 census, Mabel's husband-to-be, Frank Sheaf, was born
nearby Cleeve Prior. His father was a "Farmer and Malster" [*sic*]. In the 1911
census, Frank Sheaf was an unmarried market gardener living with his widowed
mother. Mabel and Frank Sheaf had at least one son, John Sheaf (1920-1968), so
we can assume they married by 1920 at the latest (Haines-Bellamy). Knowing

Mabel Moore's Home, The Manor, in Hinton-on-the-Green
(Google Earth)

Old country: John Sheaf with his grandmother, Betsy Moore
(Haines-Bellamy)

the family, Edith would certainly have met Mabel's mother, pictured above, and her son, John.

Having been "sent away" by her grandmother, Mrs. Jane Bratt (*TFA* 27), Edith was unlikely to go back to Birmingham for school holidays. If she stayed in Evesham, it is probable some of her new friends at Dresden House, including Molly Field and Mabel Moore, invited her to spend some of these holidays with their families. Being accepted and welcomed by other people now that her parents' shame was unknown, might have been an important experience for Edith.

At Dresden House, Edith began to enjoy playing the piano and probably had her first friends with whom she maintained contact for years (*TFA* 30, 67, 27). Edith could begin to see what choices and opportunities she might have, given her financial security as an heiress and with her past hidden. Edith may have stayed at Dresden House until she was 18, i.e. through the spring term of 1907. By January, 1908, Edith was living at the Faulkners' house in Birmingham. That move marked the beginning of another complete and exciting change in her life (*Bio* 38).

The Faulkners', Birmingham, 1908-1910

Edith probably left Dresden House School in 1907 after she turned eighteen. Stephen Gateley, then her guardian, faced the problem of finding a safe and respectable residence, where he could keep an eye on her. From Gateley's point of view, Edith was a marriageable young heiress who needed careful supervision to protect her from any unscrupulous fellow who would be interested in marrying her only for her money. As Edith Bratt's guardian, he appears to have taken a somewhat avuncular role, as opposed to maintaining a purely business relationship with Edith. Edith's keeping a photograph of Gateley (*TFA* 27) and Gateley's later sharing with Edith a letter written to him from her "Uncle" Jessop indicate a closer relationship.

Gateley chose a boarding house on Duchess Street run by Mrs. Faulkner, "an active member of the [Birmingham] Oratory parish" (*TFA* 26), where Father Francis Morgan resided (*Bio* 38).[1] Father Francis also chose this same residence when he decided his wards, the two young Tolkien brothers, needed a better home than the one provided by their Aunt Beatrice Suffield (*Bio* 38, *TFA* 25). Gateley, a solicitor, who had handled both Alfred Warrillow's and Fannie Bratt's wills, was almost certainly Roman Catholic as he was married in St. Chad's Roman Catholic cathedral in Birmingham. He also was a solicitor for

---

1 Mrs. Faulkner was previously the manager of the Dorothy Restaurant on Oxford Street, London (1891 census). Several of Madame Blavatsky's Theosophy disciples owned this restaurant and used it to promote Theosophical doctrines from 1890 until 1895 (A.L.C. 533). It was unique and almost-revolutionary in serving only women. Mrs. Oscar Wilde was a frequent customer. *The Theosophist* reports Mrs. Faulkner joined the Theosophists at that time.
Carpenter writes that Louis Faulkner was "a wine-merchant with a taste for his own wares" (*Bio* 38). Bru reports rather that Mr. Faulkner was a partner in Faulkner & Co., Continental Carriers (88). This was probably a shipping company which carried consignments of wine. Carpenter's aside of "a taste for his own wares" may have been a way of introducing Mr. Faulkner's drinking habits. Tolkien is likely to have noticed this consumption as he seems to express his poor opinion of his Uncle Walter Incledon's drinking in his comment, "drinks like a fish," in *Roverandom* (74, Bunting, "*Roverandom*, Part II" 7).

the Roman Catholic Archdioceses of Birmingham.[2] With a history of persecution, Catholics tended to associate and favor business with other Catholics. This may have been part of why Gateley chose this "genteel" residence, run by a Catholic whose reputation was vouched for by his co-religionists.

The bankruptcy notices of 1907 list Mr. Louis Faulkner of 37 Duchess Road, Birmingham as going out of business.[3] Mrs. Faulkner probably started taking in boarders to help make ends meet.

By January 1908, Edith was a boarder, living at the Faulkners' house in Birmingham (*Bio* 38). Edith was not particularly happy at the Faulkners after all the friends and fun of Dresden House in Evesham. Mrs. Faulkner was happy to have Edith accompany soloists at her musical soirees, but she objected to actual piano practice (*Bio* 38-39). Edith would retreat to her room and her sewing machine. Any outing had to be chaperoned or circumspect, for example when Edith went to a matinee at Birmingham's Theatre Royal she was instructed to take a book to read during the intermission to discourage strangers from talking to her (*TFA* 28). Edith would have been pleased to have some other young people as boarders. Otherwise, there was only the fifty-four-year-old Mrs. Louisa Faulkner; her sixty-four-year-old husband Louis Faulkner; their unmarried daughter, twenty-nine-year-old Helen; and Annie Gollins, the maid (*Bio* 38, 1911 census). Edith was still in touch with her "substitute mother," Jennie Grove (*TFA* 36), in 1911, and she was able to ride her bicycle to visit her (Bio 41) as Jennie was working as a domestic and a boarder in Handsworth not far from the Warrillow house on Heathfield (1911 census). Because of her close relationship with Jennie, Edith may have been open to considering Annie Gollins, someone about her own age, (*C&G* 2.458), as more than just a maid.

In January 1908, the Tolkien brothers arrived from their Aunt Beatrice Suffield's house and were given the bedroom directly above Edith's at the Faulkners' (*Bio* 39-40). Young Ronald Tolkien would have just turned sixteen in 1908 and he

---

2 "Stephen Gateley." The Archdiocese of Birmingham Archives, last viewed on 6/9/2020. https://www. birminghamarchdiocesanarchives.org.uk/archives_index.asp?searchstring=Stephen%20Gateley&searchs tringand=%&searchparishlo=0&searchparishhi=99999999&searchcollectionlo=0&searchcollectionhi= 99999999#results.

3 Announcement in *London Gazette* Jan. 4. 1907 issue 27983 p. 150. "Louis Faulkner." London Gazette, last viewed on 6/11/2020. https://www.thegazette.co.uk/all-notices/notice?service=all-notices&text=Louis+Faulkner.

was already in the First or Senior Class at King Edward's School. He is likely to have taken notice of Edith immediately. She had the same name as his Catholic godmother and aunt, Edith Mary Incledon. His ears also would probably have perked up hearing Edith had been at Dresden House in Evesham. Ronald knew his mother's family, the Suffields, had lived in that area for generations. Ronald Tolkien cherished that heritage and identified himself strongly with his Suffield background (*Letters* 54, 213). Ronald's brother, Hilary, had musical interests and played the flute.[4] Hilary and Edith may have shared musical interests or performed duets. Edith had been an orphan for five years and Ronald Tolkien for four years. Ronald may have seen her as a friend (*Bio* 39), like his Incledon cousins, Mary and Marjorie. With Ronald Tolkien, Edith Bratt could have fun, namely throwing sugar lumps from a tea shop balcony down into the hats of unknowing pedestrians (*Bio* 40). They went for bicycle rides and had fireside chats (*Bio* 40).

They became friendly (*Bio* 39), but their serious relationship seems to have been sparked by Edith's reaction to Ronald and Hilary seemingly not getting quite enough to eat and being hungry (Grotta-Kurska 24). This report of persistent hunger is puzzling, though growing teenage boys have proverbially been known to eat their families "out of house and home." However, it is very hard to believe the kind Father Francis Morgan, whose caring and generosity were well known (Bru 59, 65), would have placed Ronald and Hilary in a house where they would have been persistently underfed. Father Francis Morgan had inquired about the happiness of the Tolkien boys at their Aunt Beatrice's house so it is likely he continued to monitor their happiness at the new lodgings on Duchess Street.

---

4 This information is from notes on Angela Gardner's paper on Hilary Tolkien given at "The Return of the Ring" conference, Loughborough University, 2012. Hilary was a skilled and talented musician playing several instruments: flute, small trumpet, piano (personal email from Elizabeth Currie 3/26/16). Flute playing appears in some of Tolkien's earliest work, e.g. the poem, *Tingfang Warble*, and the 1915 Gnomish Lexicon entries: Dairon "the fluter," (29) and 'thimli' 'whistle or piccolo' or earlier 'thimpa' 'a whistle' or 'flute', 'thimpion' or 'thibinweg' 'a piper', 'thimpa-' 'to play a flute or whistle' 'thimp' 'the stop on a flute', and' 'thibindon' 'flute-playing' (73).

Suffield Family Funeral Plaque of 1706/1713 in the Evesham Church
(Courtesy of Steve Ponty)

The likely answer is that in early 1909 the Tolkien brothers had become involved in the new Boy Scout troops sponsored by the Birmingham Oratory: "three patrols of Scouts under the Brothers Tolkien" marched in the Easter Monday Parade in May 1909.[5] The Tolkien brothers' Boy Scouts activities would have brought about a change in their situation at the Faulkner boarding house. Ronald and his brother were the leaders of three patrols, and there would be six to seven boys in a patrol (Baden-Powell 35). The Boy Scouts were to build "endurance" as a scout was to be "strong, healthy, and active. It means a lot of exercise, like playing games, running, walking, cycling, and so on" (Baden-Powell 26-27). Recommended games included building snow forts or huts or clearing snow from pavement in the winter and going miles on patrol or following previously laid trails, not to mention camping or hiking fifteen miles to earn a badge (Baden-Powell 53, 87). Ronald Tolkien also had joined the King Edward's School Officer Training Corps by April 1907 at the age of fifteen, though he is not known to have gone on summer field exercises until 1909

---

5 "Tolkien." The Oratory, Birmingham, last viewed on 6/3/2020. www.Birmingham-oratory.org. uk.TheOratory/Tolkien.

(*C&G* 1.14, 1.17). This kind of exertion, tramping through woods, marching and camping, would have left Ronald ravenous.

Ronald Tolkien's hunger may have recalled painful memories from his mother's illness. The period of time, before Ronald's mother went to the hospital and was diagnosed with diabetes, could have left memories which combined a time of hunger with his mother's impaired mental functioning (Bunting, "Spiders. Part I and II"). Tolkien's writings are filled with episodes of great hunger which could reflect his personal, childhood sufferings which "records do not record" (*Letters* 420): Beren, with whom Tolkien explicitly identified, journeys through Taur-na-Fuin where there is "no food" and "death only" (*S* 164); Thorin's party suffers hunger and thirst in Mirkwood, a doppelgänger of Taur-na-Fuin (Rateliff 219); the child-like Bilbo Baggins is hungry in the Elvenking's halls; and Sam and Frodo endure painful hunger and thirst crossing Mordor over the plateau of Gorgoroth. Repeated episodes of hunger at the Faulkners' may have triggered a recall of Ronald's painful and probably traumatic memories with their intense and contradictory feelings concerning his mother from the hunger time of 1904.

In early 1904, young J.R.R. Tolkien came down with the measles and whooping cough which his brother had. Consequently, he could no longer go to the store or get groceries as he had since approximately late November 1903 when his mother became housebound due to her undiagnosed diabetes (*Bio* 28-29). By March 1904, Ronald Tolkien, his brother Hilary and his mother, Mabel Tolkien, were all likely to be suffering from hunger. Mabel Tolkien, as her calorie intake dropped below 1200 calories, would have gone into an ongoing, protracted state of diabetic hypoglycemia (or low blood sugar). The clinical literature on diabetes reports diabetic hypoglycemia can result in mental disturbances, including unexplained outbursts of anger, periods of detachment, bizarre fugue-like states as well as episodic confusion (Jefferson and Marshall 167).[6] In a fugue state,

---

6 A "fugue state," in recent terminology, has been redefined to include only "purposeful travel or bewildered wandering that is associated with amnesia for identity or for other important autobiographical information" (DSM-5 298). In this new nomenclature, the effect of the diabetic psychosis would now be a "dissociative amnesia" to highlight the inability to recall important autobiographical information, inconsistent with ordinary forgetting. This amnesia can be "localized" for forgetting events of a circumscribed period of time or "generalized" when a person forgets their own identity. With the establishment of a normal level of blood sugar, the amnesia of a diabetic psychosis, resolves.

or a state of dissociative amnesia as it would be labeled now, Mabel Tolkien would not have known she was Mabel Tolkien, but rather would have believed she was someone else who would not have recognized Ronald and Hilary as her own children. "Tremor, irritability, increasing confusion, delirium, or frank psychosis may follow" in this state (Kaplan and Sadock 199).

With today's well-controlled insulin treatment, most people with diabetes run the risk of high blood sugar levels due to the overabundance of sugary calories in the modern diet. Blood sugar swings with hypoglycemia can create scenes which have almost disappeared. Something as simple and seemingly innocuous as skipping or delaying a meal could be enough to induce hypoglycemia. Old case records, like this one from the early 1920s, document what it was like: a patient

> during a meal, pressed his friends, to help themselves to more pepper. Then in a loud voice, he insulted his wife, who, realising he was hypoglycemic, asked him to take some sugar. He replied that, of course, she wanted him to take sugar, so that she could get rid of him and marry someone else. Eventually he was forced to take sugar, became normal within a few minutes, and had no recollection of what had happened. (Tattersall 69)[7]

---

7 Tolkien repeatedly depicts this kind of dramatic recognition of someone after an altered state of consciousness throughout *The Lord of the Rings*. The first instance of this reorientation occurs when Merry awakens in the tomb of the Barrow wight saying, "The men of Carn Dum came on us at night, and we were worsted. Ah! The spear in my heart!" Then, "What am I saying? I have been dreaming" (*FR* I 8 154). This scene is parallel to the scene in the tombs when Denethor, emerging from his "trance" of "madness," recognizes his son Faramir, and "the flame died in his eyes" just as Gandalf promised: "Your father loves you, Faramir, and will remember it ere the end" (*RK* V 7 128, V 4 90). The other examples of fleeting lack of recognition because of a "passing madness" occur in relation to the Ring. When Bilbo asks to see the Ring in Rivendell, Frodo, "feeling a strange reluctance" finds suddenly "To his distress and amazement [...] that he was no longer looking at Bilbo, a shadow seemed to have fallen between them and through it he found himself eyeing a little wrinkled creature with a hungry face and bony groping hands. He felt a desire to strike him" (*FR* II 2 244). Boromir levels paranoid accusations at Frodo: "Miserable trickster! [...] You will take the Ring to Sauron and sell us all. You have only waited your chance to leave us in the lurch. Curse you and all halflings to death and darkness!" (*FR* II 10 415-16). He then "passed his hand over his eyes, dashing away the tears. 'What have I said? He cried. 'What have I done? [...] A madness took me, but it has passed.'" (*FR* II 10 416). When Sam returns the Ring to Frodo in the Tower of Cirith Ungol: "Sam had changed before his very eyes into an orc again, leering and pawing at his treasure, a foul little creature with greedy eyes and slobbering mouth. But now the vision had passed" [...] "The hideous vision had seemed so real to him" (*RK* VI 1 188).
   An attenuated version of this effect occurs when Gandalf releases Théoden from the spell of Wormtongue's "twisted tales and crooked promptings," which had blinded and disabled Théoden. This enables Théoden to recognize the reality of his situation (*TT* III 6 119). This motif reoccurs when Théoden breaks the spell of Saruman's rhetoric and voice after the Battle of Helm's Deep, by proclaiming the reality of Saruman's evil and corruption (*TT* III 10 185).

Not all intermittent episodes of hypoglycemia lead to forgetting, but the modern physician is trained to watch for this. However, imagine this situation with Mabel Tolkien, except she had not been diagnosed with diabetes and hypoglycemia and no one knew the appropriate management. Her sons could have only felt confused, helpless, bewildered, and frightened by her sudden anger and later forgetting and/or vehement denial of such an episode. Mabel Tolkien's unpredictable lashing out would have left troubling memories. She could have leveled unfounded, paranoid accusations like the patient in the case history, i.e. "she could get rid of him and marry someone else."

Edith probably had gone hungry at her foster home. As a result, she was likely to have known the telltale signs of hunger: how one watched the clock for mealtime; the pinched, pained look, occasioned by hunger; and how anxious eyes followed the filling of the plates. Also, Edith may have been disciplined by the popular method of withholding of food (Rose 231). In response to Ronald's situation, Edith persuaded Annie, the maid, to bootleg food from the kitchen via the dumbwaiter (Grotta-Kurska 24). Also, when "the Old Lady," Mrs. Faulkner, was out, the Tolkien brothers would go to Edith's room for secret feasts (*Bio* 39).[8] Not only was the initial friendship augmented by a conspiracy against adult authority, consistent with Tolkien's known dislike of being "bossed around" (Morton and Hayes 51), but Edith was very likely to be genuinely concerned about Ronald's distress. The clandestine supplemental food arrangement reportedly "worked well for months" (Grotta-Kurska 24).

How could Ronald, an orphan, not be touched by such an act of unselfish caring? Edith's creative and surreptitious response to Ronald's hunger was probably needed during the busy summer of 1909. Ronald Tolkien had late spring/early summer Boy Scout exercises, as well as field exercises during Summer term and the camp of July 27 to August 4 with the King Edward's School Officers' Training Corps (*C&G* 1.27-28). Finding in Edith someone he could depend on may have been part of what "led to their decision" in the summer of 1909 that they were in love (*Bio* 40). In 1909, Edith gave Ronald a picture of herself at the

---

8 Later in life, Edith expected "the [Tolkien] children to eat up every scrap," and Carpenter labels this as "authoritarianism" (156). However, not only was the expectation children would clean their plates common in the 1920s and 1930s, "because think of all those starving children in China," but this may also reflect a different context given Edith's likely history of deprivation growing up.

age of seventeen, "as a keepsake at the beginning of their romance" (McIlwaine 146-7). She was Ronald's "first – and only – love" (Grotta-Kurska 23).

Something else was likely to be leading to a closer relationship: Edith may have learned about Tolkien's nightmare of the "Great Wave" (*Bio* 23; *Letters* 213, 347). The Victorians and Edwardians placed great faith in the powers of fresh air, and bedroom windows were habitually left open.[9] With the windows open, Tolkien could hear Edith's "private whistle-call" and they had "absurd long window talks" (*Bio* 40). In the same way, Edith could have heard the young Tolkien repeatedly cry out in his sleep as he awakened gasping from his nightmares (*Letters* 347). Edith had noticed and then responded to Ronald's hunger, and her kind and sympathetic concern about the unhappiness evident in his nightmares may have fostered Ronald's trust in her. By that summer of 1909 when Ronald Tolkien felt he was in love, he may have confided some of the painful experiences which resulted in his suffering "a terrible chaos which darkened my youth and early manhood" (McIlwaine 170, *Bio* 31). Edith's ability to arrange and maintain an illicit food operation is likely to have convinced Ronald he could trust Edith to keep a confidence. Given Edith's empathy and concern, Ronald is likely to have believed she would guard his own previously unspoken secrets.

Sharing secrets was likely to be a big step for Ronald. Tolkien was a private person and knew how to keep a secret: he learned to be careful about "giving myself away" ("Secret Vice" 213) or revealing his "mad hobby" of invented languages which began in childhood (*Letters* 8). Neither Tolkien's family nor his friends knew about Edith or the meaning of Tolkien's 1912 Christmas play, *The Bloodhound, the Chef, and the Suffragette* (*Bio* 61). Tolkien only revealed the complete surprise of Edith's existence to his amazed friends in his literary group, the TCBS (Tea Club Barrovian Society), in late December 1913, when the couple was to be betrothed in the Catholic Church on January 8, 1914. Even then Rob Gilson had to write on January 5, 1914, to ask if Tolkien would "reveal the lady's name" (*C&G* 1.56, *Great War* 33). Again, Tolkien was so close-mouthed with his Aunt Jane Neave that when *The Hobbit* was published

---

9   Florence Nightingale extolled the virtues of fresh air. British Library, Victorian Britain. "Health and Hygiene in the 19th century." Last viewed on 6/3/2020. https://www.bl.uk/victorian-britain/articles/health-and-hygiene-in-the-19th-century.

in 1937, she wrote "to all but demand instant enlightenment" as she knew
nothing about this book (Priestman 50).

Another of Tolkien's secrets was his polished manuscript of "The New Lay
of Gudrún" or "Guðrúnarkviða en nýja," published as part of *The Legend of
Sigurd and Gudrún*. This work from the early 1930s had an audience and an
interested publisher. It could have been the solution to academic and financial pressure on Tolkien to publish. However, Tolkien uncharacteristically
destroyed most of his drafts, never quoted from or referred to the "New Lays"
as he did with many of his other unpublished works, and tucked the manuscript away for more than thirty years (*Legend* 4-5), possibly because it was
linked too closely with memories and thoughts about his mother (Bunting,
"Finding Tolkien" 80-82).

Several others saw Tolkien as guarded and evasive, though they described it in
different ways, i.e. the way someone might act if they were avoiding talking
about certain topics. Brace described Tolkien as "cagy" in interviews. Tolkien
redefined words and recontextualized what he said (Lee 160-61, *Letters* 372-78)
and avoided some topics (Lee 133-34). Tom Shippey points out Tolkien's claim
that "more than one poem in recent years [...] has been inspired by the dragon
of *Beowulf*" ("Beowulf: the Monsters" 16). But Tolkien's misleading phrase,
"more than one," actually meant "exactly two, his own *Iumonna Gold Galdre
Beweunden* and C.S. Lewis' *Once the worm-laid egg*" (Shippey, *Roots* 3). This is
just one example of "Tolkien's mind [...] of unmatchable subtlety, not without
a streak of deliberate guile" (Shippey, *Road* 5). C.S. Lewis wrote to his brother
in 1939 that "Tolkien's trials, besides being frequent and severe, are usually of
such a complicated nature as to be impenetrable" (Kilby 33). Clyde Kilby wrote:

> Tolkien was like an iceberg [...] with much more below the surface [than
> above]. In this one was aware of a single totality but equally aware at various
> levels of a kind of consistent inconsistency that was [...] developed, almost
> deliberate, even enjoyed. (4)

The idea of a "secret" would agree with what Tolkien wrote when discussing
himself and his wife: "someone close in heart to me should know something about
the things that *records do not record: the dreadful sufferings of our childhoods*, from
which we rescued one another, but could not wholly heal wounds that later often

proved disabling" (*Letters* 421, italics added). Tolkien's literary executor and editor, his son, Christopher Tolkien, required the biographer, Humphrey Carpenter, to rewrite his original draft of the official biography. Carpenter stated he "cut out everything which was likely to be contentious." He added that asking someone to write a biography is "a bit like inviting a private detective to investigate your family secrets" ("Learning" 270, 271). Carpenter does not and cannot explicitly say writing Tolkien's biography led to unearthing family secrets, as he was almost certainly bound by a Nondisclosure Agreement as is everyone who has access to the Tolkien archives (Testi 97). Carpenter repeatedly implied there were omissions or possibly "secrets" ("Review", *Bio* 260). If Ronald Tolkien shared his dark and painful childhood memories, then Edith is likely to have reciprocated, but not to the extent of sharing her darkest secret, her illegitimacy. Edith only revealed this to him after they were married and when exposed by her inability to complete the marriage register (*Bio* 79).

This 1909 relationship with Edith seemed to help Ronald thrive. In the fall term of 1909, Ronald Tolkien became more outgoing and involved in school, making his maiden Debating Speech on October 8, 1909, advocating for "the Militant Suffragette," "with much wordplay," though "marred by a faulty delivery" (*C&G* 1.18-19, *Bio* 40). This unexpected topic for a debate at an all-male school may have reflected his new relationship with Edith. This suspicion is supported by Tolkien's play of December 1912, *The Bloodhound, the Chef, and the Suffragette*, based on his anticipated reunion with Edith Bratt (*Bio* 59). The lost heiress of the play, Gwendoline Goodchild, is an avatar of Edith and is almost certainly the play's eponymous "Suffragette." The name 'Gwendoline' is Welsh for 'Fair Browed', and Tolkien fondly remembered his wife's bright eyes (*Letters* 420). Ronald Tolkien would have known the name 'Edith' is from Middle English and means 'happy', 'blessed' or 'prosperous'. Consequently, it was quite appropriate for the name of an heiress. Food, a reference to the link which first brought them together, figures in the play as there is "the Chef." This last character is possibly the penniless student (a thinly disguised J.RR. Tolkien), who lived in the same lodging-house as Edith/Gwendoline and with whom she has fallen in love.

Tolkien also played in King Edward's School Rugby First XV for the first time on October 26, 1909 and received "2nd Team colours" (*C&G* 1.19). Tolkien wrote years later that his relationship with Edith spurred his performance on the field: "Having the romantic upbringing, I made a boy-and-girl affair serious, and made it the source of effort" (*Letters* 52).

However, "[t]oward the end of the autumn term of 1909," that is around late November or even in early December (*Bio* 41), before the December 13-17 Oxford scholarship examination (Priestman 25), Ronald Tolkien and Edith Bratt colluded to leave the Faulkners' on their bicycles at different times and gave notice of different destinations.[10] After meeting away from watching eyes, they rode together at least ten miles to and through the Lickey Hills and had tea at a house in Rednal where Ronald had stayed previously when he was working on his scholarship (*Bio* 41). The lady who served tea told Mrs. Church at the Rednal Oratory House. Mrs. Church knew the Tolkien boys from 1904 when they and their mother lived at the postman's house in Rednal (H. Tolkien 26). Mrs. Church then told the Oratory cook, who, of course, told Tolkien's guardian, Father Francis Morgan.

When upon further inquiry, Father Francis Morgan learned of Edith and Ronald's other meetings, he realized the extent of young Tolkien's deception and his clandestine relationship with Edith, if only through Ronald's silence, and demanded the "*affair* should stop" (*Bio* 41, italics added). Whatever else Father Francis Morgan might have learned from Ronald Tolkien or the other parties at the Faulkners', knowing Ronald Tolkien had seen Edith in her "little white nightgown" was probably enough to make the good man choke figuratively, if not literally (*Bio* 40). A confession of kissing would have created a demand for immediate action (*Bio* 40). The standard of the time, a chaperoned visit would have only allowed a fleeting touch of a sleeve or fingertips (*Bio* 9). At that point, we can infer that it is likely Father Francis Morgan would have seen the sexual aspect of Ronald and Edith's relationship as the explanation for

---

10 In the Victorian period until the advent of the "safety" bicycle in the 1890s, women's "lives were very circumscribed – they were supposed to stay home and take care of the family." But soon women were 30 percent of all cyclists, riding bicycles to visit friends and travel the countryside. *The Minneapolis Tribune* wrote, "A woman awheel is an independent creature, free to go where she will." The 1896 *Scientific American* observed, "As a social revolutioniser it has never had an equal." In 1896, the suffragist Susan B. Anthony said, "I think [bicycling] has done more to emancipate woman than any one thing in the world." Women finally could go where they wanted, on their own. Rather than being chaperoned at home, young women could meet potential partners without supervision. *Smithsonian Magazine*, last viewed on 6/3/2020. https://www.smithsonianmag.com/innovation/fight-scooters-common-19th-century-battle-over-bicycles-180973510/#VAWyiWSs3rcXlLzT.99.

Ronald's reticence and deception. We have no reason to believe Father Francis Morgan, a man who regularly heard confessions as part of his duties, was so naive as to underestimate the rashness of impassioned adolescents.[11] There is no indication that either of the pair gave any sign of regret except for getting caught. It is probable that, to Father Francis Morgan's specifically Catholic religious mind, Ronald had succumbed to the sin of lust, a gateway to depravity, risking a downward spiral beginning with some kind of carnal knowledge and dishonesty which could lead to mortal sin.[12]

While Carpenter's biography emphasizes Father Francis Morgan's fears about Tolkien's academic future (*Bio* 41, 43), this presentation of the episode spins Father Francis Morgan's probable real concerns, namely that a pretty, Protestant temptress might be leading young Tolkien away from his Catholic faith and a requisite Catholic marriage (*Letters* 52). This is not to mention the dread of an unplanned pregnancy which would require Ronald to marry and have no chance of getting the education he needed in order to provide a middle-class life for his wife. Carpenter's shift of focus is too narrow and consequently misleading about the full picture of what was happening in Tolkien's life.

Father Francis Morgan probably took the reasonable step of informing Stephen Gateley, Edith's guardian, about this predicament. As "the adults in the room," the two Catholic guardians would have been focused on heading off what they would have seen as a predictable, slow-motion train wreck. Cognizant of the mores and realities of Edwardian England and sincerely concerned about the long-term best interests of their respective wards, Father Francis Morgan and Stephen Gateley would almost certainly have consulted, collaborated, and coordinated their plans to hopefully avert this crisis. We can infer that Mrs. Faulkner, a member of the Oratory parish, would have been informed of the situation. She is likely to have been alarmed at the risk of any hint of impropriety marring the reputation of her new establishment. As a result, she would have been relieved to hear of Father Francis Morgan's

---

11 "Fathers and Brothers. Father Francis Morgan." Birmingham Oratory, last viewed on 6/4/2020. https://www.birminghamoratory.org.uk/francis-morgan/.

12 See an earlier, but comparable, Protestant view of this evolution in William Hogarth's (1697-1764) popular *A Rake's Progress*.

plans to promptly remove the Tolkien brothers. She was probably enlisted in safeguarding Edith in the interim.

Stephen Gateley would have been in a difficult position given the history of Edith's mother. As Alfred Warrillow's solicitor, Gateley would have known Fannie Bratt and Alfred Warrillow's affair led to Alfred leaving the bulk of his estate to Fannie and to the birth of Edith Bratt. Gateley may have also known more details about the Warrillow separation. One can imagine that, in spite of the handsome fee he received for serving as Edith's guardian, Stephen Gateley regretted ever agreeing to accept Edith as his ward, given this fiasco with Ronald Tolkien which might sully his reputation. While Gateley is likely to have blamed Edith for her provocative behavior, he may also have suspected young Tolkien was nothing but an opportunistic gold digger, i.e. planning to compromise Edith in order to marry her for her money. Gateley also knew his options were limited as Edith would soon be of age in January, 1910. While Edith might say she was in love and Ronald had made "declarations and promises," possibly of a future marriage (*Bio* 61), Gateley could sagely point out Ronald was not of legal age to marry. Edith, however, had not made any reciprocal "vow" to Ronald Tolkien (*Letters* 53). Given that Ronald was a Catholic with a priest of the Oratory as his guardian, the probably Catholic Gateley may not have been opposed to a Catholic marriage for Edith.

As a lawyer practiced in assessing liabilities, Gateley would have pointed out that Mrs. Faulkner would have been within her rights to press charges of theft for the food Edith stole. Gateley could assure Edith he would handle that problem with a generous reimbursement. He could have continued that since Edith had now made herself unwelcome at the Faulkners' boarding house due to her unacceptable behavior, Gateley would have to find another residence. He may have tapped the network of Alfred Warrillow's friends to find the solicitor, Charles H. Jessop, as a suitable, out-of-town escape from such an alarming debacle with young Tolkien. Whether Edith was willing to wait for Ronald to become twenty-one to marry her was her decision.

The speed with which Father Francis Morgan acted to arrange new accommodations for the Tolkien brothers is an indication of how seriously he took the situation. Ronald Tolkien left Birmingham to go to Oxford to sit for his entrance examination of December 13-17, 1909. He "was not allowed to return to Duchess Road [i.e. the Faulkners'] afterward" (Priestman 25). Father Francis Morgan may have lodged him at the Oratory to keep him "quarantined" during the Christmas holiday. Or since there were probably already plans for the Tolkien brothers to spend part of the Christmas holiday with Ronald's godmother and aunt, May Incledon, and her family in Barnt Green, that visit may simply have been extended. The Tolkien brothers then spent "a few days in January 1910 at 11 Frederick Road" (Priestman 25) before moving to lodgings with Thomas and Julia McSherry on Highfield Road, Edgbaston (*C&G* 1.21). Ronald Tolkien's level of distress about his situation can be judged by his later report that "the combined tensions" of "work for (a very necessary) Oxford scholarship" and the "absorbing and nervously exhausting" uproar over his relationship with Edith "nearly produced a bad breakdown" (*Letters* 52). In his first surviving diary, Tolkien wrote, "Depressed and as much in dark as ever" on January 1, 1910 (*Bio* 42). However, the McSherrys' house was not far from the Faulkners' house on Duchess Street (*Bio* 42), 0.9 miles according to Google, creating a situation where Ronald and Edith could still be in contact.

Carpenter's comments that Ronald Tolkien did not simply disobey Father Francis Morgan by openly continuing the romance and that he was not "a rebellious young man" seem disingenuous (*Bio* 41). Rebellion and open disobedience, of course, would have been folly given Ronald's legal and financial situation. However, Ronald employed deception to hide his defiance of repeatedly meeting and writing to Edith. There is no evidence Ronald Tolkien saw anything that he and Edith had done as wrong. Nor is there evidence he was either repentant or contrite. Ronald Tolkien did not like being "boss[ed] about" (Morton and Hayes 51).

On January 20, 1910, Edith and Ronald met secretly in the afternoon, "taking a train into the countryside and discussing their plans" (*Bio* 42, *C&G* 1.21). They also stopped at E.H. Lawley and Sons, a jewelry shop in Birmingham. Edith bought Ronald a pen as a belated birthday present and he bought Edith a wristwatch as a twenty-first birthday present, both gifts costing 10 shillings 6 pence. The matching costs could have been the result of Edith's intervention. Ronald was acutely aware of her status as an heiress, particularly on her twenty-first birthday. Edith could certainly afford to pay far more than Ronald could. Edith appears to have created an arrangement which spared Ronald any embarrassment about his financial situation. The result was that Ronald got a handsome pen and Edith got a modest watch.

The next day Ronald and Edith met at a tea shop to celebrate Edith's twenty-first birthday (*C&G* 1.21). Edith was now free of her guardian, Stephen Gateley. She had decided to accept an invitation to live in Charlton Kings, near Cheltenham, with Charles H. Jessop, a solicitor, and his wife, an "elderly family friend" (*C&G* 1.21). It would be surprising if this invitation, a *deus ex machina*, arrived just at the right time without some nudge from Stephen Gateley, who knew the gravity of Edith's position in relation to Ronald Tolkien. In persuading Edith to accept this solution, Gateley's best argument probably would have been that Ronald Tolkien was in no position to marry Edith for three years and that she needed to be in a new setting which would preserve her reputation and provide a respectable cover story for her parentage.

Father Francis Morgan, via the quite efficient Edwardian grapevine, learned of their meeting at the tea shop and demanded Ronald not see or write Edith again except on the day of her departure, March 2 (*Bio* 43). However, Ronald Tolkien saw Edith "accidentally" on February 16 at the Prince of Wales Theatre and again on February 21 and 23 (*Bio* 43).[13] Could all of these rendezvous be "accidental?" This last occasion occurred when Edith was coming from the (presumably) Anglican Cathedral where she had gone "to pray for [Ronald]" (*Bio* 43). Tolkien continued to be defiant and "in bad faith," as one might say now, in relation to Father Francis Morgan. Ronald was pushing the limits of his guardian's patience and tolerance and was risking being found out. On February 26, Father Francis Morgan wrote Ronald that he had been seen again with Edith, which was "evil and foolish" and threatened that his university career would be cut short if he continued to see or write her (*Bio* 43). Again, ignoring the limits set by Father Francis Morgan, Tolkien wrote Edith about his guardian's demands. In response, Edith wrote, "Our hardest time of all has come" (*Bio* 43).

---

13 Maggie Burns argues that "Prince of Wales" here refers to the Prince of Wales Theatre on Broad Street, which was on the route from Tolkien and Edith's residences as opposed to any of the several Prince of Wales pubs in Birmingham. It would have been inappropriate for a single, middle-class young lady to enter a pub, and Tolkien would not have gone to any of these establishments at lunchtime on a school day (*C&G* 1.819).

Later in 1941, faced with his own son's struggles with romance, sexuality, and Catholicism, Tolkien was not proud of his behavior of 1909 and 1910. He wrote that his early history with Edith Bratt was "so exceptional, so wrong and imprudent in every point" (*Letters* 52). Referring years later to their separation, Tolkien wrote, "it was very hard on *my lover*" (italics added). He notably did not refer to Edith as "my beloved" or "my dear one" or "my intended" or "your mother." Tolkien also wrote, "I did not see or write to *my lover*" (*Letters* 53, italics added). Tolkien's repeated characterization of his relationship with Edith as his "lover" changes the context of his other statements that this was an "affair" or a "love-affair" (*Letters* 52-53). The couple's relationship was in some way a physical relationship, "evil and foolish," if only based on a few kisses. What matters here is Tolkien's views, both in 1909 and 1910, and in 1941 and later. In his 1972 letter to his son Christopher, Tolkien wanted him to know "things that records do not record: […] the sufferings that we endured after our [Ronald and Edith's] love began – all of which (over and above our personal weaknesses) might help to make pardonable, or understandable, the lapses and darknesses which at times marred our lives" (*Letters* 421). Tolkien here wrestles with "personal weaknesses" which resulted in "lapses and darknesses" which he hopes are "pardonable or understandable." Tolkien struggled with the need for the "painful and bitter" separation, justifying it by writing "probably nothing else would have hardened the will enough to give such an affair (however genuine a case of true love) permanence" (*Letters* 53).

The twenty-first century reader has a very different frame of reference about what constitutes acceptable dating and sexual behavior. This modern understanding cannot be used to judge Ronald Tolkien's and Edith Bratt's behavior in 1909/1910. Further, the contemporary reader should be cautious in assessing this story as there is presently only scanty and inadequate information on which to base an informed opinion about this situation.

Tolkien's heirs evidently agreed with their father's judgment, expressed from a perspective of maturity, on the early relationship between their parents. Ronald Tolkien, raised as a Victorian whose society did not mention sexual or execratory subjects in polite company, would not want his sexual behavior scrutinized or discussed by anyone. Further, he would want to protect Edith, whose illegitimacy and its stigma had stunted and overshadowed her life. One can hardly blame the Estate for not wanting to expose such an impetuous history of youthful and passionate indiscretion. As a result, it is not surprising Carpenter's first draft of the biography was "unacceptable," and he then eliminated what was likely to be contentious (270).[14]

To render the romance of Edith Bratt and Ronald Tolkien sufficiently conventional, Carpenter would have had to cut and/or minimize almost all mention of Edith's wealth, which made her a vulnerable target of inappropriate advances. He then would have replaced that information with repeated statements about Edith's plans for a music career which was, in fact, unnecessary for her financial security. Carpenter deleted any mention of the sufferings of Edith and Ronald's respective childhoods which brought the two together. He hid Edith's reality with the statement: "Edith's childhood had been moderately happy" (*Bio* 39). Carpenter avoided stating directly the risqué and socially unacceptable level of Edith and Ronald's intimacy in 1909. He reinterpreted Tolkien's stubborn and repeated defiance of, and dishonesty in relation to his guardian by describing Father Francis Morgan's opposition as implicitly an autocratic overreaction. Carpenter blurred the specifics of the crucial time sequence of the date of the fateful bicycle ride and when Father Francis Morgan precipitously moved the Tolkien brothers with a vague "[t]oward the end of the autumn term of 1909." He appears to have been instructed to downplay Ronald Tolkien's intense, ardent, and amorous relationship with Edith and consequently redacted any impact it might have on his writing. Carpenter's "During the summer of 1909 they decided they were in love" (*Bio* 40) becomes a decorous fig-leaf for a blazing ardor, which in 1909/1910 was socially and morally unacceptable.

This change in the official biography does not seem to be the result of Carpenter's bias due to his own experience with the Oxford community, his feelings toward his subjects or their religion, his own historical context, or his methodology (duPlessis 44). The result of Carpenter's omission of the passionate context of Ronald and Edith's relationship has been to create skepticism about the suitability of the couple's match, the "trite" explanation of their mutual attraction based on their both being orphans (duPlessis 47) and suspicions about the ac-

---

14 Rayner Unwin confirms this report writing Christopher Tolkien "tore Humphrey's draft to pieces," and Humphrey "re-wrote the whole book, which in its revised form, Christopher approved" (249).

tions of Father Francis Morgan in separating the couple and thereby creating a scenario of a "thwarted romance" (*Bio* 44). Only the most careful reading of the available biographical materials reveals Tolkien's own mature opinion of his defiance, his willingness to deceive Father Francis Morgan in 1909/1910, and his emotionally fueled blindness to possible consequences of his conduct in 1909. A fuller, but probably still incomplete picture emerges of Edith Bratt and Ronald Tolkien's early relationship.

At the Faulkners' boarding house, Edith had the pivotal and decisive experience of meeting and then falling in love with Ronald Tolkien. From what we know about Ronald Tolkien, falling in love with Edith contributed to his taking on new activities and risks in his debut with the Debating Society and on the rugby field. But Edwardian society would have found their kisses and Ronald Tolkien's seeing Edith in her nightgown unacceptable. The almost inevitable discovery of their complicity of stolen food and bicycle rides precipitated their initial separation and Ronald's seemingly determined maneuverings to stay in contact with Edith. Stephen Gateley's likely persuasive appeal to Edith, to wait safely in a setting which could disguise her origins until Ronald came of age, seems to have prevailed. Her leaving Birmingham for the home of Charles Jessop marks the beginning of another stage in her unpredictable life.

Chapter Five

Charlton Kings, 1910-1913

The move to Charlton Kings created a complete break between Edith and her past. The concealment of Edith's origins and of her recent scandalous involvement with Ronald Tolkien offered the opportunity for new community involvement, but within the confines of a rather tyrannical household headed by "Uncle" Charles Jessop. Edith appears to have been willing to wait for Ronald Tolkien, counting on his "promises and declarations" (*Bio* 61).

"Edith was taken off to" her new life in Charlton Kings on March 2, 1910 (*TFA* 29). This phrase suggests someone escorted Edith on the train as it would be improper for her to travel without a chaperone. Stephen Gateley, legally her guardian until January 21, 1910, would be the most likely person to escort Edith. Having probably been in touch with his co-religionist, Father Francis Morgan, Gateley is likely to have been very relieved to finally put a definite end to the continuing contact between Edith and Ronald. Ronald Tolkien caught one last glimpse of Edith on her bicycle in Birmingham on her way to the train station that day (*Bio* 43).

While the city of Cheltenham has now absorbed Charlton Kings, the town was a separate entity in 1910. Edith settled into the spacious house owned by the seventy-five-year-old Charles H. Jessop, a solicitor (*TFA* 30), and his fifty-two-year-old wife, with a resident cook/general domestic and another housemaid (1911 census).[1] The couple had only been married nine years and had no children. In the 1911 census, Edith is listed as a visitor, implicitly a guest, and not a boarder.

---

1 GA/D2428/2/38 - Hereditament Number 724 for Charlton Kings, Income tax parish: Charlton Kings. Date when served: 26/04/1912 occupied and owned by Charles Hale Jessop. Description: house of 1 rood 34 perches (A Perch was 16.5 feet.). "Duties on Land Values." Gloucestershire, last viewed on 6/8/2020. https://www.glos1909survey.org.uk/code/data.php?id=3984.

One of these semi-detached homes was 2 Lyefield Lawns,
home of the Jessops, in 1910. (Google Earth)

If Charles Jessop was a "family friend" (*C&G* 1.21), he would not have been a friend of the working-class Bratts, but rather of the middle-class Alfred Warrillow. Jessop was doing bankruptcy filings in 1869, the year of Warrillow's bankruptcy. Given that the solicitor Stephen Gateley, from the many references online, did mainly real estate law, especially for the Catholic Church, Alfred Warrillow may have sought out a separate bankruptcy lawyer. Alternatively, Warrillow may have known Jessop from his stationery business, the office supply stores of their day, with legal firms as regular clients. Jessop's willingness to provide a home and to lie by telling everyone Edith was his "niece" is striking as he had nothing to gain by doing so. It is very hard to imagine a man of Jessop's class knowingly accepting an illegitimate child into his house. However, this magnanimous act of charity, namely giving Edith the status of "niece," created a cover story with which she was familiar and which would allow her to "pass" as a typical middle-class young lady.

With Father Francis Morgan's permission, Ronald Tolkien wrote Edith for Easter, on Saturday, March 26, 1910. He wrote a "long letter" which ended with his earliest surviving, but unpublished, poem, *Morning*. He also enclosed two devotional pamphlets (*C&G* 1.23). Edith replied saying she was happy with the Jessops and "all that horrid time at Duchess Road seems only a dream now" (*Bio* 44). This last statement seems to refer not only to the petty constraints on Edith's piano playing and the limits on her social activities by Mrs. Faulkner, but also shocked recriminations about Edith's conduct by any knowledgeable parties. Mrs. Faulkner had probably become even more vigilant and restrictive after she learned about Edith's relationship with Ronald Tolkien.

Two weeks later, on April 11, 1910, Ronald Tolkien saw *Peter Pan* at the Prince of Wales Theatre in Birmingham and wrote in his diary "Wish E[dith] had been with me" (*C&G* 1.23, *Bio* 46-7). Ronald had one of his last encounters with Edith less than a month earlier on February 16, 1910 at the Prince of Wales Theatre so he would have, of course, thought of her. Tolkien turned to writing and wrote poems including *Woodsunshine* and later *Sirens* (*C&G* 1.24, *Bio* 47).

For Edith, Charlton Kings was an improvement over the Faulkner boarding house. Edith practiced daily as much as she wanted to on a grand piano, took organ lessons, and began to play for the local Anglican church (*Bio* 44, *TFA* 30). Edith regularly attended church at the Anglican St. Mary's and volunteered to help with the Boys' Club and the choir outings. This impressive church, with a Norman tower dated from around 1190, additions from 1390-1400, and much remodeling in the 1800s, became an important venue for Edith's activities.

At church, the Jessops were probably acquainted with the family of Henry Liddell, who had been the dean of Christ Church College in Oxford. Liddell built a three-story, five-bedroom house on Cudnall Street in 1862. The Rev. Charles Lutwidge Dodgson – also known as Lewis Carroll – visited the Liddell girls, Alice, Lorina, and Edith, who lived with their grandparents, governess, and two maiden aunts, there in the 1860s. Carroll is believed to have been inspired by the house's giant, ornately framed "looking glass".[2]

---

2 https://www.dailymail.co.uk/news/article-2591691/Five-bedroom-three-storey-house-real-Alice-Wonderland-lived-market-time-three-decades-1million-complete-looking-glass.html, last viewed on 6/4/2020.

St. Mary's Cheltenham (Google Earth)

While the Jessops had few visitors aside from the local vicar, Edith took the train to see her friends from Dresden House in Evesham. Molly Field is named (*Bio* 44), but it is likely Edith also saw Mabel Sheaf, her "oldest" friend (*TFA* 67). Cheltenham, Hinton-on-the-Green, and Evesham were all on a loop line of the Midland Railway. The distance to Hinton was twenty miles and given the stops at other stations on the way, it probably took 35 to 40 minutes for Edith to go see her friends.[3] Molly's family had probably entertained and hosted the orphaned Edith multiple times during the years at Dresden House. With Edith living in Charlton Kings, the visits could begin again.

Edith also participated in the Primrose League. This activity suggests Edith enjoyed being an outgoing, social person who wanted to be involved in her community. The Primrose League's main drawing card was a program of social events, including day excursions, winter evening entertainments, the

---

3 "At the beginning of the twentieth-century railroads had an average speed of 40 mph."
"The development of the railway network in Britain 1825-1911." Dan Bogart, Leigh Shaw-Taylor and Xuesheng You, last viewed on 6/4/2020. https://pdfs.semanticscholar.org/beca/ae2e1cf76dca3ecc5a252d529e583806ecec.pdf.

Primrose summer fête, and the opportunity to hear and meet members of the Parliamentary Conservative Party.[4] Edith's previous interest in politics is suggested by Tolkien's maiden debate speech on the suffragette and his epithet of "Suffragette" for Edith in his 1912 play.

Edith's social participation is now possible because no one would question the solicitor's "niece" about her background. This level of social engagement is a marked contrast to the official biography. Carpenter labels Edith as "shy," and shows her to be reluctant to return the visits needed to join Oxford society (*Bio* 154). However, this description seems to be a ploy to avoid an explicit discussion of the pariah status of bastards in polite English society which Edith faced. Carpenter evokes the class consciousness involved in these Oxford University visits describing how the other faculty wives lived in "awesome college lodgings" or "their turreted mansions." Carpenter appears to be ignoring the typical interactions of a gathering of university faculty wives. After the obligatory discussion of the weather, compliments on the hostess's dress and décor, remarks on the health of family and the King, comments on the recent move and the new house, there would be the standard questions of "where was Edith Tolkien from?" and "who was your father?" and "what did your father do?" The answers to those questions would almost certainly determine Edith's standing in the "pecking order" or social hierarchy of university wives. What was she supposed to say? "My mother's employer seduced her and I'm a bastard." Or should she lie about who her father was and eventually be found out; or give her father's name and occupation correctly, only to have the gossip mill discover he did not marry Edith's mother? The stigma of being illegitimate seems the most likely reason why she had "a very limited social life in childhood and adolescence" (*Bio* 154), and in married life as a university wife.

Further, Carpenter's report of Edith's "shyness" is undercut by his noting that in the "informal" atmosphere at Leeds University, Edith was happy and "made friends with other wives" (*Bio* 105, 155). Edith visited with Ronald's students

---

4 The Primrose League, founded in 1883, was an organization for spreading the principles of the Conservative Party in Great Britain. See Seldon and Snowdon. When founded, women had the same status and responsibilities as men, until a separate Ladies Branch was established. "Founders of the Primrose League." Alistair Cooke. Oxford Dictionary of National Biography, last viewed on 6/4/2020. https://www.oxforddnb.com/view/10.1093/ref:odnb/9780198614128.001.0001/odnb-9780198614128-e-42172.

at Leeds and "[m]any of these pupils became family friends who kept in touch with her in later years and often came to visit" (*Bio* 155). Carpenter then adds Ronald and Edith shared many friends, who were part of Ronald's academic world, including Rosfrith and Robert Murray, Simonne d'Ardenne, Meredith Thompson, Elaine Griffiths, Stella Mills, and Mary Salu (*Bio* 158, *TFA* 67-69). When any questions about Edith's background could be safely eliminated, her sociability was evident.

Unfortunately, Edith's new social life in Cheltenham in 1910 came at the expense of a soon revealed limitation in the Jessop household. Mr. Jessop was a "martinet with a strong temper" (*TFA* 30). He dominated his wife and Edith. Mrs. Jessop could only beg Edith not to upset her husband. Edith consequently had "too much time on her hands" and few friends. She filled the time with piano playing and copying music. This situation is likely to have worsened when she hurt her back trying to play the pump organ or harmonium (*TFA* 30).[5]

Edith had one last instance of contact with Ronald Tolkien. Ronald Tolkien broke his promise to Father Francis Morgan and telegraphed Edith on December 17, 1910 on learning he had obtained an Open Classical Exhibition at Exeter College (*C&G* 1.27). Edith telegraphed her congratulations on the same day (*C&G* 1.27). She sent Ronald an unsigned Christmas card a week later (*C&G* 1.27).

Turning our attention from Edith in Charlton Kings, we can examine the silent impact of her loss on Ronald Tolkien. Carpenter only briefly acknowledges Ronald Tolkien's depression and grief over Edith's departure (*Bio* 44). Ronald had already been wrestling with bouts of depression since his mother's death (*Bio* 31). Ronald described these as "a terrible chaos which darkened my youth and early manhood" (McIlwaine 170). The experience of being in love and having that love reciprocated could have created a counterbalance to Tolkien's psychological turmoil. Now, that psychological ballast was gone.

---

5 The pump organ, reed organ, harmonium, or melodeon is a type of free-reed organ. It creates sound when air flows past "the reed," a vibrating piece of thin metal placed in a frame. Harmoniums were most popular in the West in the late nineteenth and early twentieth centuries. They were especially preferred by small churches where a pipe organ would have been too large or too expensive. Some harmoniums had two keyboards and pedal keyboards, like a regular organ, but this arrangement required an assistant to operate the bellows. Edith played this kind of harmonium (*TFA* 30). The required pumping may have been what hurt her back.

Carpenter's presentation suggests Tolkien turned his attention to absorbing academic challenges and accomplishments at King Edward's: the excitement of rugby, the formation of TCBS (Tea Club Barrovian Society), and the pleasures of Edwardian male camaraderie and fun including debates and plays (*Bio* 53). This seems to be too narrow a picture. Ronald Tolkien might have complied, mastered and enjoyed the expected role of Edwardian schoolboy with its sports, debates, plays, OTC (Officers' Training Corps), and classes. But his heart was in the stolen hours when he was in control and chose freely what he wanted to create: "the satisfaction of a personal pleasure" in a "private" language and its "concomitant" world and mythology ("Secret Vice" 199, 207). Tolkien was not a person who focused on conventional success except as a means to an end, as in earning a degree so that he could get a job and marry Edith. Throughout his adult life, he was more interested in languages and stories, and especially his own invented languages and stories, which expressed his intense inner life, than in money or external success.

Tolkien already had a rich, inner life at King Edward's in 1910 with his history of inventing languages and drawing. Feeling imprisoned by his legal guardian, Ronald Tolkien took what he later termed the Honorable Escape of the prisoner: Fantasy (OFS 148). Three independent, primary sources report Tolkien writing a mythology by 1910. Clyde Kilby reports Tolkien "told one of his closest friends that he had the whole of his mythic world in his mind as early as 1906. He told me that he was writing some of *The Silmarillion* [...] about 1910" (47). George Sayer reports Tolkien "had in a sense planned them [the stories of *The Silmarillion*] before he went to school [Oxford] and actually written one or two of the poems while he was still at school," meaning King Edward's (8). In an annotation on his poem, *East of the Moon West of the Sun*, Tolkien wrote, "First poem of my mythology Valinor thought of about 1910" (McIlwaine 204). The catalyst to Tolkien's writing seems to be as much, if not more, a response to the loss of Edith Bratt, "my lover" (*Letters* 52-53), than his involvement with the TCBS.

Tolkien wrote, "The [mythological] 'stories' were made rather to provide a world for the languages than the reverse" (qtd. in *C&G* 2.632, *Letters* 231). By 1908/1909, Tolkien knew, from Wright's primer, languages evolved. Ronald "found it necessary to construct at least in outline a mythology concomitant [...]

because the making of language and mythology are related functions" ("Secret Vice" 210-11). Tolkien continues: "[I] invented several languages when I was only about eight or nine, [...] but I destroyed them. My mother disapproved. She thought of my language as a useless frivolity taking up time that could be better spent in studying" (Grotta-Kurska 18; see also Plimmer and Plimmer, Plotz, Resnik 41). By 1905/1906 when Tolkien and his brother resumed regular visits with the Incledon family and prior to the Incledons' move to Barnt Green outside of Birmingham, Tolkien discovered Mary and Marjorie Incledon, his cousins, like a number of Edwardian children, had "concoct[ed] their own sub-culture of a secret language," Animalic (Rose 227-28). Mary Incledon and Ronald Tolkien then collaborated on Nevbosh or New Nonsense, a language of mostly disguised English, French, and Latin words (*Bio* 36). Sometime around the autumn of 1907, probably after the Incledons had moved (*C&G* 2.568 no source is given), Tolkien created Naffarin, based mostly on Latin and Spanish (*C&G* 2.631). On June 10, 1909, Tolkien devised a code, *The Book of Foxroot*, with an invented alphabet, using English and Esperanto as the basis of the code (*C&G* 1.17-18, Priestman 18). This language and its alphabet are likely to have been sparked by Tolkien's involvement in the Boy Scouts (Bunting, "Boy Scouts" 76-77). About this time he also acquired a copy of Joseph Wright's *Primer of the Gothic Language* which traced Gothic to what is now called Proto-Indo-European (QL x).

Tolkien admired Gothic not only for introducing him to "modern historical philology," but enjoyed "for the first time the study of a language out of mere love: I mean for the acute aesthetic pleasure derived from a language for its own sake" (*Letters* 213). Now, in 1910 with Edith gone, he focused on Gothic "often putting Gothic inscriptions in his books" (*Letters* 357) and learned enough to play the part of a barbarian envoy who spoke seemingly fluent Gothic (*Bio* 48). Tolkien knew enough about Indo-European to lecture the First Class at King Edward's for hours on the derivations of modern languages in the spring of 1910 (*Bio* 48). He began an "attempt to invent an 'unrecorded' Germanic language, and my 'own language' – or series of invented languages" (*Letters* 214). Tolkien's "first imaginary language," invented while he was still a schoolboy, i.e. at King Edward's High School, was based on Wright's *Primer* (Priestman 24). Tolkien was likely to have continued working on his "private lang" during the first year and a half at Oxford (1911/1912) as Tolkien wrote he nearly failed his Honour Moderations because he was "studying something else: Gothic and what not" (*Letters* 52), which may include his invented Gautish (QL x) or "Gautisk" (*Great War* 17) as well as the Finnish *Kalevala* (*Letters* 214-15). Tolkien must have been in Birmingham studying at King Edwards' when he started this new, invented language as he was "shar[ing] a room with [his brother] Hilary" and wrote in his diary, "Did a lot of private lang" (*Bio* 37).

Tolkien was "inventing" extra words in Gothic/Gautisk following the rules of language construction he had learned (*Bio* 37) not only from Wright's primer, but also from his copy of *Chambers's Etymological Dictionary* which he had acquired in approximately late 1903.[6] Tolkien's acquisition of *Chambers's Etymological Dictionary* seems to have been partly in response to his teacher, George Brewerton, lending Ronald a primer to learn Old English in the fall of 1903 (*C&G* 1.10). Joseph Wright, between 1916 and 1919, held classes in Gothic at Oxford so he may have also coached Tolkien in this area (E.M. Wright 19). Gautisk's vocabulary and grammar may be in the large mass of Tolkien's yet unpublished notebooks and papers (Garth, "Book Reviews" 233).

At Oxford, Ronald Tolkien kept a diary for Edith in which he recorded his misdemeanors and failings (*Bio* 58), including not studying, spending too much money, and not going to mass.[7] He treasured Edith's picture at the age of 17 "as a keepsake" (McIlwaine 146-47, *Bio* 61).[8] He arrived at Oxford in October 1911 after being part of a seven-week walking excursion in Switzerland organized by the Brookes-Smiths (Lewis and Currie, *Tolkien's Switzerland* 269-70). Ellen Brookes-Smith had become Tolkien's Aunt Jane Neave's business partner in the Phoenix and Manor Farms in July 1911 (Morton and Hayes 34).

---

6 In Tolkien's "battered" copy, Tolkien noted, "This book was the beginning of my interest in Germanic Philology (& Philol. in general) [about 1904]. Unfortunately, the 'introduction [...] became so well-worn & tattered it has become lost" (Priestman 16). Certainly, a book he consulted a lot.

7 Tolkien came to Oxford in 1911 on a £60 scholarship which paid £20 of his college bills for each of the three terms in an academic year (*Exeter* 35). Father Francis Morgan provided additional funds. In June 1912, Ronald Tolkien was transferred to the Loscombe Richards Exhibition for one year (*Exeter* 15). This scholarship was for a student in financial need who was already a member of the college. The Loscombe Richards endowment was £707 8s 11d (Boase 203). However much money it provided, Tolkien acted as if his income had increased by renting a different room. The new room's rent was an increase from £10 10s in the 1911/12 school year to £16 16s in the 1912/13 school year. Similarly, furniture rent increased from £3 14s to £5 (*Exeter* 15).

8 The Carpenter biography states Ronald Tolkien had "a few photographs of [Edith] as a child" (61). This information is incomplete.

The following summer Ronald went on a walking tour with a new sketch book in the Berkshires. He drew villages and scenery with three ink drawings of Eastbury (August 27-28, 1912), three watercolors of the Lambourn countryside, and two pages of ink drawings of the Lambourn church (August 21, 23, 30-31) (*C&G* 1.40). The tour also included sites in Buckinghamshire (*A&I* 17) and even Wales as attested by two views of Trwyn Llanbedrog on Cardigan Bay (*A&I* 33). This tour seems similar to an earlier art holiday which included visiting Whitby in 1910 where Ronald drew several landscapes (*A&I* 16). Tolkien seems to have had a benefactor helping him to pay for travel expenses, an activity of the privileged and leisure class. Given that Tolkien was unlikely to be trekking across the countryside by himself, a likely candidate, who could act as a chaperone and companion, would be Tolkien's Aunt May Incledon. Her oldest daughter, Marjorie, who was one year older than Tolkien, had an interest in painting, especially landscapes, like Tolkien, and portraits (*C&G* 2.568). Tolkien's sketching tours would certainly fit with the Incledons' affluent lifestyle.

At Oxford, Ronald Tolkien kept up an almost frenetic level of social activity, such that one visitor, seeing the display of cards on Tolkien's mantel, remarked Tolkien seemed to have signed up for every single college association (qtd. in *Great War* 31). Ronald also joined the Exeter College unit of King Edward's Horse, a unique and prestigious organization with units in London, Liverpool, Oxford, and Cambridge.[9] King Edward's Horse was administered directly by the Horse Guards in London and had the cachet of royal patronage. It was only open to Colonials, those born in the colonies like Tolkien.

Tolkien's participation in King Edward's Horse has received little attention. Nevertheless, this organization expressed the ethos of the British Empire at the time, so a short digression to review this group seems useful. King Edward's Horse's presence in Oxford gives a good idea of the color and flavor of what it was like when Great Britain was at the apex of her power. This mindset included the celebration of Empire Day on May 24, Queen Victoria's birthday, beginning in 1902 with its saluting of the Union Jack, concerts, parades, patriotic

9 See "King Edward's Horse (The King's Overseas Dominions Regiment)." Last viewed on 11/17/2020. http://kingedwardshorse.net/

songs and inspirational speeches, calculated to instill in the youth a pride and appreciation of the glories of British Empire. Britannia ruled not only the waves, but had had the heady experience of world dominion for generations: the empire on which the sun never sets.

Presumably, Tolkien attended the "Freshers'" [Freshmen's] Fair at the beginning of the academic year at Oxford when all societies compete with one another for new members. King Edward's Horse would have had representatives present. Some of the senior undergraduate members might have been dressed in striking full dress uniform: khaki serge with scarlet braiding and narrow scarlet piping on the turn-down collar and cuffs and scarlet double stripes on the khaki cord breeches. The headdress was a wide-brimmed slouch style hat of khaki felt with a large drooping plume of black/green cocks' feathers modelled on that of the Italian *Bersaglieri*. This was worn only on ceremonial occasions as can be seen in a film of the King Edward's Horse unit in the 1910 funeral procession of Edward, the Seventh.[10] The young Tolkien, who ordered tailor-made suits in 1913 (*Bio* 68), was likely to be impressed by such style and panache. The service uniform, which Ronald typically would have worn, sported the increasingly standard peaked cap.[11]

The senior members would have highlighted the regiment's reputation and bravado. The impressive cavalry skills of the troops were extolled: mounting and dismounting from a barebacked horse, at the trot or canter; jumping a high bar without stirrups or even saddle, sometimes with hands clasped behind one's back; and jogging bareback at a fast trot (Asher 112). King Edward's Horse maintained a band, though that was not likely to be based in Oxford.[12] However, more appealing to Tolkien might have been the unit's de facto existence as a dining and drinking club. King Edward's Horse competed with the Oxford University OTC [Officers' Training Corps] which still today boasts "a fantastic social calendar, from glittering dinners and cocktail parties to the more

---

10 See "Funeral of King Edward VII The Peacemaker (1910)." Last viewed on 11/14/20. https://www.youtube.com/watch?v=CHKyY6kej10. King Edward Horse can be seen on foot around the 1 minute 10 second mark.

11 "Aldershot 1911 & Dibgate 1912." The King's Colonials, last viewed on 11/12/2020 https://www.kingscolonials.com/aldershot-1911-dibgate-1912.

12 There is a recording of "KING EDWARD'S HORSE BAND: Chocolate soldier - 1910/11 UK Velvet-Face 78rpm 204" at https://www.ebay.co.uk/itm/KING-EDWARDS-HORSE-BAND-Chocolate-soldier-1910-11-UK-Velvet-Face-78rpm-204-/124146206193, last viewed on 11/16/2020.

casual fancy dress events, the OUOTC has everything you need to enhance and complement your time at university in Oxfordshire and Buckinghamshire."[13] The swashbuckling appeal of the regiments was seen in their names, like the City of London Yeomanry's The Rough Riders, and The 3rd County of London Yeomanry's The Sharpshooters.

King Edward's Horse reflected the Empire. It was composed of four squadrons. A Squadron was limited to "British Asians" (mostly from India), and their badge was a large elephant. B Squadron included "British Americans," meaning Canadians, with a badge showing a beaver against a maple leaf. C Squadron was Australians and New Zealanders whose badge showed a kangaroo and tree fern with a rising sun background. D Squadron was reserved for "British Africans" from Rhodesia and South Africa, entitled to a badge with an ostrich against a rising sun.[14] Ronald would be in D Squadron.

Ronald probably had further instruction in riding a horse during King Edward's Horse's Summer Camp on Dibgate Plateau near Folkestone July 27 to August 10, 1912 (*C&G* 1.36, James 52). Tolkien was likely to recall Major General Edmund Allenby, who was one of the generals who inspected the troops at the Summer Camp in 1912. Allenby, later Field Marshal, Edmund Henry Hynman Allenby, 1st Viscount Allenby, GCB, GCMG, GCVO, High Commissioner for Egypt and Sudan (1919 to 1925), achieved fame for his successful campaign in Palestine and Syria in World War I. T.E. Lawrence, known as "Lawrence of Arabia," was under his command. General Allenby memorably dismounted at the Jaffa gate of Jerusalem and entered the city on foot when he took possession of it in December 1917.

Prior to that training, Ronald was unlikely to have had more than fleeting experiences with horses, limited perhaps to a work horse at his Aunt Jane's

---

13 https://www.google.com/url?q=https://www.army.mod.uk/who-we-are/corps-regiments-and-units/university-officers-training-corps/oxford-uotc/&sa=U&ved=2ahUKEwjllPDCgYrtAhVwThUIHbE1A04QFjAAegQICRAB&usg=AOvVaw1VHTpkzQt0lntMJlIfA5sd, last viewed on 11/17/2020.
14 "4th County of London (King's Colonials) Imperial Yeomanry." Unofficial history of the Australian and New Zealand Armed Service, last viewed on 11/15/20. http://www.diggerhistory.info/pages-asstd/kings-colonials.htm.

farm, because horses are expensive animals and Tolkien was poor (*Bio* 58).[15] Some cadets in the unit may have owned their own mounts. Garth reports the members borrowed "good mounts from local hunts," though this information is not in the *Amon Hen* 13 article which he cites (*Great War* 24). This statement seems inaccurate because hunts themselves owned very few horses, as these mounts were provided only for the use of the professional Huntsman and one or two Whippers-in. Perhaps Garth means they borrowed from the members of the local hunts. The Army Act, however, specifically allowed one shilling nine pence per day for the maintenance of horses.[16] That would be £31 and 2 shillings per year. Comparing that expense to the £60 Tolkien paid for three terms of his college bills in an academic year (*Exeter* 35), we see that sum is slightly more than half of Tolkien's yearly college bill. Basic upkeep on a horse was a significant cost.

Horses were everywhere in 1911, and easily hired. There were numerous options including the possibility of an Army stable of mounts. If the subsidy of the Army Act was extended to the King Edward Horse troops, Ronald may have hired a mount from the local Cathedral Stables on St. Aldgates (Street) only a few hundred yards from Exeter College (*Oxford Journal,* Saturday, December 15, 1900; 1911 OS map). Exeter College did keep a pack of hunting hounds, beagles that hunted hares, but the Huntsman and Whippers-in would have been on foot.[17] The local Yeomanry unit, Queen's Own Oxfordshire Hussars, may have been a source of a mount.

---

15 Working horses were employed for agricultural duties at Phoenix Farm until the 1920s when they were replaced by tractors. Horses pulled wagons and harrows and were ridden as a form of transportation, rather than for sport. Morton and Hayes have pictures of Phoenix Farm from that time period, showing two horses or ponies (Morton and Hayes V, VII).
　　Garth's report that Tolkien was skilled enough to break horses for the unit seems unrealistic (*Great War* 24, 318). It takes years of experience to be able to train a horse to accept a saddle and rider. Garth cites an account by Michael and Priscilla Tolkien from the October, 1974 *Amon Hen* as his source, though this account also stated erroneously that Tolkien was on the *Lusitania* when Tolkien returned to England (*Amon Hen* 13, 9). Tolkien sailed on the *Asturias* (*C&G* 1.102).
　　At Oxonmoot 1990, Mrs. Helen Armstrong, a former Secretary of the British Tolkien Society, asked Priscilla Tolkien about her father's history of riding. Priscilla told Helen Armstrong "that her father had indeed learned to ride while he was in the army, not as a cavalryman but as part of his basic officer training. He had had little opportunity to ride since then" (31). Priscilla Tolkien's statements are inconsistent with each other and other facts, suggesting a fading recall of family stories, heard in passing and mentioned rarely years ago.
16 Great Britain 1910, 8.
17 "Sport" British History Online, last viewed on 11/10/2020. https://www.british-history.ac.uk/vch/oxon/vol2/pp351-372. A film, "1927 Eton College Beagles," last viewed on 11/15/20 is available at https://www.youtube.com/watch?v=rQliIysT6nk. This gives an idea of what this activity was like.

When not in a whirl of social activities, Tolkien had periods of dark ruminations (*Great War* 29) as seen in his art of 1911-1912, i.e. *Before, After,* and *Wickedness* (*A&I* 34, 36, 37, 65). Daniel Grotta-Kurska reports Tolkien began writing about Númenor at Oxford but abandoned the story as "too grim" (40).[18] This Oxford attempt at a mythology may be the origin of the unpublished prose tale, "The Fall of the Númenóreans and the Change of the World," which was submitted to Stanley Unwin in November, 1937, along with "The Gest of Beren and Lúthien" (McIlwaine 218, *Letters* 25). For "The Fall of the Númenóreans and the Change of the World" to have been submitted to a publisher, it must have been a polished manuscript. That indicates that it is not the same as the published fragmentary versions of "The Fall of the Númenor" (*Lost Road* 11-38). "The Fall of the Númenóreans and the Change of the World," must be a previously unknown Tolkien work, stored in the archive.

Further evidence of Tolkien's creation of an earlier mythology, which presumably included a story of Númenor, appears in two other references to earlier legends. Tolkien wrote, "Before 1914 I wrote a 'poem' upon Earendel who launched his ship like a bright spark from the havens of the Sun. I adopted him into my mythology" (*Letters* 385) and "I found my real interest was only in the upper end, the *Akallabêth* or *Atalantie* ('Downfall' in Númenórean and Quenya), so I brought all the stuff I had written on the originally unrelated legends of Númenor into relation with the main mythology" (*Letters* 347).

Christopher Tolkien states his "father erred" in the Bretherton letter cited above as did Carpenter when he wrote, "Tolkien's legend of Númenor, the great island in the West [...] was probably composed some time before the writing of 'The Lost Road'" of 1937 (*Bio* 170, *Lost Road* 8-10). Commenting on the annotation, "First poem of my mythology, Valinor, thought of about 1910," Arden Smith writes, "the second phrase may mean merely that Valinor (glossed as 'Asgard' in the Lexicon) was thought of previously, and the date may be very approximate" (QL xiii). Ronald Tolkien, however, did not work by just making up a name in isolation, but rather by creating a whole network of an invented language, i.e. Gautisk, with other names and attached

---

18 See Bunting's "Apologia for Daniel Grotta" for a discussion of why Grotta should be considered a useful source.

stories. The year 1910 is significant because it is before the watershed of going up to Oxford in 1911. The specification of 1910 means Tolkien is indicating his mythology was written before he went to Oxford. Three statements from Tolkien; three other, independent, supporting sources; the existence of "private lang" in Birmingham when Ronald was in school at King Edward's, and the drawings of seemingly mythical characters and settings point to Tolkien's troika, his typical modus operandi of intertwining invented languages, artwork, and mythical or legendary stories. This evidence points to a new conclusion: it was the suppressed and redacted impact of the loss of Edith which propelled Ronald Tolkien into writing and creating a mythology. This means Tolkien's mythology started before the isolated Elvish words and the Qenya lexicon in 1915 and Gnomish lexicon in 1916 and 1917.

Ronald Tolkien's artwork suggests illustrations for an undocumented mythology. Tolkien routinely illustrated his own mythological stories as seen in his illustrations for *The Hobbit* and *The Lord of the Rings*. As early as 1915, Tolkien was creating illustrations for his poems. The March 1915 poem, *Water, Wind, and Sand*, is labeled as an "Illustration for *Sea-Song of an Eldar Day*." The April 1915 painting, *Tanqui*, seems to be the visual analogy of his poem, *Kôr: In a City Lost and Dead (The City of the Gods) (C&G* 1.67, 1.71). In the same way, the 1911 red and black pencil drawing, *Before*, has the "megalithic doorway" of Númenor which appears later in one of Michael Ramer's dreams in "The Notion Club Papers" (*A&I* 35). The drawing, *Thought*, dated 1912, is a possible portrait of one of various Valar, including Varda or Manwë, suggesting Tolkien is again illustrating an early mythology (*A&I* 38, 37). Wayne Hammond and Christina Scull regard Tolkien's drawings of *Before* and *Afterwards* as expressing early images of Tolkien's mythology (*A&I* 36).

With Edith having had no contact with Ronald for almost three years, she became engaged to Molly's brother, George Alwin Field, a promising young man and a farmer. George was born February 4, 1890 in Bengeworth, Evesham, Worcestershire. He had attended a boarding school, The Larches New School, in Bishampton (1901 census). George enlisted in the Worcestershire Yeomanry on April 24, 1915, noticeably not at the outbreak of World War I in August,

1914.[19] The Worcester Yeomanry was a Territorial Force regiment, rather like the American National Guard.[20] The yeomanry units were cavalry units formed from the nobility or landed gentry with their tenants. Most cavalry units in the Great War fought as infantry. George Field "re-enlisted" joining the Regular Army, the Army Service Corps (ASC) and quickly rose to the rank of Acting Staff Sergeant. He became a Temporary 2nd Lieutenant in the now Royal Army Service Corps (RASC) on July 3, 1916.[21] This corps was responsible for all transportation by rail, motor, or horse for men and all material. Due to the high casualty rate among young officers, especially after 1915, "temporary" officers were appointed from candidates who previously would not have been considered as they did not have the pre-war qualifications of being proper gentlemen, i.e. with the necessary private income, public school education, or upper-class family background. Further promotion did not come to these men.

In contrast to Edith's doubts and fears, Ronald Tolkien was certain Edith was waiting for him. Ronald's writing and drawings of December 1912 show this (*Bio* 60). There was something special in the relationship of Edith and Ronald as can be seen in the fact that Annie Gollins, the maid at the Faulkners' who helped Edith pirate food to the Tolkien brothers, named her own children Ronald and Edith (*C&G* 2.458). Ronald had made "declarations and promises" (*Bio* 61) when they lived at the Faulkners', and Edith was his inspiration and hope for the future.

In December 1912, Ronald Tolkien contributed a play, *The Bloodhound, the Chef, and the Suffragette*, for the Christmas entertainment when he spent the holidays with his cousins, aunt and uncle Incledon at Barnt Green (*Bio* 59). Tolkien's Aunt May Incledon continued the Suffield family tradition of putting on dramatic programs at Christmas which May's father, John Suffield, who may have been present, would have fostered as he was an active member of the Birmingham Dramatic and Literary Club (Burns, "Jane Suffield"). Both of Ronald Tolkien's parents had participated in amateur theatricals as young people (Priestman 23).

---

19 "George Alwin Field." The Auxiliary Division of the Royal Irish Constabulary, last viewed on 6/8/2020. http://theauxiliaries.com/men-alphabetical/men-f/field-ga/field.html.
20 Windrow 74.
21 "George Alwin Field." The Auxiliary Division of the Royal Irish Constabulary, last viewed on 6/8/2020. http://theauxiliaries.com/men-alphabetical/men-f/field-ga/field.html.

Mabel had participated in amateur theatricals in Bloemfontein, South Africa (Gorelik 7). Ronald's play patently referred to his relationship with Edith Bratt whom he saw as an heiress whom he met as a "penniless student" while they were sharing the same lodging house. Ronald Tolkien would be turning twenty-one on January 3, 1913. Ronald was brimming with the expectation of being able to write Edith again and propose on his twenty-first birthday when he would be free of his guardian, Father Francis Morgan.

By naming Edith as the probable suffragette, Ronald was poking fun at her because the suffrage movement was built largely of spinsters, of every class.[22] The predominance of single women was partly due to the fact husbands and fathers had the legal power to forbid women from participating in the suffrage movement. Ronald could easily have been aware of the general view that Edith, at the age of twenty-four, would be beginning to be seen as a spinster in the eyes of others. He was going to remedy her status.

In Tolkien's drawings – *The End of the World*, *The Back of Beyond*, and *Undertenishness* with *Other People* on the verso, all dated December 1912 – his anticipation of contacting Edith emerges (Bunting, "Tolkien in Love"). *Undertenishness* with its bright colors and symmetry expresses "the freedom and vision of youth, when everything invites and colours seem more brilliant than they are in reality" (*A&I* 37), or perhaps rather the joy of a young Ronald Tolkien in love anticipating the long-awaited reunion with his beloved. On the reverse of *Undertenishness* is the drawing *Other People*. This picture shows: "A tall, tunnel-like space with a small figure setting out to walk down a narrow path towards a lighted opening; but he is menaced at the sides by huge figures like chessmen [...] the implication is clear that others were preventing Tolkien from reaching his goal" (*A&I* 40). While Ronald was now free of Father Francis Morgan, his guardian, who had required him to break off contact with Edith, he anticipated and portrayed his apprehension of his family's opposition. Middle-class men were expected to be providers for their wives and children. They tended to marry late as did Ronald Tolkien's father at the age of 34 to a twenty-one-year old. Ronald knew of Edwin Neave's long courtship and engagement to his Aunt Jane Suffield (*Bio* 29). This sentiment was well

---

22 Jeffries 90-92.

expressed in a letter from Edith's "Uncle" Jessop to Stephen Gateley: "I have nothing to say against Tolkien, he is a cultured gentleman (gentm. in original), but his prospects are poor in the extreme, and when he will be in a position to marry I cannot imagine" (*TFA* 34.).

Further, Ronald's family almost certainly knew that Father Francis Morgan's sudden removal of the Tolkien brothers from the Faulkner boarding house in December 1909 had at least something to do with Ronald Tolkien's behaving inappropriately with a young lady whose name the Incledons most probably knew. Ronald had been at the Faulkners' since January 1908, and at some point would have mentioned the young lady who played the piano there. Ronald's Catholic Aunt May Incledon probably also had some contact with Father Francis Morgan. Aunt May was likely to have inquired about the character of the new residence and would have known that an Edith Bratt lived in the house. She may have even visited the Faulkners to see how suitable it was and may have met Edith. How could Ronald Tolkien now tell his aunt and her family he was proposing to that siren, the older woman, the instigator of that scandal?

Ronald probably delayed telling Edith's name to the members of the TCBS because they were in contact with Mrs. Incledon (*C&G* 1.109) and might let Edith's name slip. If any of the TCBS mentioned Edith's name, Ronald Tolkien might face a likely repeat of the harangues and lectures about his foolish and ill-advised behavior, which he had probably endured in December 1909 and January 1910. There would probably have been reproaches and allegations of how Ronald was just like his mother, who fell in love at the age of eighteen, accepted a proposal, and defiantly exchanged secret *billet doux* with Ronald's father-to-be, Arthur Tolkien in 1888 (*Bio* 9). Ronald's other Suffield aunt, Aunt Jane Neave, had served as the teenage go-between for her older sister, Mabel, and her intended Arthur Tolkien, delivering notes from Mabel and probably receiving letters from Arthur. Jane Neave was likely to see parallels between young Ronald and his impetuous mother.

In the drawing, *The End of the World* (McIlwaine 37),

> a tiny stick-figure blithely (bravely?) steps into the abyss. [...] But what glories lie beyond the world's end: the Sun, the Moon, a star, all essential elements in

Tolkien's mythology and frequent motifs in his art, here in a restless sky drawn as if by Van Gogh. (*A&I* 40)

Ronald Tolkien, by making a commitment to marriage and family with his proposal, was facing "The End of" his blithe world of irresponsible student life. The drawing's "restless sky" could well reflect conflicting emotions of hope for love, a family, and stability in the face of an uncertain future and his own family's disapproval. "On its verso is a complementary image, *The Back of Beyond*, in which [...] a small man peers over the edge of the picture to whatever lies 'below'" (*A&I* 40, McIlwaine 41). Here Ronald seemingly can only gaze into an unknown future. The colloquial phrase, "the back of the beyond," first appeared in print in Sir Walter Scott's 1816 novel *The Antiquary*. It meant "a distant place, beyond human experience" or "any real or imagined remote region".

This theme of disapproval is further treated in "*Grownupishness* [...] [with] the inscriptions 'Sightless: Blind: Well-Wrapped-Up' [...] Could *Grownupishness* show, then, next to the colourful picture of youth, the black and white view of a particular grown-up, or adults in general – a narrow vision, an inward-looking attitude" (*A&I* 38)?[23] A number of indications in *Grownupishness* suggest Tolkien is referring to his Aunt Jane (née Suffield) Neave, a sister of Tolkien's mother, Mabel Suffield Tolkien, who was likely to oppose Tolkien's marriage plans (Bunting, "Tolkien in Love"). The figure's tonsured head could suggest the well-known picture of Tolkien's aunt in her graduation gown, and the exclamation points and question marks echo the ones which peppered Aunt Jane's correspondence. The geometric figures seem to refer to Aunt Jane's teaching Tolkien geometry in 1900 (Bunting, "Tolkien in Love" 7-8, 9). The "serried ranks of amphitheater seats" (Bridoux, "Book Reviews" 152-53) could refer to Jane Neave's role as a teacher and also suggest she may have continued in that role outside of the classroom.

This artwork does not show Ronald Tolkien looking forward to a reunion with a remote "shining ideal" (*Bio* 66). Ronald anticipated a mutual relationship

---

23 Scull and Hammond change their dating of *Wickedness* to December, 1912 from the previous broader and more uncertain date of 1911-1912 (*A&I* 65) (*C&G* 1. 42). They offer no reason or information for why they have changed their previous dating. *Wickedness* does not fit with the rest of the pictures of December, 1912 which are connected in terms of the paper used and the themes presented. Previously, Hammond and Scull had argued persuasively that Wickedness fits both chronologically and thematically with *Before, Afterwards* (dated 1911), and *Thought* (dated 1912) (*A&I* 35-37, 65).

of affection, passion, and understanding with "*my lover*" (*Letters* 52-53, italics added). Only that potent combination made the obstacles and changes, which he knew he faced, worthwhile.

In response to Ronald Tolkien's January 3, 1913 letter of proposal, Edith replied she was engaged to George Field because "he had been kind to her and she felt 'on the shelf' [...] and she had given up believing that Ronald would want to see her again after three years [...] 'I began to doubt you, Ronald [...] and to think you would care for me'" (*Bio* 61). However, with Ronald's renewed vow of love and marriage, she indicated "everything had changed" (*Bio* 61). Ronald wrote back, and they arranged a meeting (*C&G* 1.42).

A woman, who was "left on the shelf," was a spinster. Married women were higher up in the social hierarchy, regardless of class or age, than spinsters, who were regarded with suspicion.[24] Marriage was the primary goal for most

Charlton Kings Station with the sign to left (June 1962)
(Geoffrey Skelsey. Wikipedia Commons)

---

24 "Corsets, Cutlass, and Candlesticks" Sharon Biggs Waller, last viewed on 6/5/2020. https://corsetsandcutlasses.wordpress.com/2013/02/14/romance-and-courtship-in-the-edwardian-era-it-wasnt-much-fun/.

women. Spinsterhood was often taken as an indication there was something wrong with a lady.

On January 8, 1913, Edith met Ronald at the Charlton Kings station. If Ronald Tolkien came to "Uncle" Jessops' house, there would always be a chaperone present in the room so that there would be no questions about Edith's character.[25] This convention meant they could not have a private conversation. Even if they had gone out in the garden, there would still be surveillance, and the yard may not have been large enough to be out of anyone's hearing. Besides, Edith's entertaining a single young man when she was already engaged would have aroused suspicions of impropriety.

Edith and Ronald walked from the station into the country and sat under the viaduct, perhaps partly to avoid the prying eyes and gossip which had previously caused them so much trouble. Ronald was likely to have had an overnight bag: pajamas, dressing gown, slippers, and wash-kit. He may have carried that with him or stashed it in some bushes as a railway station of that size was not likely to have a Left Luggage Office. Ronald may have been unwilling to leave all his belongings with the station attendant or porter.

Ronald and Edith also probably needed to get out of the wind and possibly rain, so they could hear each other talk. The weather for January 8, 1913 had "unimportant" gales in some parts of the British Isles and the temperature during January was generally above 50 degrees Fahrenheit (10 degrees Celsius).[26]

"By the end of the day Edith had declared that she would give up George Field and marry Ronald Tolkien" (*Bio* 62). What this bloodless summary does not tell us is that this couple must have experienced a reigniting of the passion and commitment which they had previously discovered on Duchess Street, a mutual engagement which they had found nowhere else. While Ronald Tolkien believed his name meant "foolhardy" (*Bio* 19), he appears to have met someone willing to match his risk-taking in Edith Bratt. Edith, like her mother, was willing to bet on earnest promises and a passion which put her reputation at risk. They

---

25 Emily Post (1873–1960). Chapter XIX . "The Chaperon and Other Conventions." Etiquette (1922), last viewed on 6/5/2020. https://www.bartleby.com/95/19.html.

26 "Monthly Weather Report." National Metrological Library and Archives, last viewed on 6/6/2020. https://digital.nmla.metoffice.gov.uk/SO_7498a04d-6a40-4207-a27f-772663ffd2fc/.

agreed that at present they would tell no one except Father Francis Morgan (*C&G* 1.42).

This was the Viaduct outside of Charlton Kings. It no longer exists.
(*Gloucestershire Echo* 01/31/2019)

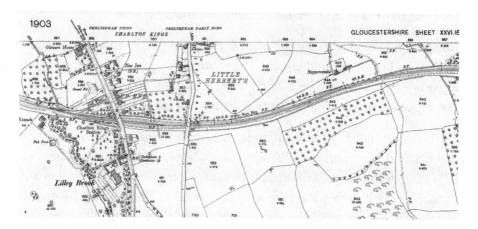

"They walked out into the country and sat under a railway viaduct while they talked" (*Bio* 61). This 1903 OS map from the National Library of Scotland shows the FP (footpath) alongside the railway tracks that the couple took. There was a distance of 3.4 miles between the railway station and the viaduct.

The local paper, *The Cheltenham Looker-On* of January 13, 1913, announced Tolkien's overnight stay at Moorend Park Hotel.[27] Because the main resort season was May to October, Ronald's January visit during the off-season probably meant he had a reduced room rate at this impressive and fashionable establishment built for an affluent spa clientele. The same paper also had a notice for a "Mr. Tolkien" staying at Moorend Park on March 1, 1913.

```
Moorend Park.
  CHARLTON KINGS.
  Channer, Miss
  Coates-Carter, Mr. and Mrs.
  Coates-Carter, Miss
  Elliott, Mr. T.
  Elliott, Miss
  Gwynne-Hughes, Mr. and Mrs.
  Johnstone, Mrs.
  Lilley, Mr. and Mrs.
  Shortrede, Mr. and Mrs.
  Tolkien, Mr. J. R. R.
```

Cheltenham Looker-On
Announcement of January 13, 1913

Ronald Tolkien's January meeting with Edith seems to have left him elated. His quick and rough drawing of *Xanadu* from early 1913, done on the back of a tailor's bill, reflects his new mood (*A&I* 41). This drawing features the "stately pleasure dome" and a plunging river, the River Alph, and its chasm, with ceaseless turmoil seething, a "deep romantic chasm" from Coleridge's *Kubla Khan*. The juxtaposition of the Kubla Khan's exotic "pleasure dome" and a "deep romantic chasm" with "ceaseless turmoil seething" could express Ronald Tolkien's emotional and physical state. Here the young Ronald Tolkien's thoughts of the sensual pleasures attendant on having been united with "his lover" in January 1913 draw on the extravagant opulence or luxury of an Oriental

---

27 "Tolkien at the Moorend Park Hotel 1913." Morgan Thomsen, last viewed on 6/5/2020. https://mythoi.tolkienindex/. An image of the impressive Moorend Park Hotel may be viewed at https://www.hippostcard.com/listing/cheltenham-ukcharlton-kingsmoorend-park-hotel-postcard-1950s/15272555, last viewed on 7/6/2020.

"pleasure dome." "Luxury" could discretely refer to sexual indulgence, as seen in the poetry of Emily Dickinson.[28]

This rekindled passion seems to have inspired Ronald's ingenious incentive plan, created the week following his reunion with Edith, for improving his lax, to non-existent, study habits. Ronald wrote on January 15, 1913: "I am going to send you in a 'bill' at the end of each week for the amount of work done to be paid for at the rate of a kiss an hour as soon as I see you again" (McIlwaine 148, 149). The fact Ronald can require this kind of payment is a marker for the level of intimacy in their relationship, as kissing was a big step past chaperoned courting. Both of them seem ready to resume the relationship near the level of 1909/1910.

This work-diary bore the title and dedication, "JRRT and EMB in account together, AMDG [ad majorem Dei Gloriam or to the greater glory of God]." It not only tracked Ronald Tolkien's study hours, which would provide the means for their eventual marriage, but also Ronald's performance of religious duties and observance of saints' days, marked in red, recommitting himself to his Catholic faith (Priestman 27). What the work-diary entries seem to mean is that now Ronald Tolkien was carefully framing his passion for Edith within the context of his Catholic faith as part of holy matrimony. Ronald would now channel his love for Edith in a way which made it acceptable to his Catholic moral scruples. He seemed determined he was not going to repeat the conflicts among romance, sexuality, and Catholicism which he experienced in 1909/1910 (*Letters* 52-53).

Ronald wrote to Edith on January 17, 1913 saying he was "determined to put all 'lawless and bachelor like things' behind him," i.e. the "End of the [old]

---

28 Emily Dickson used this sense:

> Wild nights – Wild nights!
> Were I with thee
> Wild nights should be
> Our luxury!

One would not expect the rather Anglo-centric *OED* to quote American authors. The *OED* lists only one use of the word "Luxury," and that sense is from Crabbe, a century before and using it as a conscious archaism. However, Tolkien has not been known to think poorly of an archaism.

World" of pranks, sports, and clubs (McIlwaine 148).[29] He confessed in a letter of January 24, 1913, "I am so dreadfully tempted by sloth" (McIlwaine 150).[30] Ronald had to try to make up for lost time as Honour Moderations were to begin Thursday February 27, continued on Friday February 28 and probably finished on March 1 (C&G 1.44).[31] His borrowing of Greek plays, *Oedipus Tyrrannus*, *Elektra*, *Eumenides*, *Agamemnon*, and *Choephoroe*, from the library in the weeks before the exam may indicate last minute cramming (*Exeter* 23).

Ronald wrote Edith frequently. On January 26, he wrote to say how he was waiting just for her (McIlwaine 148). On February 1, 1913, Ronald Tolkien sent Edith a picture postcard of the Exeter College dining hall, marking the place where he sat (C&G 1.43, *TFA* 35). On the card, Ronald wrote: "I have been so busy all day that I have not had any time to write and have now to go to an Old Edwardian meeting [...] Went to H[oly] Comm[union] this morning and am going again tomorrow" (*Exeter* 23).[32] On February 17, Sydney Cohen,

---

29 Ronald was not completely successful with this resolution. The *Chronology* places the quote from the Carpenter biography (54) about "a university rag against the town, the police, and the proctors" in the academic year of 1913-1914 (C&G 1.53). This dating does not seem likely, given Tolkien's new attitude and seriousness about his future with Edith, though he continued to attend Stapeldon Society meetings, partly because he was the Secretary. The most likely occasion was on May 12, 1913 when, "Tolkien describes confrontations between Town and Gown which he had been involved the previous night [...] [and] describe[s] his arrest and subsequent release" (C&G 1.49). Given that Ronald Tolkien had hijacked a bus and addressed a "huge mob" (*Bio* 54), an arrest would seem likely. Consequently, the episode in the Carpenter biography seems more likely to have occurred in May 1913 than in the following academic year.
    Garth places this event after the advent of motorbuses (*Exeter* 20), but there is nothing in the Carpenter biography that indicates this was not a horse drawn vehicle. Given that Tolkien "drove" the bus, it was likely to be horse drawn as Tolkien was familiar with horses from being part of King Edward's Horse. There is no evidence Tolkien knew how to operate a motor vehicle in 1913 or 1914. The November 1913 Exeter College Smoker shows continued involvement in college activities, but Tolkien is preparing for his January 1914 betrothal.
30 McIlwaine writes, "Actually [Tolkien] was never slothful but his conscience was so well-developed that he was inclined to chastise himself for any hours not spent on his studies or for any small lapse in religious observance" (150). While this statement may be true, it misses the point. Ronald Tolkien had no difficulty finding ways to have fun and be busy at Oxford. In 1913, Tolkien was in serious danger of losing his scholarship as he had partied for two years. The sub-rector's report card notes that the first year Ronald Tolkien was "V[ery] lazy & warned re exhib[itio]n," i.e. he is in danger of losing his scholarship (McIlwaine 144-45). Tolkien perhaps puts it best himself: "I was clever, but not industrious or single-minded; a large part of my failure was due simply to not working (at least not in classics) [in 1911-1913] [...] because I was studying something else: Gothic and what not" (*Letters* 52).
31 Ronald Tolkien took three-hour examinations in Latin Prose, Tacitus, Greek verse, translation of Virgil, Latin verse composition, and Comparative Philology (C&G 1.44). If he took one each morning and afternoon, he would have completed his examinations by Saturday afternoon March 1.
32 Garth dates the postcard as February 2, 1913.

who had entered Exeter the same year as Ronald and who lived on the same staircase in the Swiss Cottage as Ronald, committed suicide (*Exeter* 23-24). Ronald Tolkien presumably shared this shocking news with Edith. The dread of disgraceful failure has been known to drive students to suicide, and the possibility of that ignominious fate is likely to have been apparent to Ronald, who had recurrent episodes of depression (*Bio* 31) described as "a terrible chaos which darkened my youth and early manhood" (McIlwaine 170). On the second day of the Honour Moderations, February 28, he wrote, "I realize how hazy are my prospects, and how very small my talents," probably after realizing how barely adequate some of his examination responses were. Ronald also resigned from King Edward's Horse on February 28, eliminating one more activity which drained his time and created one more expense (*C&G* 1.44).[33]

After finishing his papers and without knowing the final outcome of his examinations, a narrowly squeaked Second Class result, Ronald Tolkien seemingly caught the train to Charlton Kings to arrive on March 1. Ronald was, we think, a man on a mission: a Ring-bearer.[34] Ronald was not careful with money and had a habit of running up expenditures (*Bio* 53, *TFA* 32, *C&G* 1.822, Priestman 24). He may have returned to Birmingham's E.H. Lawley and Sons to buy an engagement ring as he would be less likely to be known there. The couple did not want to announce their engagement (*Bio* 62). Further, it was time to cash in on the "bills," charged at one kiss per hour, the fee Edith must pay Ronald for his time spent studying for his examinations.

Edith had sent George Field's engagement ring back as she had promised, and Ronald needed to replace it to seal the status of the relationship.[35] Etiquette, of course, had rules to cover the contingency of the broken engagement: the

---

33 See Bunting's "Tolkien in Love" for a discussion of the possible financial support of this activity, given by Tolkien's Aunt Jane, who would likely have disapproved of his plans to marry (7-8).
34 On April 8, 1913 on page 6, the *Times* published the April 7, 1913 results of Honour Moderations. The *Oxford University Gazette* posted the results on April 17, 1913 (*C&G* 1.45). Garth puts Tolkien's Class II result in the context of three other Classics candidates at Exeter achieving the same results, two doing worse, and only one obtaining a First (*Exeter* 24). However, this is a small sample. The question remains not only how did Tolkien do in relation to all the other candidates, but was this an acceptable result for someone with a serious academic career in mind.
The *Cheltenham Looker-On* documents "Mr. Tolkien" stayed at the Moorend Park on March 1, 1913. "Tolkien at the Moorend Park Hotel 1913." Morgan Thomsen, last viewed on 6/5/2020. https://mythoi.tolkienindex.net/2013/12/04/.
35 Edith's engagement ring was later stolen (*C&G* 1.132).

woman had the privilege of terminating an engagement without offering any explanation other than her will, though arbitrary caprice would cast a shadow on her reputation and character. For example, Clementine Hozier broke three engagements before marrying Winston Churchill. The rules proscribed the young woman's return of all letters and gifts from the young man. The man would know that the return of his gifts was final, and he should send hers back also. Social expectation dictated the man was to make no explanation, even privately, as to the reason for the breaking of the engagement. He was honor bound to show great reserve, and not to cast any shadow upon the woman's reputation, whatever she or his friends might say.[36]

About the time Edith replaced George Field's ring with one from Ronald Tolkien, C.H. Jessop wrote Stephen Gateley to let him know that the importune young man, Tolkien of the Birmingham boarding house, had popped up again three years later. Jessop wrote that Ronald's "prospects are poor in the extreme, and when he will be in a position to marry I cannot imagine" (*TFA* 34). The tone of the letter suggests Jessop wrote sometime probably in late March to early April 1913. That would be before Edith's announcement of her intentions of converting to Catholicism. Given Jessop's antipathy to Catholicism, Jessop's tone would be expected to have been much more negative after Edith's declaration.

Stephen Gateley was no longer Edith's guardian in 1913 and a busy man.[37] The fact C.H. Jessop wrote Gateley indicates a kind of "Old Boys" network of social contacts based on business and presumably a previous joint relationship with Warrillow. Jessop may also have thought poorly of the whole situation given

---

36 "Victorian and Edwardian Etiquette for Romance, Chaperons, and Engagements." Last viewed on 6/7/2020. http://etiquipedia.blogspot.com/2013/02/victorian-and-edwardian-era-etiquette.html.
   George was understandably upset and his family was probably insulted and angry at the breaking of the engagement (*Bio* 62). The family may have felt used and that Molly's orphan friend had abused all their kindness and attention. If a date had been set, his family may have had to deal with the return of any wedding presents already received from friends. Any accompanying explanatory note with the returned gifts should mention nothing beyond the fact the engagement had been broken.
   George and Edith "became friends once more" (*Bio* 62), but that was probably after the war when everyone realized how lucky they were to be alive and able to pick up the pieces of their lives.

37 *Tolkien Family Album* refers to Gateley as Edith's guardian. This statement is true, but it is important to remember Gateley's guardianship ended in January 1910. Nevertheless, Edith appears to have had some later contact with Stephen Gateley even after 1913 or how else would she have come to possess this card from Charles Jessop? When and how Stephen Gateley gave this note to Edith Bratt would be a worthwhile story.

that the return of George's ring constituted a "Breach of Promise," something an old school solicitor would take very seriously and which would have damaged Edith's reputation in many eyes.

Ronald Tolkien wrote Father Francis Morgan about his marriage plans when he returned for the start of the school year on January 12, 1913 (*Bio* 62). Father Francis Morgan would have impressed on Ronald the need for Edith to convert. Father Francis Morgan's own Catholic mother, María Manuela Osborne-Mann, married the Protestant Francis Morgan. This marriage required a papal dispensation which was only obtained due to the Osborne-Mann family's influence with the Church and their significant connections (Bru 25-27), none of which Ronald had. Edith must convert to have their wedding blessed by the Catholic Church.

Edith was open to converting to Catholicism, partly because she believed her family had previously been Catholic (*Bio* 65). There is, of course, a trivial sense in which everyone in England had family long ago that had been Catholic, i.e. before Henry VIII's creation of the Church of England in 1534. Edith's father, Alfred Warrillow, had been married in an Anglican church, but his employing a Catholic solicitor may suggest some sympathies toward Catholicism. Prejudice against Catholics among Anglicans was very strong at the time in England, as can be seen from the reaction of Ronald Tolkien's relatives to his mother Mabel's conversion. It would be unusually tolerant for an Anglican to engage a Catholic solicitor.

Edith must have known conversion to Catholicism would result in the loss of her immediate social network in Charlton Kings which she had built up over the past three years. Becoming a Catholic would mean the end of all of her involvement at the local Anglican church of St. Mary's including playing the organ and helping with the Boys' Club and the choir outings. It would also affect her participation in the Primrose League, many of whose members would share "Uncle" Jessop's strong anti-Catholic views (*Bio* 65). Further, Edith had probably already alienated her old friend, Molly Field, by ending the engagement to Molly's brother, George. It is unknown how Edith's other friend from Dresden House, Mabel Sheaf, would have taken the news of a broken engagement plus conversion to Catholicism. Edith expected Mr. Jessop to order her to leave as soon as she could "find some other accommodation" (*Bio* 66). Finding some other accommodation in Charlton Kings, whose small town sensibility would rally around the established and respectable Charles Jessop, would make no sense. To convert meant she would be moving elsewhere.

Edith wanted to delay telling "Uncle" Jessop until a time nearer the wedding date because of her dread of confronting his outbursts. However, Ronald Tolkien demanded Edith act quickly, calling the despised Church of England "a pathetic and shadowy medley of half-remembered traditions and mutilated beliefs" (*Bio* 65). Ronald had mended his slack church attendance since his reunion with Edith in January 1911, as part of his recommitment to his faith as documented in his work-diary. Ronald recalled his mother's example of endurance when persecuted for her faith. Carpenter speculates, without providing any evidence, Ronald Tolkien may have felt Edith needed to prove her love by converting after having been engaged to George Field (*Bio* 66).

So, Edith told the Jessops of her plans "to pope," and unsurprisingly Mr. Jessop ordered Edith to leave as soon as she could find some other residence (*Bio* 66). Given that Edith moved by June 14, 1913, she probably told him in April as it would take at least a month or two to decide where to move and how and to arrange all the details (*C&G* 1.49). While Edith may have dreaded the confrontation, there is nothing to indicate she regretted leaving the Jessop home. Rather, Edith may have been so eager to leave the stifling control of the Jessop residence that her previous engagement to George Field may have been in some way a conventionally acceptable, back-up exit plan from her confinement at the Jessops'.

With "Uncle" Jessop providing a veil which hid her birth, Edith became more outgoing and social. But the need to cater to "Uncle" Jessop's temper fueled a desire to escape into a marriage, hopefully with Ronald Tolkien, but possibly with George Field. While separated from Edith, Ronald had escaped into fantasy and student pranks, but now he was ready and eager to commit to a new life with Edith. The move to Warwick would create a new beginning for both of them. Things were moving fast for Edith Bratt.

Waiting in Warwick, 1913-1915

The hopes Edith had placed in the "declarations and promises" of the teenage Ronald Tolkien in 1909/1910 were brought to fruition with the engagement ring Ronald presented her in 1913 (*Bio* 61). The now impending marriage brought with it a new life with a new name which would bury the shame of her illegitimacy. There was, however, a catch. Her agreement to convert to Catholicism prompted a move which in effect burnt her bridges to the Anglican church and the safe-haven which "Uncle" Jessop had offered her in Charlton Kings. In Warwick, Edith would be free, for the first time, of the supervision, intimidation and control of others and could be reunited with the one sympathetic family member she had, her "substitute mother," Jennie Grove (*TFA* 36). Her life was increasingly bound up with Ronald Tolkien whose artwork, poetry and invented languages began to reflect her presence and importance.

It was Edith's decision to move to Warwick, but we do not know why she chose that destination (*Bio* 66). Stephen Gateley, previously her guardian, dealt in real estate transactions and may have pointed her to Warwick as a place where she could find a good house. That does not seem like a strong explanation. As a solicitor for the Roman Catholic Archdiocese of Birmingham, Gateley may have known that Father William Murphy, who was born and raised in the Birmingham area (1881, 1891 census), had been placed in Warwick in November 1912.[1] If not moving for a job, people usually move to someplace where they know someone. Consequently, the prospective Catholic convert, Edith, may have been encouraged by Gateley to seek out a Catholic contact in Warwick, Father William Murphy.

---

1 "Stephen Gateley." The Archdiocese of Birmingham Archives, last viewed on 6/9/2020. https://www.birminghamarchdiocesanarchives.org.uk/archives_index.asp?searchstring=Stephen%20Gateley&searchstringand=%&searchparishlo=0&searchparishhi=99999999&searchcollectionlo=0&searchcollectionhi=99999999#results. Notice in *Warwick and Warwickshire Advertiser* Saturday 23 November 1912, p. 5.

Edith moved to Warwick with her cousin, Jennie Grove, and Jennie's dog, Sam, in June 1913 to "temporary rooms" (*TFA* 36, *Bio* 66).[2] They rented a house, and when Ronald arrived on June 14, he spent time with Edith "searching for a house for Edith and Jennie" (*TFA* 36, *Bio* 66). While Carpenter has only vague references to Edith having money, i.e. she "had inherited a small amount of land [...] and this produced just enough income to keep her" (*Bio* 39), she was "the lost heiress" of Tolkien's December 1912 play, *The Bloodhound, the Chef, and the Suffragette* (*Bio* 59). Edith, the heiress, was now in control of her own funds. She could easily afford to rent a house at 15 Victoria Road, Warwick, from Mrs. Annie Arnold (*Bio* 66). Recently built in 1906, it was an attractive, three-story mid-terraced Edwardian home situated close to the town center as well as shops and parks.[3] The house today still has its original terracotta tiles on the front path and hall and there is a yard in the back. This is not the house pictured in *Tolkien Family Album* which sits farther down Victoria Street (37). That house may have been the house Edith rented when she first moved to Warwick (*Bio* 66).

Edith established a household with her own piano, which she kept all her life, as well as a valuable set of hand-painted Staffordshire china (*TFA* 37). At this time, she probably also purchased the small oak desk with an Edwardian harp-shaped chair, which her children remember (*TFA* 27). Unlike Ronald, Edith was a good money manager as seen by her meticulous account book (*TFA* 46).[4] In Warwick, she showed good judgment and spent her money on investments which would last. She gave up this pleasant house in Warwick "with some regret" when she moved in 1916 to follow Ronald to his camp in Staffordshire (*TFA* 38).

---

2 Tolkien appears to be fond of Sam and asked about him in the November 29, 1914 letter to Edith: "How's the poor dog? Please give my love to Jennie" (McIlwaine 155). Sam was probably a faithful companion and protective of Jennie, traits another Sam, Sam Gamgee, would share.

3 What is often presented as "common knowledge" about Tolkien should be viewed with caution. Despite two feature articles in major newspapers, i.e. June 19, 2017 *Birmingham Mail* and June 23, 2017 *The Sun* (https://www.thesun.co.uk/news/3872003/jjr-tolkien-house-for-sale-warwickshire-lord-of-the-rings-hobbit/, last viewed on 7/3/2020.), the claim that this residence was Edith Bratt's is ambiguous. The two major newspapers did not do "due diligence" as the tax records show Mrs. Arnold is the owner and Edith Bratt is the renter. Likewise, there is an unsubstantiated real estate announcement for the house where Tolkien supposedly lived in Great Haywood, the "Rock Cottage," which has no clear documentation of his staying there.

4 Keeping an account book may have been one thing Edith learned from her mother, Fannie Bratt, as Fannie almost certainly had to keep the account books for her business.

The fact Edith had an independent income and was not financially dependent on Ronald Tolkien, contrary to the picture implicit in the official biography, created a relationship unusual for the time, as opposed to an "average marriage" (duPlessis 71). The dynamic of their relationship did not follow the typical pattern of the woman as "the little wife." Rather it was Edith who was providing a home and the stability which Ronald Tolkien had not had since perhaps even as long ago as the period in Sarehole living with his mother and brother. Ronald, the Oxford student, was still dependent on Father Francis Morgan's generosity to pay for school (*Bio* 49, *Letters* 52) and had "always been desperately poor" and "always had something of a wanderer's life" (qtd. in *Great War* 44, 130). Carpenter portrays Tolkien as considering his rooms at Oxford as "his home" (*Bio* 52), and Garth repeats this (*Exeter* 7). This statement does not seem accurate nor does Carpenter substantiate the claim. On January 6, 1914, two days before their betrothal, Tolkien wrote about their being "two homeless children" (McIlwaine 148). Having a home meant a lot to him.

Number 15 Victoria Street is the unit on the left in this picture with a dog in the window. (Google Earth)

Ronald Tolkien came to visit Edith in Warwick June 14-28, 1913 (*C&G* 1.49), presumably to help with the move, i.e. unpacking, putting up boxes, hanging pictures, etc. Jennie Grove functioned as a necessary chaperone because otherwise Edith and Ronald could not visit (McIlwaine 170).[5] It is not surprising that in the stress and disorder of setting up Edith's first independent household, Edith and Ronald "were not always happy together" as Ronald "found the hours that passed in domestic concerns to be rather irritating" (*Bio* 66). "[W]hen they were together their tempers would often flare," but they also went punting down the Avon like any typical couple (*Bio* 66). It was normal for Edith to order servants around, but Ronald, who did not like being "bossed around" (Morton and Hayes 51), had not had a woman "boss" him around since his mother's death when he was twelve. He would not have been accustomed to taking orders, even if he was trying to be helpful. Edith had no reason to let Ronald tell her how to spend her money or where to live, especially with his less than stellar track record in money management (*Bio* 53), and she is likely to have made that clear. She was an intelligent woman who had learned that "Aunt" Jessop's example of cowering in response to her husband's demands was not a good one to follow, so she was not inclined to repeat such a mistake in her own life.

Ronald Tolkien knew how lucky he was to have Edith. She was the beautiful, accomplished, well-to-do heiress who would have been a prize for many, but Edith chose Ronald, a student with an income of £20-40 a year (*Letters* 53), casting aside the financially more promising George Field. Ronald could see her as the *Kalevala*'s Maid of the North, rejecting the more established suitor for the Smith. Perhaps like the knight often identified as Sir Gawain in *The Canterbury Tales*' "The Wife of Bath's Tale," a variant of the medieval poem *The Wedding of Sir Gawain and Dame Ragnell*, Tolkien may have chosen Sir Gawain's path of allowing women their own sovereignty or the ability to make their own decisions. Tolkien would have known Sir Gawain already from his academic work on *Sir Gawain and the Green Knight*.

When things were more settled, Ronald sketched *Pageant House Gardens* on June 28, 1913 (*Bio* 67, *A&I* 19). This handsome building was part of the rebuilding of Warwick in the 1700s and was acquired by Warwick Town Council. The

5 "Victorian and Edwardian Etiquette for Romance, Chaperons, and Engagements," last viewed on 6/7/2020. http://etiquipedia.blogspot.com/2013/02/victorian-and-edwardian-era-etiquette.html.

name 'Pageant House' comes from the fact the costumes for the very successful Warwick pageant of 1906 were made here. The pageant raised enough money

Pageant House, Vauxford, May 2018 (Wikipedia Commons)

to purchase the back garden, which then became the first public garden in Warwick. It was named Pageant Gardens. This garden is still open to the public and is a popular setting for wedding photographs. Tolkien wrote on the back of the drawing: "We spent a very happy morning here Mary [Edith's second name]: do you remember in the dear early sweet days of our first liberty" (*A&I* 19). Tolkien sounds very happy to be with Edith in Warwick in June 1913, contrary to the difficulties Carpenter highlights.

Most importantly for Ronald Tolkien, in June 1913, they attended Benediction at the local Roman Catholic church, St. Mary Immaculate, "from which we came away serenely happy, for it was the first time that we had ever been able to go calmly side by side to church" (*Bio* 66). Edith took instruction in the Catholic Catechism from the recently arrived Father Murphy, in preparation for her reception on January 8, 1914 into the Catholic Church and formal betrothal with Ronald.[6] The banns for the Catholic wedding would have been read aloud in

---

6 Notice in *Warwick and Warwickshire Advertiser*, Saturday 23 November 1912, p. 5.

St. Mary Immaculate the three Sundays before the wedding to allow time for anyone with a just cause to voice an objection to the marriage.

Ronald could only stay in Warwick briefly as Edith was a secret he had not revealed to his friends and family. One wonders if, like the Victorian Algernon

St. Mary Immaculate Roman Catholic Church, Warwick
(Google Earth)

Moncrieff in Oscar Wilde's *The Importance of Being Earnest* (1895), Ronald Tolkien might have created his own fictional Bunbury to explain his visit to Warwick.

Ronald Tolkien then left Warwick to briefly visit his school friend, Robert Gilson, at his home, Canterbury House, in Marston Green, a village southeast of the center of Birmingham in late June 1913 (*C&G* 1.50). Then he saw his Aunt May Incledon (née Suffield) and family in Barnt Green for at least ten days in July. His cousin, Marjorie Incledon, was interested in landscapes. When at Barnt Green, Ronald may have gotten feedback, encouragement, and suggestions on technique and composition for his new artworks done in a new large sketchbook (*C&G* 1.50). He painted *King's Norton from Bilberry Hill, Foxglove Year* (*A&I* 21), *The Cottage, Barnt Green* (*A&I* 18), and two other paintings with different views of the garden and a pencil drawing of the garden (*A&I* 33). Then Ronald went to his Aunt Jane's (née Suffield) Phoenix Farm where he probably saw his brother, Hilary, as well as his Aunt (*C&G* 1.50). Here he continued his burst of artwork: *Phoenix Farm, Gedling* (*A&I* 20), *Phoenix Farm from Gedling*, and probably *Lamb's Farm Gedling, Notts* [Nottinghamshire] (*C&G* 1.50). This burst of artwork was consistent with Tolkien's pattern of drawing on previous holidays in 1910 and 1912, and presumably in 1911 when he was in Switzerland. But like the art of December 1913 with its bright palate, it appears to spring from Tolkien's potent happiness after the June 1913 visit to Warwick, knowing Edith had committed to him and they would have a future together.

Ronald Tolkien then assumed his responsibilities for his first job as an escort and tutor for three Mexican boys on a tour of France with the boys' aunts from July 29 to September 1, 1913 (*C&G* 1.50-52). Ronald and Edith wrote each other during this separation, with Ronald sending letters July 29, July 30, (*C&G* 1.50) probably August 10, August 18 (*C&G* 1.51), and August 29 (*C&G* 1.52). There may be more letters which serve as sources of the information for the vagaries and crisis of this tour. Ronald also wrote "lovingly of [Edith's] 'little house'" in Warwick (*Bio* 67).

Tolkien returned to visit Edith in late September (*C&G* 1.52), probably after a visit around September 16, 1913 to Norwich (Garth, *Worlds* 192). Tolkien's familiarity with Norwich's Gothic church of St. Peter Mancroft and its rivers, Yare and Nen, resurfaces in his poem *The Man in the Moon Came Down too Soon* (Garth, *Worlds* 65). Nen also seems to reemerge in 'nenn' 'river' in Tolkien's Gnomish lexicon of 1917 (60).[7] Ronald then revisited Birmingham probably for the September 27 and possibly October 1 meetings of the TCBS proposed by Christopher Wiseman (*C&G* 1.52). Tolkien again stayed in Warwick in early

---

7 See Hooker, *Tolkien and Welsh* 51-4

October returning to Oxford by October 10 for the October 12, 1913 start of Michaelmas Term (*C&G* 1.52). He hardly seems to be able to stay away from Warwick and Edith.

In the fall of 1913, Ronald and Edith were still not officially engaged or betrothed, and they had not told anyone besides Father Francis Morgan about their engagement. As a result, Edith was on her own and alone. Ronald Tolkien was busy at school, and Edith would have needed a chaperone to visit him (McIlwaine 170). This was difficult to arrange, although Father Francis Morgan, now reconciled to the marriage as it would be a Catholic union, stopped in Warwick on his way to Oxford and chaperoned Edith on at least one occasion (*TFA* 35). After the close call of Honours Moderations, Ronald Tolkien was working harder at school as seen in his winning £5 (or £566.73 in 2018 money or $750.12) by successfully competing for the Skeat prize for English in the spring of 1914 (*Bio* 69).[8] This prize was for an essay demonstrating knowledge of a portion of English literature prescribed annually by Exeter College.

With the betrothal ceremony imminent, Ronald Tolkien had to reveal Edith's existence to his friends in the Tea Club Barrovian Society (TCBS). He wrote Rob Gilson and Christopher Wiseman at Cambridge and also informed G.B. Smith, who was at Oxford with Tolkien (*Bio* 68). Tolkien, however, was still so discreet, if not secretive, about the engagement that Rob Gilson had to write on January 5, 1914, to ask if Tolkien would "reveal the lady's name" (*Great War* 33). At first glance, the mores of Edwardian society might have dictated Tolkien's hesitation because a commitment to a woman might distance him from his all-male writing group (*Great War* 33). The patriarchal Victorian/Edwardian society in which Tolkien lived fostered all-male bonding in all-male schools, with all-male activities. The segregation of boys and girls started early and did not allow the sexes to mix.

---

8 "Inflation Calculator." Bank of England, last viewed on 5/31/2020. https://www.bankofengland.co.uk/monetary-policy/inflation/inflation-calculator. An average 2018 rate multiplier of 1.3236 is used to convert to dollars. Garth gives a slightly different view of finances (*Great War* 129).
   Only two candidates took this test at the end of the 1914 Easter vacation. The questions were on the medieval literature of Chaucer and Langland. Tolkien's library request for Langland's *Piers Plowman* may have been part of his preparation for this exam (*Exeter* 26).

Tolkien appears to have referred to these factors to explain his reticence as indicated in both Wiseman's and Gilson's replies. Christopher Wiseman wrote, "The only fear is that you will rise above the TCBS," and Gilson replied, "I have no fear at all that such a staunch tcbsite as yourself will ever be anything else" (qtd. in *Great War* 33). The TCBS knew nothing of the scandal of 1909/1910 involving Edith and Ronald.

However, it is likely Ronald had a more personal and compelling reason for not revealing Edith's name to the members of the TCBS. He wanted to prevent them from revealing Edith's name to his Aunt May Incledon or any of the Incledon family before the die of the betrothal was irrevocably cast. Ronald Tolkien knew his "astonished family" (*Letters* 53) would have to accept the *fait accompli* of an official Catholic betrothal, cutting short any unpleasant discussions of his and Edith's previous audacity and troubles.

His family would have been astonished partly because Ronald Tolkien had recapitulated aspects of both of his parents' courtship. Like his mother, Mabel Suffield, Ronald had fallen in love at eighteen. Mabel then committed to Arthur Tolkien at the age of twenty-one when she set sail to South Africa to marry him. For Ronald, this commitment took the form of a proposal to Edith at the age of twenty-one, formal betrothal at the age of twenty-two once Edith had been received into the Catholic Church, and marriage at the age of twenty-four due to the need to complete his degree in 1915 and then the interruption of the war.

Arthur, like his son Ronald, may have failed to ask the guardian of the beloved for consent to marry. Arthur Tolkien's proposal was accepted by the eighteen-year-old Mabel Suffield, but Carpenter states John Suffield, Mabel's father, "would not permit a formal betrothal for two years because of her youth" (*Bio* 9). In the context of Victorian custom, this statement makes no sense. If Arthur Tolkien had asked John Suffield for Mabel's hand in marriage, the father could have easily stipulated there be no marriage until she was twenty-one. John Suffield knew Victorian etiquette allowed the woman the uncontested privilege of terminating an engagement without offering any explanation other than her will. If Mabel changed her mind, she was free to terminate the commitment.[9] In contrast to his father, Ronald not only failed to ask Edith Bratt's guardian, Stephen Gateley, for permission, but he himself did not ask his own guardian, Father Francis Morgan which, given his age of only eighteen, would have been a requirement. At the time of his 1888 proposal, Arthur Tolkien was only a bank clerk, and like his son Ronald, had minimal financial security to offer his intended and her family. Given Arthur's financial status, he could logically anticipate a rejection by Mabel's father. Arthur's ultimately successful pursuit of a substantial position as a bank manger allowed him to support Mabel in a manner her father would find acceptable. Arthur Tolkien's unorthodox courtship may explain the report of John Suffield's begrudging "tolerance" of his son-in-law (*Bio* 10).

The couple's exchanging secret letters would have been seen as rebellious and defiant behavior in 1882, and a warning of a possible elopement. Such things were not done in respectable families. Faced with fear of scandal and a possible elopement, John Suffield, a Victorian father, would have been forced to act as Mabel's flaunting of convention would have fueled gossip and ridicule which would have affected not only the family's reputation, but also his business. John Suffield would have taken steps to separate the pair in a way very similar to the way Father Morgan separated Ronald Tolkien and the object of his affection, Edith Bratt. Mabel's father could have sent her to stay with other family elsewhere, for example, her older brother, Roland, in Manchester (Morton and Hayes 14). The history of how Sigmund Freud arranged a secret engagement in 1882 with the twenty-year-old Martha Bernays illustrates the thinking of that time. When Martha's widowed mother learned of this, within the year the Bernays family decamped from Vienna to the hinterlands of Wandsbek near Hamburg (Burke 47). Mrs. Bernays was not going to have rumor, innuendo, or the vagaries of hormones besmirch her family and Martha's future, especially as a result of a penniless medical student, Sigmund Freud, whom she found unimpressive.

At this point, Edith and Ronald Tolkien are a couple and their lives have meshed. Consequently, to understand what is happening with Edith, we often need to fill in the background about Ronald Tolkien as those were the experiences they were sharing and talking about. Also, we will see Edith

---

9 "Victorian and Edwardian Etiquette for Romance, Chaperons, and Engagements," last viewed on 6/7/2020. http://etiquipedia.blogspot.com/2013/02/victorian-and-edwardian-era-etiquette.html.

more and more through Ronald Tolkien's eyes as he incorporates Edith into his invented languages and mythology and expresses his feelings about her in his artwork.

Michaelmas Term at Oxford ended on December 6, 1913. Tolkien went to Birmingham to visit friends and participate in Old Edwardian activities at King Edward's High School in mid-December. He visited his cousins and Aunt and Uncle Incledon at Barnt Green in late December up to January 4, 1914 (*C&G* 1.55). There is no mention of Ronald's seeing Edith during the Christmas break. However, given his happiness "in the dear early sweet days of our first liberty" (*A&I* 19), his wish for contact with Edith possibly seen in the letters sent during the 1913 summer tour of France, and his repeated visits; it is hard to believe Ronald Tolkien did not spend time during this holiday with his Edith. The first week in December is a possibility.

Tolkien had his twenty-second birthday on January 3, 1914. On January 6 anticipating the reunion with his soon-to-be-betrothed Edith, Tolkien drew a romantic fantasy house, *Untitled* (*Northern House*) with rounded walls, an ornamental door and windows, and a seashell roof in a forest with a shaft of moonlight beaming down, a delightful hideaway for a newly united couple (*A&I* 42-43). On January 8, the Catholic Church received Ronald's fiancée, Edith Bratt and formalized their betrothal. Edith was now officially Ronald's intended. The date of January 8 marked the one year anniversary of their reunion under the viaduct in Charlton Kings (*Bio* 68). Tolkien celebrated this occasion with the poem *Magna Dei Gloria* (*Warwick*) or *To the Greater Glory of God* (*Warwick*) dedicated "To EMB" (Edith Mary Bratt) (*C&G* 1.56). Historically, betrothal in Roman Catholicism was a formal contract considered as binding as marriage, with marriage to another being forbidden.[10] The Church regarded betrothed couples as husband and wife – even before their wedding and physical union.

"[T]he question of Edith becoming a Catholic was an emotional matter" for Ronald Tolkien (*Bio* 66). The meaning of Catholicism to Tolkien was deeply tied to his memory and view of his mother whom he believed had been persecuted for her Faith. In November 1913, Tolkien wrote:

---

10 "Betrothal" New Advent, last viewed on 6/10/2020. https://www.newadvent.org/cathen/02537c.htm.

My own dear mother was a martyr indeed, and it is not to everybody that God grants so easy a way to his great gifts as he did to Hilary and myself, giving us a mother who killed herself with labour and trouble to ensure us keeping the faith. (*Bio* 31)

Tolkien closely associated his mother with his own membership in the Catholic Church and in some ways after Tolkien's mother died, Catholicism or perhaps rather The Blessed Virgin Mary, "took the place in his affections that she [Tolkien's mother] had previously occupied," providing a consolation which was "emotional as well as spiritual" (*Bio* 31). The "deep and passionate nature" of Tolkien's faith was "entwined" with the memory of his dead mother (*Bio* 68) and also very likely with Tolkien's veneration of Mary. Tolkien's guardian, Father Francis Morgan, was known to have a special veneration of Mary.[11]

Given the close association of Catholicism and Ronald's memories of his mother, Edith's conversion to Catholicism was likely to summon up memories of Tolkien's mother, creating a "Shadow of the Past" which intruded into Tolkien's happy present and promising future plans. Before Ronald Tolkien returned to Oxford for the start of Hilary term on January 18, while still in Warwick, Tolkien painted a watercolor entitled *Eeriness* between January 6 and January 12, 1914 (*A&I* 43-44). *Eeriness* appears to be an attempt to express and try to come to terms with a variety of intense feelings in response to Edith's conversion.[12] The *Eeriness* "wizard" can be interpreted as a representation of Tolkien's mother, Mabel, in need of the praying guardian angel behind her and the three trees of Calvary on the hill for her salvation (McIlwaine 168, Bunting, "1904" 64-66).

---

11 "Father Francis Morgan." The Oratory, last viewed on 6/3/2020. https://www.birminghamoratory.org.uk/francis-morgan/.

12 In this scene, "tall, straight trees that line and shade the road appear to stretch out menacing arms toward a wizard-like figure with a staff," and with "a cat design on the back of the robe" (*A&I* 44), recalling the cat lurking between the curtains in Tolkien's earlier drawing, *Wickedness* (*A&I* 37). Behind the wizard and just outside the wizard's circle of light, is a guardian angel with hands raised in prayer. The hill with three trees is almost certainly a variant of the standard representation of Calvary as the three crosses are referred to as "trees" in the New Testament, i.e. Acts, 5:30. Mabel Tolkien died "too ill for viaticum" (*Letters* 354) and therefore in Tolkien's Catholic view she would have died with sins still unforgiven so that she would be placed in Purgatory ("What is Purgatory?" Catholic Answers. https://www.catholic.com/tract/purgatory, last viewed on 6/9/2020). In this picture with its praying guardian angel and the light of Calvary, we see Tolkien's deep concern for the salvation of his mother's soul.
The unpublished illustration, *Childhood Memories of My Grandmother's House*, dates from this period in January, and it may also recall memories of Tolkien's mother as Tolkien began visiting his Tolkien grandmother at the age of 3 or 4, probably in the company of his mother (Grotta-Kurska 20, *Bio* 18). Tolkien would identify this house as belonging only to his grandmother as his grandfather Tolkien died by August, 1896 when J.R.R. Tolkien was only four (*Bio* 18; Bunting, "*Roverandom* Part 1" 3).

In response to the discordant and somber mood evident in *Eeriness*, on January 12, Tolkien then drew a bright watercolor, *Beyond* (McIlwaine 170), with a narrow road rising into the air. It resembles the frontispiece of *East of the Sun and West of the Moon, Old Tales from the North* (1914), done by Kay Nielsen, an illustrator Tolkien liked (*C&G* 1.56, *A&I* 42, 57, 116).[13] The Nielsen illustration depicts the title story's happily united couple successfully escaping the castle of the Trolls as a result of their being aided by Christians and the girl's being a Christian. This theme would certainly fit with Edith's recent conversion to Catholicism and their betrothal. *Beyond* has an inscription: "Alas! In dreadful mood" (*A&I* 44), but the "dreadful mood" is due to the previous painting *Eeriness* and "a terrible chaos which darkened [Tolkien's] youth and early manhood" reflected in *Eeriness*. McIlwaine associates this turmoil with Tolkien's mother (170; see Bunting, "Spiders Parts I and II").

The images of *Beyond* present a story. In the foreground, Tolkien repeats the cluster of the three fir trees as an allusion to Calvary from *Eeriness*. However, the three trees now also symbolize Edith and Ronald in two of the trees, as named in his poem of January 1915 *As Two Fair Trees*. The central tree would be the tree/cross of Christ. One of the trees is smaller, seemingly weaker, perhaps reflecting Ronald Tolkien's despondent mood which was crushing him. The road leaps a barrier and heads to magical mountains with a full moon and a star/sun. The moon is on the right and the star/sun is on the left suggesting we are in the transformed Warwick (Kortirion), part of Faërie, as the Warwick coat-of-arms has the moon on the right and sun on left. In Tolkien's early stories, 'Kortirion', the ancient dwelling of the Fairies, came to be known in English as 'Warwick' (*LT2* 293). *Beyond* also appears in some ways as a reply to his early drawing of late 1912, *The Back of the Beyond*. In *The Back of the Beyond* the future was a complete unknown, but now in *Beyond* there is an inspiring destination.

Shortly after painting *Beyond*, Tolkien painted the watercolors, *Here* and *There*, with a similar choice of colors and a relevant annotation, "[...] same mood

---

13 Hammond and Scull state this may recall the 'Olórë Mallë', the 'Path of Dreams', in *The Book of Lost Tales* (*A&I* 66, *LT1* 211). Hammond and Scull document Tolkien's use of two drawings of Nielsen from Arthur Quiller-Couch's *In Powder and Crinoline* (1913) (*A&I* 57, 116).
Tolkien's 1915 poem, *The Shores of Faery*, which starts with the line, "East of the Moon/West of the Sun" plays with the title of "East of the Sun and West of the Moon," showing his familiarity with this story.

getting milder" (McIlwaine 170-71). *Here* has an unusual circular frame and is annotated "in an exciting place." The circle represents unification, totality, wholeness, and inclusion, and in the mid-nineteenth century, a Celtic revival led to an increased use of the ringed or Celtic cross. The priest at the Warwick church was Father William J. Murphy. He was born in Birmingham, but his father was from Ireland where these crosses were common (1881 census). Father Murphy may have promoted the ringed cross. Tolkien's mother's grave at St. Peter's in Bromsgrove was marked with a Celtic cross. The circular composition also embodies the Sun or Son who brings Light and Hope, a verbal pun which Tolkien, well known for his puns and verbal jests, will use in his 1915 poem about himself and Edith, *As Two Fair Trees* (McIlwaine 146). The equation of the Sun of Righteousness and the Son of God, Christ, was also made in Catholic litany and theology.[14] The watercolor again shows the three fir trees of *Beyond* "with concentric circles swirling around the central tree, perhaps conveying the dizziness of excitement" (McIlwaine 170). The three trees should be seen as a reference to Calvary, given Tolkien's deep Catholic faith and the recent betrothal ceremony, with the large central tree as Christ and the two adjacent trees, now of equal size, as Ronald and Edith. The topmost circle could be a halo marking the Christ. The giddy excitement concerns Edith's reception into the Church, the assurance of her salvation, and their union with each other and the Church. The three concentric circles could be Edith's engagement ring and a set of wedding rings, which echo the trinity seen in the trees. Edith's report, that her first confession and first communion were "a great and wonderful happiness," would have delighted Ronald Tolkien (*Bio* 68).

There, annotated "when you don't want to go from here," "depicts a distant mountain" indicating "a barrier that had to be crossed in order to continue the journey" (McIlwaine 170-71). *There* suggests Oxford, which was taking Ronald Tolkien away from Edith and his present happiness, but whose hurdles Tolkien had to surmount to obtain the degree which would let him marry and support

---

14 "As the divisions of the secular year are made by the Earth's revolutions around the sun, so the Church marks her seasons by reference to Christ, the Sun of Righteousness" (Grafton 225). In "The Litany of the Most Holy Name of Jesus," Jesus is "Jesus, Son of the living God [...] Jesus, Sun of Righteousness; Jesus, Son of the Virgin Mary" (Anonymous, *Vade Mecum* 59-60.)

Edith.[15] However, in the painting, the mountain's peak pierces through a night sky suggesting a transcendent future.

The excitement of the January betrothal and reception into the Catholic Church began to fade for Edith. Going to mass and taking communion became more difficult at the "sordid" and unappealing Catholic church, especially when compared to the handsome church in Cheltenham which Edith had previously attended (*Bio* 68). Although Edith helped with a church club for working girls, she made few friends (*Bio* 68). In Charlton Kings, "Uncle" Jessop's status and network of acquaintances had eased her way into a social life. She was now on her own, and the process of building a social network was much slower and harder. Edith was not needed as an organist at the Catholic church, and she had less incentive to practice, though not because, as Carpenter wrote, she "knew now she would never make a career as a musician" due to the demands of family and marriage (*Bio* 69). Edith could afford, but only permitted herself to occasionally attend, the theater or concerts, while Ronald's letters were full of dinner-parties, fun, and movies (*Bio* 69). Ronald's money from his summer tutoring job seemed to have been "burning a hole in his pocket:" he probably paid off what he owed on Edith's ring, but then went on a spending spree which included two tailored suits, furniture, Japanese prints for his rooms in Oxford, and custom rugby boots (*Bio* 68).[16] Edith, careful with her money, was leading a quiet life waiting for Ronald (*Bio* 69).

Carpenter states Edith's life was "dreary" in Warwick because of Ronald Tolkien's limited visits, but this statement seems unsupported (*Bio* 69). On

---

15 A related picture in this series, *Everywhere*, has not been published (*C&G* 1.49). Forty years later, another young Englishman, Paul McCartney, would express the feelings of love, not in a painting, but in a song, "Here, There, and Everywhere."

16 "On 11 October 1913, an Oxford undergraduate bought a pair of black leather football [rugby] boots for 14 shillings and sixpence and spent an extra sixpence on a pair of brown laces." "Rare ledgers reveal shoe-buying habits of Tolkien and Waugh," last viewed on 6/9/2020. https://www.theguardian.com/uk-news/2017/mar/22/rare-ledgers-shoe-buying-habits-of-tolkien-waugh-ducker-son. Using the Bank of England Inflation Calculator, 1 pound was worth £116.26 in 2019. That would yield a cost of £84.29 for the shoes today or £87.20 with laces. Using an average 2018 rate multiplier of 1.3236, that would be $111.57 for the shoes and $115.18 for shoes with laces.

Ducker & Son had been an Oxford custom shoemaker since 1898. Tolkien finally paid for the rugby boots in April 1914. The date suggests Tolkien had gotten carried away and was not watching his money carefully when he made this purchase (https://www.tolkienguide.com/modules/newbb/vi/viewtopic.phps, seen 9/1/02019, but no longer available). Tolkien was not careful with money and had a habit of running up expenditures (*Bio* 53, *TFA* 32, *C&G* 1.822, Priestman 24).

the contrary, Warwick would have been a desired escape from Edith's having to "walk on eggshells" at the Jessops' to mollify "Uncle" Jessop's temper. Edith finally was free of other people's rules in her own household. Edith was doing what many other women did at the time, namely waiting for their sweetheart to be in a financial position to marry. Her relative social isolation due to her recent move may have made this more difficult.

Marrying for love was not the norm in Edwardian society, but a love match could happen among the working and middle-class where property and social status were not so compelling as in the upper class. Girls usually met their sweethearts through friends, family, or at work. Because it took a while for men to save up enough to be able to afford a wife and family, middle class and upper working-class men tended to marry later in life.[17] Carpenter's implication that Edith had regrets as indicated by "she had little incentive to practice as she now knew she would not have a career in music due to the demands of family and marriage" is misleading (*Bio* 69, qtd. in duPlessis 54). Edith, the heiress, enjoyed music and played well and was happy as a volunteer at the Cheltenham church, but she was not giving up a career.

Edith kept her letters from Ronald and we assume Ronald kept Edith's letters also. These are now in the Tolkien Archives in the Bodleian Library in Oxford (Mathison 7). Ronald repeatedly expresses how important Edith's letters are to him and how he looks forward to them, as in "You do write splendid letters to me" (*Letters* 7) and "I read your letter again last night before blowing out my candle, and it was a very dear one" (McIlwaine 155). A great deal of what we know about Tolkien comes from his letters to Edith. Ronald appears to have written twice a week if the dates of August 5, 8, 11, 14, and 16, during his 1914 Cornwall excursion are typical. After their reunion in January, 1913, there are published pieces from letters of January 15, 17, 24, 26, and February 1 and 28 (See Chapter 5). Ronald wrote Edith detailing his 1913 trip to France as a tutor (*Bio* 67-68), what he was reading (*Bio* 70), what Oxford was like after the declaration of World War I (*Bio* 72), his decision and his experience of joining the Officers' Training Corps (*Bio* 72-73; *Letters* 7, 8; *C&G* 1.62, McIlwaine

---

17 "Corsets, Cutlasses, and Candlesticks." Sharon Biggs Waller, last viewed on 6/9/2020. https:// corsetsandcutlasses.wordpress.com/2013/02/14/romance-and-courtship-iardian-era-it-wasnt-much-fun/.

139, 155), the inception of the Kullevo story (*Letters* 7), and his experience training in Staffordshire (*Bio* 77-78). He shared with Edith his passion for his "mad hobby" of "nonsense fairy language" and his new poem, *Kortirion* (*Letters* 8). It was more important to Ronald Tolkien to send a copy of his new poem, *Kortirion*, to Edith immediately and "keep the TCBS waiting" (*Letters* 8). This underscores Ronald Tolkien's shift in priorities from male companionship to his "lover" and future wife, Edith.

Carpenter characterizes Ronald Tolkien's relationship with Edith as limited to a "self-chosen role of sentimental lover," wrapped "in amatory cliché" (*Bio* 67). None of that is evident in the letter excerpts we have. Ronald's published salutations include an unsurprising "My Edith darling" (*Letters* 7), and another is "My own dearest" (McIlwaine 155). But Tolkien addressed his son, Christopher, during World War II as "My dearest" (*Letters* 102, 103, 106) or "My dearest Chris" (*Letters* 108), and his son Michael was addressed as "My dearest Michael" (*Letters* 54). Ronald called Edith "little one" (*Bio* 67) elsewhere, but it was partly because she was shorter than he was (*TFA* 41, 65). He usually signed his letters to Edith with a simple "Ronald" or "R." or sometimes "John" (*Letters* 434).

Ronald is frank and open in his letters to Edith, writing: the call to the Rector was "boring" and his wife "appalling" (*Letters* 7) and "Gentlemen are non-existent among the superiors [...] and even human beings rare indeed" at the Staffordshire camp (*Bio* 77-78). Ronald appears to see Edith as someone he can confide in and share the ongoing struggles of his life, someone who is a trusted peer and a friend, an equal who understands and cares about all his various interests.

Contrary to Carpenter's assertion, Ronald Tolkien does share his "bookish" side with Edith telling her about: a required essay; reading Shakespeare; spending time with his tutor, Mr. Sisam; the *Kalevala*; writing the Kullervo story; visiting the library; "4 hours" of studying; going to the Essay Club (*Letters* 7, *C&G* 1.64); and reading *Éarendel* to that group and reporting their reactions (*Letters* 8). A letter of November 3, 1913, before the betrothal, reports Ronald Tolkien's taking the oath at the Bodleian and Tolkien's impression of the Radcliffe

Camera (McIlwaine 153).[18] It would be hard to conceive of an activity more "bookish." Edith will later copy out *The Cottage of Lost Play* in February 1917 (*C&G* 1.106). She continued to be interested in Ronald's writing and "shared the family's interest when [Ronald] was writing *The Hobbit* and *The Lord of the Rings*" (*Bio* 158). She was the "first person" who saw Ronald's stories, *Leaf by Niggle* and *Smith of Wooton Major* (*Bio* 158).

Carpenter repeatedly underlines Edith's supposedly limited education and Ronald's lack of encouragement of "intellectual activity." Carpenter writes Edith had "to make an effort to understand his preoccupation with his books and his languages, selfish as it might appear to her [...] [an effort that was] not entirely" successful (*Bio* 153, 67). This characterization of Edith is not at all evident in these letters (see duPlessis 51-52). These statements do not fit with Edith's educational record, i.e. winning "distinction in scripture and English language" in December 1904 and her likely study of Latin which had been offered at Dresden House for years. In relation to Tolkien's early poems and writing, Scull and Hammond's *Companion and Reader's Guide* only quotes letters from members of the TBCS, but Edith's letters may be as good, if not a better, source.

What we see in this correspondence is the glue that united this couple. This was especially true for Ronald Tolkien. It is true Ronald Tolkien idealized Edith, as in "[h]aving the romantic upbringing, I made a boy-and-girl affair serious, and made it the source of effort" (*Letters* 52, *Bio* 58, 61). It is also true Edith was the one person, perhaps beside his brother Hilary (H. Tolkien 62, 69), with whom he could candidly share his feelings, thoughts, past, and hopes. Brought up by his mother, a governess, to have impeccable manners, he could relax and be accepted for himself (Lee 139).

Tolkien mocked the hypocrisy of Victorian etiquette in the first chapter of *The Hobbit* when he lampooned the various meanings of "Good Morning" and the fact a repeated refusal of an offer could be a request for an offer. Edith, too, was brought up by a governess, her mother, and now she may have felt

---

18 "I hereby undertake not to remove from the Library, nor to mark, deface, or injure in any way, any volume, document or other object belonging to it or in its custody; not to bring into the Library, or kindle therein, any fire or flame, and not to smoke in the Library; and I promise to obey all rules of the Library."

she no longer needed to pretend and could be herself. With her own history of a painful past, she could respond to Ronald's "terrible chaos which darkened my youth" (McIlwaine 170). Further, as lovers, they accepted and valued each others' physical selves (*Letters* 52-53). Where else could Ronald Tolkien even hope to find the understanding and empathy for "the dreadful sufferings of our childhoods, from which we rescued one another" (*Letters* 421)? On January 6, 1914, two days before their betrothal, Tolkien wrote: "the next few years will bring us joy and content and love and sweetness such as could not be if we hadn't first been two homeless children and had found one another after long waiting" (McIlwaine 148).

Ronald's next documented visit to Edith was after Trinity term at Oxford ended on June 20, 1914, although he seems to have stayed for the June 23, 1914 Exeter College Sexcentenary Ball as he signed a program (*C&G* 1.826). This record is probably misleading. The biography and other documentation have focused on Tolkien's academic and literary work, and not his private life. It is hard to believe that, as close as Ronald Tolkien appears to feel to Edith, as seen in his letters, he did not spend at least part of his break from the end of Hilary term March 14, 1914, to the start of Trinity term April 26, 1914, with his newly betrothed Edith. The letter from November 29, 1914, indicates there must have been a recent visit which has not been documented because Ronald reassures Edith about a silence which she evidently felt concerned about: "You found I was right then and that nothing more than increasing easy-goingness was at bottom of the silence, didn't you, little one" (McIlwaine 155). As C.S. Lewis noted with disapproval, Tolkien was "the most married man he knew" (Sayer 14), and in Tolkien's Catholic eyes the betrothal was all but marriage.

Visits should now have been easier to arrange as the requirement for a chaperone was to protect the reputation of a single woman. Their public declaration of an intention to marry in January 1914 would fulfill the social requirement that Edith only be alone with a man who intended to marry her. Further, by 1910, women were increasingly appearing in public alone: going shopping, using public transportation, going to the bank, eating in restaurants, and visiting hotel lobbies.[19]

By late January 1914, after informing the members of the TCBS, Ronald would have told "an astonished" family about his engagement to Edith (*Letters* 52). As a result, Tolkien no longer needed to disguise his visits. It may have been in Warwick with Edith during the March 14 to April 26, 1914 break when Tolkien drew in *The Book of Ishness* a watercolor of "the sea, or possibly of the Great Wave" on March 15, 1914; the painting, *Everywhere*; and a design of bells and dancing lampposts titled *Tarantella* (*A&I* 66) apparently referring to a dance, the tarantella (*C&G* 1.58). The painting's title, *Everywhere*, suggests a picture which continues the sequence of thoughts Ronald painted in *Here* and *There* earlier that year in January, i.e. pictures dealing with his relationship to Edith.

Warwick: the Town and Castle from the Priory Gardens, watercolor by Giovanni Antonio Canaletto (1697-1768)

Ronald returned to see Edith in Warwick after June 23, 1914 and probably drew a view of Warwick Castle dated by Tolkien "1913-14?" (McIlwaine 15, *C&G* 1.60). Tolkien was very impressed by the beauty of Warwick with its trees, its hill and castle (*Bio* 66). He should have been, as his path, from the train station to Edith's house across Priory Park, had a view similar to one in Canaletto's (1697-1768) watercolor, *Warwick: The Town and Castle from the*

---

19 "Shopping Liberated Women." History Programming and History.com, last viewed on 6/9/2020. https://www.history.com/news/how-19th-century-women-used-department-stores-to-gain-their-freedom.

Priory Gardens from the 1740s. In 1809, John Constable sketched a similar view.[20] Warwick, home of Edith, was becoming Kortirion: "Very beautiful was Kortirion and the fairies loved it, and it became rich in song and poesy and the light of laughter" (*LT1* 16). In the following year, the budding mythology of Kortirion would encompass Ronald and Edith. This view from Priory Gardens, with strikingly different towers rising over the edge of the escarpment, may have contributed to Tolkien's creation of the "Two Towers" (Hooker, "Tolkien's First World Towers, Pt. II")

Ronald wrote Edith on August 5, 8, 11, 14, and 16, 1914, during his expedition with Father Vincent Reade of the Birmingham Oratory across the Lizard Peninsula in Cornwall. Father Vincent Reade was going to serve mass at the chapel, Our Lady of the Lizard, in Lizard Town (Garth, *Worlds* 62). As Father Reade had been a curate at Porthleven, he was familiar with the area. As a result,

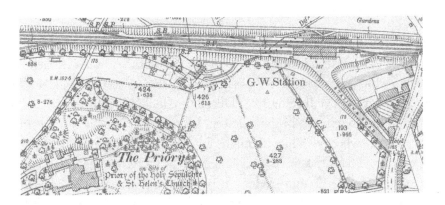

Tolkien's path, marked as a dotted line by SH-K, on a 1905 OS map from National Library of Scotland. It shows the Warwick station on the north-east corner of the Priory Park estate, which gave him a view very like Canaletto's.

he was able to take Tolkien on a number of rambles through the countryside (Garth, *Worlds* 63). On August 8, 1915, Tolkien wrote about walking on top of the cliffs to Kynance Cove (*Bio* 70). This area was already known for its remarkable geology and unique botany. This cove became popular in the early Victorian era with many famous visitors including Queen Victoria, Prince

---

20 Constable's sketch can be seen at Harvard Art Museums, last viewed on 6/9/2020. https://www.harvardartmuseums.org/art/298747.

Albert, and the poet Alfred Tennyson (Sagan-Fenton 158). Tolkien's remarks about "weird wind-holes and spouts into the cliffs which blow with trumpety noises or spout foam" (*Bio* 70) are likely to be a report of the Devil's Bellows at Asparagus Island in the cove (Garth, *Worlds* 63). On August 11, 1914, in his sketchbook from 1912, Tolkien drew a view of Cadgwith from the hill above it (*A&I* 24-25). Tolkien painted *Cove near the Lizard* on August 12, 1914 (McIlwaine 172), as well as *Caerthilian Cove* and *Lion Rock* (*A&I* 24), though Caerthilian Cove is behind Tolkien and he is at Pentreach Beach looking north (*A&I* 25). Tolkien made a third sketch that day of another cove (*A&I* 25). Ronald wrote about walking back to Lizard town through the countryside by the Helford River, the bare "Goonhilly" downs, through Ruan Minor in fading light with the flashes of the Lizard Lighthouse beacon to guide them (*Bio* 71). Tolkien wrote to Edith on August 16, "only three days until I see you" (*C&G* 1.60), a clear expression of how much he missed her. No doubt he shared all his new artworks at their meeting.

During this holiday, Great Britain declared war on August 12, 1914, and World War I began, putting an end to the boredom and self-satisfaction of the elite which seems to have characterized Oxford as seen in Tolkien's May 1914 photograph (McIlwaine 151). The picture includes Tolkien with a slight squint of disinterest and his pipe pulling his mouth into a bit of a sneer next to a student, who looks like he might fall down drunk if not supported by the window. They are behind a very expensively and fashionably dressed man of leisure. A fellow Oxford student, E.R. Dodds, who matriculated in 1912, commented on Oxford before the war, "in the last years of the Affluent Age – absurd, delightful, totally irresponsible, and totally self-assured – moulded on a way of life that appeared unshakeably pre-ordained yet was about to vanish like the fabric of a dream" (qtd, in *Exeter* 9).

Ronald Tolkien stayed probably from August 19 through August 30 in Warwick, and possibly longer (*C&G* 1.61). Ronald and Edith were now confronted by a threat to all their hopes and plans for the future: the War. The risks and costs would be particularly acute for Edith, who had already waited four years for Ronald Tolkien. She had managed to do this because of her independent financial security. While Ronald Tolkien was embedded in a network of family including his brother, his aunt and godmother May Incledon (née Suffield), and myriad other Tolkien and Suffield aunts, uncles, and cousins; Edith had no family beside Jennie Grove. Edith was probably in contact with Mabel Sheaf from Dresden House, but Edith and Molly Field were probably estranged after Edith broke her engagement with Molly's brother, George, in January 1913, a little more than a year earlier. Edith had left behind the social network she had built up in Charlton Kings in June 1913. If Ronald died, Edith would be virtually alone.

Ronald Tolkien stayed at "The White House, Northgate, Warwick" in August 1914 as he wrote his Aunt May Incledon and another lady, Mrs. Stafford, from that address (*C&G* 1.61). Again in November 1915 he stayed on Northgate Street (*C&G* 1.82). However, there is no listing for "The White House" in the Warwick census or in its Trade directories. The Punch Bowl Inn, a white building, had been at the junction generally referred to as "Northgate" for

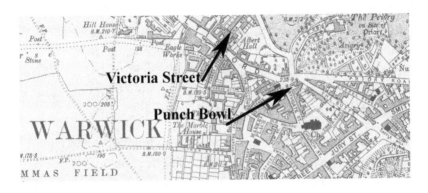

1912 OS Warwick Map (National Library of Scotland) annotated by SH-K to show
Edith and Ronald's Residences

many years, although its address is 1 The Butts. It was located close to a handsome, substantial eighteenth-century building housing Army personnel so it had a name calculated to appeal to a local clientele. While The Punch Bowl could provide affordable lodging for Tolkien on his visits to Edith, it was an establishment whose name might alarm someone with a proper middle-class upbringing like Tolkien's Aunt May or Mrs. Stafford. Consequently, Tolkien displayed his "unmatchable subtlety, not without a streak of deliberate guile" by saying somewhat truthfully he was writing from "The White House," but a white house whose name was "The Punch Bowl" (Shippey, *Roots* 3).[21]

In 1914, The Punch Bowl would soon be filling up with young men, just like Ronald Tolkien, in new uniforms, who had enlisted for the war in "Kitchener's Army," in response to his famous exhortation: "Your Country Needs You!" Ronald too would be dealing with the military, its culture and its rules soon enough. However, before returning to Oxford for the October 11, 1914 start of Michaelmas term, Ronald visited his brother Hilary and Aunt Jane Neave (née Suffield) at Phoenix Farm in late September writing his poem, *The Voyage of Éarendel the Evening Star* (*C&G* 1.61). At Oxford, Tolkien joined the Class II OTC (Officer Training Corp) with its weekly military lecture and 6 ½ hours of drill. This was a less rigorous schedule than the men in Class I whose goal was to enter the Army as soon as possible (*Exeter* 36).

Certainly by Michaelmas term 1914, Ronald Tolkien was keeping his "eyes on the prize," his final examinations in June 1915. With a good degree from Oxford, he could be assured of getting a teaching job which would support Edith and allow them to marry (*Bio* 77). It is assumed that both Edith and Ronald Tolkien knew Ronald could not pull off six weeks of cramming for this examination as he had with his Honours Moderations in February 1913.

Ronald Tolkien moved from Exeter College to St. John Street in October 1914 where he shared rooms with Colin Cullis. This relocation may have been part of an effort to decrease socializing and its attendant expenses and propensity to distract Ronald from much-needed study. In the preceding 1913/1914 academic year, Tolkien's college bills for food and coal showed a debt of £8 9s 7d for the 1913 Michaelmas term, £26 8s 3d for the 1914 Hilary term, and £25 16s 6d from Trinity term (*Exeter* 35). Carpenter intimates Tolkien ran up his bills by entertaining beyond his means (*Bio* 53) with "expensive dinners" (*Bio* 59) and "dinner parties" (*Bio* 69). The exponential increase in bills coincided with the Sub-Rector giving Tolkien and Cullis permission "to have supper for nine

---

21 https://www.ourwarwickshire.org.uk/content/cataloguewow/warwick-punch-bowl-hotel, last viewed on 6/9/2020. The website also has a postcard from about 1920 showing a white Punch Bowl Inn.

on Sat. nights in the rooms of one or the other this term" (C&G 1.57).[22] The £60 14s 4d in debt for the 1913/1914 academic year is equivalent to £7056.69 in 2019 goods and services or $8,866.66.[23] Tolkien only had £20 to £40 of income yearly (Letters 53).

Ronald could not expect Father Francis Morgan, who had contributed to cover the costs of Tolkien's education at Oxford, to pay for this extravagant "lifestyle." Ronald had already run through the money he had earned in the summer of 1913, because he was in debt during the fall 1913 Michaelmas term. The absence of a delay in Tolkien's graduation suggests these debts were paid. These amounts suggest someone vouched to pay them as Tolkien certainly did not have the funds. The most obvious candidate would be Tolkien's Aunt and godmother, May Incledon, who could certainly afford this expense and who may have wanted to reward her godson and nephew for his successful completion of Honours Moderations. While it is possible Edith could have paid this debt as she had the money, it seems utterly unlikely. Ronald needed to use his performance at Oxford as a way to prove his worth, after she cast aside George Field, and to have a way of earning a living which could support a family. Ronald Tolkien would not have wanted any suspicions he was marrying Edith for her money.

Ronald Tolkien's lecture and drill timetable for Michaelmas 1914 indicated a new level of organization and focus which he needed to keep up with his studies (McIlwaine 176). In his letters, Ronald was careful to let Edith know he was getting work done as when he talked to Sisam about a delay in writing an essay and doing four hours of work (Letters 7). While Tolkien continued to be involved with the now decimated Stapledon Society, his term as president had ended on March 8, 1914 (Great War 36, C&G 1.45). Despite his academic demands, Tolkien's imagination was productive. Ronald worked on his Kullervo story; his poems, Eärendel, The Bidding of the Minstrel, and The Grimness of

---

22 As a member of King Edward's Horse Tolkien was likely to have enjoyed convivial dinners. Beginning in the fall of 1913, he may have decided to replicate that pattern of social dinners, but among friends with more literary interests.

23 "Inflation Calculator." Bank of England, last viewed on 6/16/2020. https://www.bankofengland. co.uk/monetary-policy/inflation/inflation-calculator.
"XE Currency Converter." last viewed on 6/16/2020. https://www.xe.com/currencyconverter/convert/.

the *Sea/The Tides*; presented a lecture on the *Kalevala*; and read his *The Voyage of Eärendel* at the Essay Club. Tolkien arranged to meet with the TCBS on December 12-13, 1914 (*C&G* 1.65).

In Tolkien's November 16, 1914 letter to Christopher Wiseman, one sees Ronald Tolkien's rededication to Catholicism consistent with his commitment to Edith. While Tolkien was Catholic and Wiseman was a Methodist, Tolkien wrote to Wiseman that their friendship, "the great twin brotherhood," was based on "more fundamental matters" as "for both of them religion is at once their moving force and their foundation" (*C&G* 1.63).

Again, neither the Carpenter biography nor the *Chronology* mentions Ronald Tolkien visiting Edith when Oxford's Michaelmas term ended on December 5, 1914. However, it is not credible Tolkien would leave Edith to be alone at Christmas now. He did go to a meeting of TCBS at Christopher Wiseman's family home in London on December 12-13 (*C&G* 1.65). But, both his artwork and poetry during his Christmas break center on themes connected with Edith, strongly suggesting he was with her. The typically narrow focus of the official biography and Garth on only the TCBS obscures the importance of Edith as an audience, an inspiration, and an anchor. It is likely, given the depth of feeling evident in their letters, Ronald Tolkien spent most of his December, 1914 break in Warwick. That was when he wrote his late December poems, *Dark* and *Ferrum and Sanguis: 1914* [Latin for 'Sword and Blood'], *As Two Fair Trees*, and a revision of *The Tides*, now titled *Sea-chant of an Elder Day* (*C&G* 1.65-66).

On December 27, 1914, Ronald Tolkien created the intricate watercolor, *The Land of Pohja* (*C&G* 1.65; *A&I* 44, 45; McIlwaine 44). The land of Pohja or Pohjola is found in the Finnish epic, the *Kalevala*, which had been a focus for Tolkien while rewriting its Kullervo story and giving a lecture on the *Kalevala* that fall. The *Kalevala*, the Finnish national epic, was written much in the same way the Grimm brothers in Germany had collected and then edited German folk and fairy tales. All these mythological stories were grist for the mill for a philologist like Tolkien, and that is how he identified himself professionally (*Letters* 23, 56). He was also enamoured of Finnish which he found "quite intoxicating," like wine (*Letters* 214).

In the *Kalevala*'s Land of Pohja, Väinämöinen's music lures the Moon to settle in a birch tree and the Sun in a fir-tree from which they will be captured by Louhi and hidden away resulting in unending night. In his writing, Tolkien would revise this myth in Morgoth's destruction of the light of the Two Trees in *The Silmarillion*. In his artwork, Tolkien represented this change by means of a diagonal flap. With the flap closed, there is a purple background (McIlwaine 177), and with the diagonal flap open, there is a blue-gray background with a border of icicles (*A&I* 44).

In Tolkien's watercolor, *The Land of Pohja*, the sun in the top of the three trees appears to be in eclipse.[24] This is probably a reference to the famous solar eclipse of August 21, 1914, seen throughout much of the British empire, though not in England, and also in central Europe where World War I ignited. Like Halley's comet of ill omen of April 10, 1066, presaging the invasions of Norwegians and Normans in England, the heavens appeared to be announcing apocalyptic destruction as Great Britain had declared war on August 12, 1914. The trees are united in the face of the overshadowing menace of the eclipse.

Image by Michael Zeiler, Great American Eclipse.com

---

24 Bridoux also sees this as an eclipse ("Book Reviews" 154).

While the watercolor is titled *The Land of Pohja*, there is not a fir and birch tree depicted as specified in the *Kalevala*. Rather there are three central evergreen or fir trees, indicating Tolkien has inserted his own elaboration and interpretation of the *Kalevala* myth. This is the *Kalevala* seen in light of Edith Bratt, as the resourceful and fair Maid of the North, rejecting in 1913 the more socially desirable suitor, George Field (or Väinämöinen in the original *Kalevala* myth), to whom she was already engaged, for the impecunious Oxford student who made promises in 1910, J.R.R. Tolkien, in the role of the Smith, Ilmarinen, who forged the vault of heaven and the moon (*Bio* 60-62).[25] Assuming Ronald knew at that time Edith had suffered in her foster family, he could easily see Edith's mother, who had left her with that family, as the witch, Louhi, the mother of the Maid of the North.

The image of three trees is found in Tolkien's January 1914 paintings, *Here*, which was a response to his earlier watercolors, *Eeriness*, with its three fir trees on a hill evoking the icon of Calvary, and *Beyond*. Evergreens, like fir trees, can represent life and its continuance. If one of the tree stands for the tree/cross of Christ, then Ronald Tolkien and Edith Bratt can be the *Kalevala*'s other two trees of the Sun and the Moon. Trees of the Sun (female) and the Moon (male) also appear in the ancient Indian (Hindu) myth of the trees of the Sun and the Moon. Tolkien, whose academic focus now was placed squarely on philology, was likely to have been familiar with this legend from his studies of Sanskrit language and literature (Hooker, *Tolkienothēca*). The validity of reading Ronald Tolkien and Edith Bratt as two trees in *The Land of Pohja* is supported by Tolkien's continued use of tree imagery in reference to himself and Edith in his poem, *As Two Fair Trees*, written one month later (*C&G* 1.66, McIlwaine 146, *Bio* 74).

Another small purple tree figures in the background of Tolkien's picture. Given that World War I had started, as signified by the solar eclipse, the other tree perhaps denotes Tolkien's younger brother, Hilary, who was already signed up

---

25 Tolkien's identification with the Smith of the *Kalevala* may be part of the source of the Smith in *Smith of Wootton Major*.

and on active duty, but still training in England.[26] Hilary too was affected by the eclipse of World War I. He was a person seemingly with no fear of death, but not in a bravado machismo way, or in the upper class, public school, "stiff upper lip" way of nonchalance which denied all emotion (H. Tolkien 32, 51). The Hilary tree is the same rich, positive color as the first optimistic background in contrast to the grey background with ice.

The suggested association of the tree with Tolkien's brother, Hilary, rests not only on his sharing the experience of being overshadowed by the eclipse of the war, but also on Tolkien's self-referential entries in the Qenya lexicon of 1915/1916. There Eriniti or Lotisse or Veneste, an avatar of Edith, is the Vali of love, music, beauty, and purity, and Tolkien has her living in a 'korin' of elms with Noldorin [Ronald Tolkien] and his brother Amillo [Hilary Tolkien] in Tol Eressëa (QL 36). The entry for 'Amillo' in the Qenya lexicon is one of the earliest entries (QL 30), and the spring of 1915 is given as the likely beginning of the Qenya lexicon (QL xii). Assuming the invention and development of the new mythology had already progressed in December 1914 to what the vocabulary contains the following spring, here we see the three, Ronald, Edith, and Hilary, facing the blight of war. The lexicon corroborates the inclusion of Tolkien's brother, Hilary, in Tolkien's writing and artwork.

In January 1915, Ronald Tolkien wrote the poem, *As Two Fair Trees*, partly to celebrate his reunion with Edith in 1913 and their betrothal in 1914 (*C&G*

---

26 Hilary, who was two years younger than his brother Ronald, was the one stable and recurring presence in J.R.R. Tolkien's early life. J.R.R. Tolkien almost certainly was a witness to his brother Hilary's near drowning around 1900 in Sarehole (H. Tolkien 6). They had few other playmates growing up in Sarehole (*Bio* 21). After the family's conversion to Catholicism and a series of moves, the brothers would have had a hard time and limited opportunities to make friends with other children. Hilary was the one consistent person in his brother's life through the death of both of their parents, a series of homes, and changes in schools, until Tolkien left to go to Oxford. Siblings, who stay together as orphans, often do not compete with one another for the favors and attention of adults because adults play so little part in what clinicians call their affective or emotional lives. Instead, siblings watch out for each other: resisting being singled out for treats, not having to be urged to take turns, never telling on one another, sharing their possessions willingly, and making sure they had both been served before they ate (Simpson 150). Tolkien may have felt he needed to look after his younger brother as his father did with his younger siblings (Grotta-Kurska 13) and as he urged his own son Michael to do with Michael's younger brother Christopher (*Letters* 22). What this history indicates is a close and important relationship which has been elsewhere passed over in silence. The brothers "remained close and wrote to each other throughout their long lives" (H. Tolkien 62).

1.66, McIlwaine 146, *Bio* 74).[27] It reads in part: "as two fair trees," "we are
[...] like planted hearts in the great Sun/of Love [...] [and we] stand utterly
entwined. [...] [and] we have become/as one deep rooted in the soil of Life."
This poem embodies Tolkien's characteristic pattern of giving expression to
his thoughts both visually and verbally. *As Two Fair Trees* reflects the visual
imagery of *The Land of Pohja*, just as the watercolor, *Water, Wind, and Sand*
(March 1915) is an "Illustration of *Sea-Chant of an Elder Day*" (McIlwaine
172, *C&G* 1.67). Tolkien can be seen doing this as early as the age of twelve
in 1904 in his rebus letter (Bridoux, "Images Speak" 1-2). Ronald Tolkien also
created the watercolor, *Tanaqui*, to illustrate his poem, *Kôr: In a City Lost and
Dead* (*C&G* 1.68, 71).

The "two fair trees," Ronald and Edith, are planted in the great Sun/(Son) of
Love, Christ, who is represented in the third tree, and they have become one
with him and the Life he promised, i.e. "I am come that they have life and have
it more abundantly" (John 10:10). The Sun/Son of Love can be seen not just in
the three fir trees of Tolkien's previous painting, *Here*, repeated here, but also
in *Here*'s circular composition, like the Sun. The poem's verse invokes the Sun/
Son with "the linkéd days whose good or ill/binds us with golden strength."
In light of Tolkien's poem, *As Two Fair Trees*, the flap of *The Land of Pohja*
can be interpreted as showing that in the days of rich purple goodness when
the Sun/Son shines or even in the days of discouraging, and even frightening,
gray and cold, they are united in the Love and Life as well as joined together
"in sickness and in health."[28]

The poem also says: we "hushed each others' fears, and known grey rain/and
lonely winds and nights [...] we two" (McIlwaine 146). This is why Edith risked
so much and waited for Ronald Tolkien. Ronald could understand Edith's
past with its fears, sadness, and loneliness. George Field might be a promising
young man, a sensible Victorian, who had an eye for a wife who could provide

---

27 Tolkien rewrote the poem *Outside* in December 1914 (*C&G* 1.65). He had initially written it in
    December 1913. This suggests it may also reflect Tolkien's feelings about his betrothal and his life
    with Edith. However, it has not been published and consequently cannot be assessed.
28 Hammond and Scull write, "*The Land of Pohja* continues the theme of darkness already expressed by
    Tolkien in the poems *Dark* and *Ferrum and Sanguis: 1914* (*C&G* 1.65). However, neither of these
    poems has been published so this assertion cannot be substantiated. The theme of *The Land of Pohja*,
    as reviewed here, is one of light and love and life, though faced with adversity. The revised title of
    Dark, Copernicus v. Ptolemy, does not necessarily suggest a "theme of darkness" (*C&G* 1.67).

him with the capital to be in business, but he could not offer this kind of bond found in the understanding of long suffering.[29]

The motif of the three trees from the 1914 paintings *Eeriness, Beyond, Here, The Land of Pohja*, and the poem, *As Two Fair Trees*, reappears in the 1916/1917 heraldry design for Great Haywood or Tavrobel, as Tolkien named it in his *Book of Lost Tales* (McIlwaine 212-13). This design forms part of a triptych which will be discussed in more detail in Chapter 10.

Ronald Tolkien spent "possibly all" of his Easter 1915 vacation, March 15 to April 25, in Warwick (*C&G* 1.68). During the preceding Hilary term, Ronald had read his poem, *Sea Chant of an Elder Day*, to the Essay Club (*C&G* 1.67). During the last week of the term, he rewrote the poem, *Dark* as *Copernicus vs. Ptolemy*, and wrote another poem *Why the Man in the Moon Came Down too Soon* (*C&G* 1.67-68).

Ronald also appears to have written a poem for Edith, *Sparrow-song* ('bilink' or 'bilinc' in Gnomish), in March 1915 (*C&G* 1.67). The title suggests Edith's love of birds seen later in her having her own aviary in Oxford (*Bio* 118). Edith may have had a pet sparrow which can be a "delightful" pet.[30] She is not likely to have had a pet at the Faulkners' or even at "Uncle" Jessop's. Once she had her own household in Warwick she could have gotten a pet, as Jennie Grove was permitted to have her dog, Sam. Sparrows have often been kept as pets. Most house sparrows emit variations on its short and incessant chirping call. However, young sparrows produce a true song, especially in captivity, a warbling similar to that of the European greenfinch, which is kept as a songbird. If Edith had a pet sparrow, it was likely to serenade her when she played the piano as there

---

29 In 1922, George Field married Annie Mary Dorothy Fowler Tovey. She was well-to-do as she was the only child of the Toveys of Church Farm in Besford. George became a hotel proprietor of the Tontine Hotel in Stourport, and in 1928 a manager at the Royal Three Tuns hotel in nearby Pershore, Worcestershire. In 1939, George Field was a manager at the Regina Hotel, Stroud. "George Alwin Field." The Auxiliary Division of the Royal Irish Constabulary, last viewed on 6/8/2020. http://theauxiliaries.com/men-alphabetical/men-f/field-ga/field.html.

30 "Keeping-sparrows – interesting species for the small bird enthusiast." The Bird Blog from thatpetplace.com, last viewed on 6/9/2020. http://blogs.thatpetplace.com/thatbirdblog/2011/04/19/keeping-sparrows-interesting-species-for-the-small-bird-enthusiast/#.Xt_7qudOncc.

are recorded instances of cello with nightingale accompaniment and clarinet and laughing thrush duet.[31]

Tolkien, meanwhile, began to work seriously on his newly invented language, Qenya, sometime in the spring of 1915 (*C&G* 1.68).[32] Its earliest entries would include 'Amillo' for Tolkien's brother Hilary (QL 30) and 'Erinti' or 'Little One' for Edith (QL 36).[33] He also included a word for 'kiss', 'kilme' (QL 46), recalling Tolkien's bill of kisses from Edith for his hours of study when preparing for Honour Moderations (McIlwaine 148). There were words indicating the centrality of his Catholic faith in his new creation: 'anusta' (QL 31) for 'monastery', 'anatarwesta' (QL 31, 89) for 'crucifixion', 'evandilyon' (QL 36) for 'gospel', 'evandl' (QL 36) for 'Christian missionary', 'qinne' for 'nuns' (QL 77), and 'tarwë ' for 'cross', 'crucifix' (QL 89). 'Faidron' or 'Faithron', for 'Francis', i.e. Father Francis Morgan, appears in the 1917 Goldogrin Lexicon (GL 33). The Gnomish root 'Faith' is glossed 'liberty' with 'faithir' as 'liberator', 'Savior', an unmistakable reference to Christ, the Savior.

Tolkien's creativity was apparent in his poetry and art during this period. During Easter break, he was in Warwick and wrote the poems: *The Two Riders* on April 15-16, *May Day* on April 20-21, and *Evening* on April 22 (*C&G* 1.70). He also painted the watercolors *Tanaqui* during this Easter Break, and *Water, Wind & Sand* may date from this time in 1915 (*C&G* 1.71, 1.67, McIlwaine 173).

---

31 "How and Why Birds Sing." The Cornell Lab, last viewed on 6/9/2020. /https://academy. allaboutbirds.org/birdsong/.
"Do birds listen when You Play Music?" *The New York Times*. Dr. DeVood reported a 2012 study which suggested bird brains respond to song in the same areas that human brains do. "As a shorthand way of thinking, if a bird song sounds musical to human ears, odds are that similar human music will sound songlike to the bird," Dr. DeVood said. "We know that with the combination of both innate and learned qualities, birds will cue into a particular frequency range, a particular tempo and that the bird then constructs his own song using those qualities." https://www.nytimes.com/2017/06/19/ science/do-birds-listen-when-you-play-music.html, last viewed on 6/9/2020.
Scull and Hammond write, "*You and Me and the Cottage of Lost Play*, which was written around this time, is evidently influenced by thoughts of Edith" (*C&G* 1.71). See Bunting's "Checking the Facts" for a discussion of why this is very unlikely. They also state the poem, *Goblin Feet*, "seems to have been merely a fairy poem to please Edith," but they give no evidence to support this assertion (*C&G* 1.71).
32 See a discussion of the spring dates for Qenya lexicon (QL. x-xvii, *Great War* 328).
33 'Erinti' is not glossed, and there is no obvious cognate in the Goldogrin Lexicon of 1917. Tolkien's "favorite name" for Edith was "little one" (*Bio* 67), and the name 'Erinti' can be parsed as a calque of 'little one'. The analysis is: 'Er(e)' ('one') + 'in(ya)' ('tiny') + '-t' (noun suffix) + '-i' (feminine suffix) (QL 36, 42; GL 18; *WJ* 392, 396).

In the first week of his return to Oxford for Trinity term before the press of classes and exam preparation mounted, Tolkien wrote *You & Me and the Cottage of Lost Play* and *Goblin Feet* on April 27-28 and *Tinfang Warble* on April 29-30 (*C&G* 1.71). *Kôr: In a City Lost and Dead* was written on April 30, 1915. On May 2 and 3, Tolkien revised the poems *Darkness on the Road* and *Morning Song* (*C&G* 1.71). On May 10, he painted *The Shores of Faery*, a view of the city of Kôr (McIlwaine 202-03, *A&I* 48). The watercolor, *Fantasy Landscape*, probably belongs to this burst of frenetic activity before Tolkien's leaving Oxford (McIlwaine 174). It was a time of transition on the threshold of an unknown and unknowable future in World War I. Finally, visiting friends and family with Edith during July 1915 before going to camp to begin his military service, Tolkien wrote *The Shores of Faery*, *Princess Ni*, *The Trumpets of Faery/Faerie* and began *The Happy Mariners* (*C&G* 1.77-78).

Garth comments, "The sudden flowering of Tolkien's creativity from late 1914 to mid-1915 doubtless had much to do with the absence of friends, the adrenaline and urge for distraction as final exams approached, and a wartime need to seize the day" (*Exeter* 42). This authoritative summary leaves out the woman behind Tolkien's inspiration: the woman who had been committed to him since 1913 and who created a longed-for home; and a denizen of Tolkien's alternative world of Kortirion/Warwick in Faërie as the Vali Erinti ('Little One').[34]

John Garth, following Christopher Tolkien's tentative reference to Francis Thompson's poem *Daisy* (*LT1* 21), writes *You and Me and the Cottage of Lost Play* is a "love poem to Edith," although Garth admits the "setting of the poem has nothing to do with the urban setting in which he and Edith had actually come to know each other" (*Great War* 72). Raymond Edwards, in his 2014 biography *Tolkien*, accepts Garth's interpretation, and expands that interpretation writing the children are now "obviously meant for Tolkien and Edith" (99).

Christopher Tolkien's reference to the two lines of *Daisy*

---

34 duPlessis notes and questions Carpenter's implied dichotomy (*Bio* 53) between "male company," associated "with much that was good in life," and the "petty routine of [...] domestic life" (118). Tolkien's evaluation of his marriage was that it was of such importance to him already that in France he "re-read all of Edith's letters," but only "glanced once again at his collection of notes" from the TCBS members (*Bio* 83). The impetus to his writing and his imaginative life, both joys of Tolkien's life, appears to lie in his relationship to Edith, not the TCBS.

does not "echo" any poetic device, e.g. rhyme, meter, or alliteration, between the two poems. The poems do have the same two words: "childish things." The *Daisy* poem presents the flirtation of an adult heterosexual couple. The narrator is a man who feels the woman is a tease. Being childish is part of this couple's flirting. In 1915 when Tolkien wrote "You and Me and the Cottage of Lost Play," his marriage was so important to him that "it was like death" when he separated from his wife to go to France in World War I (*Great War* 138). Given the depth of Tolkien's feeling for Edith, he is not likely, in a "love poem" to his wife, to quote from a poem in which the woman easily and heedlessly leaves the man who feels jilted [...] Speculating that this is a "love poem" about Edith, portrays Tolkien being in bed with his wife, when they are children, and this is unlike any other material we have from Tolkien. His reticence about sexuality is well known, and this imagery has awkward implications. (Bunting, "Checking the Facts" 53)

The poem is filled, rather, with references to what was true of Tolkien's relationship with his younger brother Hilary including: the "cottage" as a reference to the cottage in Sarehole or one by the sea on their holiday; the brothers' contrasting dark and light hair; sleeping in the same bed; walking on the sand and gathering shells during a seaside holiday; and walking hand in hand. Scull and Hammond note the similarities between the garden in Howard Pyle's 1895 *The Garden Behind the Moon, A Real Story of the Moon Angel*, a place where children go when they die, with the cottage on the dark side of the moon in *Roverandom* and the dream land of "The Cottage of Lost Play" (*Roverandom* 99). Edith does not fit Pyle's setting as Tolkien never knew her as a child nor do we know of any life-threatening experiences for her.

In April, 1915, when Ronald Tolkien wrote *You & Me and the Cottage of Lost Play*, he was planning to join the military in two months. Both Ronald Tolkien and his brother Hilary, who was already in uniform, would be facing the uncertainty of surviving the war (*Bio* 77). Hilary Tolkien would be shipping out to the front lines in France shortly as he volunteered in the first wave of war time enthusiasm (*Bio* 72). He was a bugler and a stretcher bearer. This last duty was likely to expose him repeatedly to enemy fire (Currie and Lewis, *Codemaker* 106). Ronald was likely to reflect on his close relationship with Hilary in 1915, given the stark possibility they might never see each other again. Ronald was well aware of the war's mounting casualty figures. Instead, the brothers might be reunited at "The Cottage of Lost Play" where dead children go.

This focus on Ronald's brother, Hilary, may have continued in the poem, *Tinfang Warble*, written on April 29-30, 1915, the day after Tolkien composed *You & Me and the Cottage of Lost Play* (*C&G* 1.71). While Tolkien was offered piano (*Bio* 22) and "fiddle" lessons (*Letters* 73), it seems likely Hilary had lessons also. Hilary recalls making whistles from reeds as a child (H. Tolkien 6). He later became a skilled and talented musician playing several instruments: flute, small trumpet, and piano.[35] Dairon, the 'fluter' appears in the earliest version of "The Tale of Tinúviel" (*LT2* 8). The 1915/16 *Qenya Lexicon* contains 'Amillo' [Hilary], as one of its earliest entries (*PE*13 30) and also lists a surprisingly large number of flute references (29).[36]

The all-important Examinations for Honour School of English Language and Literature began on June 10 and continued through June 15, 1915 (*C&G* 1.73). Ronald wrote Edith on June 1, 1915 about the death of Earnest Hall, who was in the same class at Exeter as Tolkien and a member of Tolkien's literary group, the Apolausticks: "The first of my real personal friends to go; but I know it will soon be a long list" (McIlwaine 160). Ronald Tolkien applied for a temporary commission on June 28, 1915, which was accepted June 30th (*Letters* 53, *C&G* 1.76). The war was near.

Life in Warwick with Ronald Tolkien's intermittent presence and letters brought Edith a stability and happiness she had never known before. Her sense of a secure future would have been ruptured in August 1914 when Britain declared war. But Ronald made his commitment clear: spending school holidays with Edith and doing the work at Oxford he needed to complete his degree in the academic year of 1914/1915. Edith became part of Ronald's imaginative life, expressed in his paintings and poems, in a magical and blessed land of Faërie. As Tolkien wrote in 1938/1939, "A real taste for fairy-stories was wakened by philology on the threshold of manhood, and quickened to full life by war" (OFS 135). Philology was certainly present in Tolkien's studies with Joseph Wright at Oxford, beginning in

---

35 Based on notes taken at the presentation of an original paper given by Angela Gardner's on Hilary Tolkien at "The Return of the Ring" conference, Loughborough University, 2012 (Elizabeth Currie email 3/26/16).
36 See Bunting and Currie's "Tolkien's *Fantasy Landscape*" for more on the importance of Hilary in Ronald's life (11-12) and Bunting, "Finding Hilary, Part II" for Hilary's presence in *The Lord of the Rings*.

1912, and his continuing elaboration of invented languages culminating in the *Qenya Lexicon* of 1915. "The threshold of manhood" would be turning twenty-one and renewing his relationship with Edith who became a central figure in Ronald's life and art. This period would be the calm before the storm of changes awaiting them in the next few years.

Chapter Seven

Waiting in Warwick, 1915-1916

Edith, after her five years of waiting, knew that, with the successful completion of Ronald's examinations in July 1915 for his Oxford degree, the wedding could now be arranged. The interruption of Ronald's military service, beginning in July 1915, put their lives on hold again. During this time, Ronald increasingly made Edith part of his imaginative world and brought her with him into the realm of Faërie.

In the summer of 1915, life was a rush, filled with milestones. Tolkien took his Examinations for the Honours School on June 10-15, 1915. On June 28, 1915, he applied for a commission with the Army. On July 2, 1915, his First Class result for the Examinations was posted.

The Army would give Tolkien his first regular paycheck. On commissioning, he would have received a grant of £50 for the purchase of his uniform and other essentials.[1] That sum is equivalent to £5,178.64 or $6491.15 for gear in 2019. Tolkien also could receive a 1s 9d a day ration allowance when on leave.[2] An officer was expected to buy a lot of his own equipment or "kit" and also that of his "batman," i.e. soldier servant. Tolkien's pay as a second lieutenant would have been 7s 6d per day or £5 5s 6d every two weeks.[3] That would be equiva-

---

1 "Oral Answers to Questions on War: Uniform and Kit Allowance," last viewed on 6/17/20. Hansard is the record of Parliamentary Proceedings https://api.parliament.uk/historic-hansard/commons/1915/feb/25/uniform-and-kit-allowance.
  Department stores, such as Army & Navy and Selfridges, stocked necessary military equipment, including guns. Harrods had a separate "War Comforts Room" (Lewis-Stempel 45).
2 "Oral Answers to Questions: Territorial Force, Rations," last viewed on 6/18/2020. https://api.parliament.uk/historic-hansard/commons/1915/feb/04/rations. This amount is what the War Office would have provided the Battalion catering manager with, to feed each soldier each day in the Battalion Messes. If, for some reason, a soldier was not with the Battalion, on leave for example, only then would he have been paid this amount because he would not have been on the Ration Strength.
3 "British Army rates of pay 1914." The Long, Long Trail, last viewed on 6/16/2020. https://www.longlongtrail.co.uk/soldiers/a-soldiers-life-1914-1918/british-army-rates-pay-1914/.

lent to £505 and some change in 2018 or at least $668.42.[4] Officers had their pay and allowances paid into Cox & Kings, the bank used for officers, once a month.[5] Once Tolkien was in the field and in command of subordinates, his pay would increase. An officer, who returned home because of wounds, did not technically have a paycut, but with the loss of allowances pay effectively was halved.[6] Tolkien would not be an exception to that rule in November 1916, when he returned home to England with trench fever.

Before Tolkien left for his first posting and unknown future, he prioritized seeing friends and family. Ronald spent some time in Warwick with Edith, but by July 9, 1915, the couple was in Birmingham, probably visiting Father Francis Morgan (*C&G* 1.76-77). Edith seems to have been with Ronald in his travels as a letter from Christopher Wiseman wanted them to join him and his mother for tea (*C&G* 1.78). As a man now in a position to marry his fiancée, Ronald probably took this opportunity to introduce Edith to his family. Curiosity about the young lady, who had spun Ronald Tolkien into an emotional maelstrom in 1909/1910 and to whom Ronald then rushed to propose to at the absurd age of twenty-one, would have been intense. Given the impending war, amnesty for breaches of propriety was likely. Both the disruptions of the war and their betrothal probably allowed the apparent relaxing of the rules so that Edith and Ronald could travel together unchaperoned.

Arriving in the Birmingham area, Edith and Ronald stayed at Ronald's Aunt and Uncle Mittons' house, Abbotsford, in Moseley. Tolkien's father's sister, Mary Jane Tolkien, married T.E. Mitton, and Tolkien and his brother Hilary had previously spent school holidays with the Mitton family (*C&G* 2.791). This visit would also be an opportunity for other friends and family from the

---

4 "Inflation Calculator." Bank of England, last viewed on 6/16/2020. https://www.bankofengland.co.uk/monetary-policy/inflation/inflation-calculator, and average 2018 rate multiplier of 1.3236.
Today the monthly pay for a British second lieutenant is £2,731.66/month, as compared with Tolkien's £1010. https://apply.army.mod.uk/what-we-offer/regular-officer/benefits, last viewed on 6/18/2020. Monthly pay for a second lieutenant in the US Army is $3,287.10 as compared with Tolkien's approximately $1337.00.
https://www.federalpay.org/military/army/second-lieutenant, last viewed on 6/18/2020.
5 "Cox's and King's, Army Agents (175801923)." Lloyds Banking Group, last viewed on 6/17/20. https://www.lloydsbankinggroup.com/Our-Group/our-heritage/our-history2/lloyds-bank/coxs--kings-army-agents/.
6 "Army Estimates, 1915-16," last viewed on 6/16/2020. https://api.parliament.uk/historic-hansard/commons/1915/apr/22/army-estimates-1915-16-progress-10th.

Birmingham area to come and meet Ronald Tolkien and his intended before he went to join the war. The Mittons would have, of course, provided separate rooms for the couple, as would have been expected for the time. Ronald Tolkien and Edith then stayed with his Aunt and Catholic godmother, May Incledon (née Suffield) and probably saw his Uncle Walter and cousins, Marjorie and Mary, in Barnt Green July 13-14, 1915 (*C&G* 1.78). Ronald Tolkien then left to report for duty at the Kempston Barracks in Bedford.

The Kempston Barracks, on the west side of Bedford, were built in 1876 of brick with stone dressings and a slate roof. It was designed to resemble a castle in what is known as Fortress Gothic Revival Style. The 1885 Kelly's Directory described the barracks as forming

> three sides of a quadrangle, and occupy 23 acres, enclosed by a high wall, 13 of which serve as encampment, drill and recreation ground; the east and west wings of the north front are connected by a central block with four massive towers, holding [...] arms and accoutrements, [...] a powder magazine, clothing and bedding stores; the west wing includes the officers' mess, and quarters for eleven officers and their servants; the east wing consists of canteen, reading and recreation rooms, sergeants' mess, four non-commissioned officers quarters, workshops and stores; the sides consist of two blocks, available for 288 soldiers (single) and eight sergeants; besides a hospital for 28 patients, four orderlies, residence for hospital sergeant and cook, and detached infectious ward and mortuary; there are also married soldiers' quarters for 31 families, with an infant school attached.[7]

As there were rooms only for eleven officers, Tolkien was billeted with a half dozen other officers in a house in town requisitioned by the Army (*Bio* 77).

The world of the British military has its own traditions, customs, and prejudices. Before World War I, the British infantry was organized in Regiments. Most of the men for a Regiment were recruited from the local county where their Depot was. For example, beginning in 1881, the Regimental Depot of the Royal Warwickshire Regiment was in Budbroke Barracks about four miles to the west of the city of Warwick. A Regiment before 1908 consisted of two battalions or combat units, each of about 800 men. As this system was developed to cover

---

7 "Kempston Keep." Bedfordshire Archives and Records Service, last viewed on 6/16/2020. http://bedsarchives.bedford.gov.uk/CommunityArchives/Kempston/KempstonBarracks.aspx. About 1982, most of the original buildings were demolished and sold, but The Keep or the main block at the front was left.

1914 postcard of Kempston Barracks

the British Empire, normally one battalion was on "Home Service," while the other was "Overseas," often in India. The two battalions rotated after about five years and generally never met or even served together (Spiers 82-94). Under the Haldane reforms of 1908, each Regiment had a 3rd (Reserve) Battalion and some a 4th (Extra Reserve) Battalion.[8]

The British military saw itself as a professional, almost semi-caste organization, which cultivated an all-male environment. They saw women and wives as draining off the strength of their fighting forces (French 128) as well as creating headaches in terms of transportation, housing, and dealing with the native servants (Riedi 236-53). Each Regiment promoted a distinct professional identity with a Regimental March; a Regimental Mascot; distinctive headgear, like Scottish bonnets and Glengarries; yearly commemorations of past glory, such as the Minden Day from 1759 in the Seven Years War for Tolkien's Lancaster Fusiliers; and carrying not only The King's Color (or flag) into battle, but also the Regimental Color. The loss of either was a disgrace.

In contrast, battalions raised by Secretary of State for War, Horatio Herbert Kitchener, formed of civilians, all volunteers at first, were designated as "Service Battalions," not Regular Army. The men of these units were only required for service until the end of hostilities. Originally, a Reserve Battalion was part of

---

8 Hamill-Keays 3.

the Regular Army, but an enormous number of Reserve Battalions were now needed to train Kitchener's New Army; as he had called for "a million men" (Simkins). Consequently, the Army's Reserve Battalions now trained men who would be joining a Service Battalion or rehabilitated those who had been wounded, or taken ill, so that they could be sent back to a Front. Tolkien was in the 11th (Service) Battalion in France (*Bio* 81). On his first stay on Cannock Chase, he was in the 13th (Reserve) Battalion (*Bio* 77). In Yorkshire, Tolkien was placed in the 3rd (Reserve) Battalion (*Great War* 232). Service Battalions were not Regular Army and were viewed with disdain by the professional members of the Regular Army, both enlisted men and officers.

Despite his training and preparation, Tolkien did not quite fit the mold for World War I officers. His classical education, his good manners, his ability to play rugby aggressively, and a basic ability to ride a horse from his days at King Edward's Horse all helped him pass as an "officer and a gentleman." However, he was not an Anglican, nor a graduate of a military college, nor did he come from a wealthy or landed family. Tolkien would be assessed carefully by his superiors for his ability to conform to military culture and to show he knew his place in the hierarchy of Mess etiquette.[9] He would be evaluated on maintaining his kit, cleaning, ironing, boot polishing, gun maintenance, and "housework," as Tolkien would later inspect his men and enforce standards for all these tasks. Drill – marching, saluting and parading – under the inevitable loud and merciless SNCO (Senior Non-Commissioned Officer) was inescapable, as well as learning to drill his own platoon (*Bio* 77). He attended military lectures (*Bio* 77), especially on Military Law, as he would have to enforce it. He would have had weapon practice: Lee-Enfield .303 rifle, Webley .455 revolver,

---

9 "Temporary Gentlemen on the Western Front: Class Consciousness and the British Army Officer, 1914-1918." Laura Root. *The Osprey Journal of Ideas and Inquiry*. University of North Florida, last viewed on 6/16/2020. https://digitalcommons.unf.edu/cgi/viewcontent.cgi?article=1071&context=ojii_ volumes.
The etiquette of the officers' mess could vary by regiment and was suitably and sufficiently byzantine and arcane enough to put any new officer in his place. Rules included: "4. When the toast to the King is drunk, don't say 'God Bless Him.' This is a Field Officer's prerogative; 5. Don't draw your sword; mention a woman's name, or discuss religion or politics in the mess," "11. When Subalterns are talking to Captains, they should not 'Captain' them, but should use their surnames. For example, 'Thanks, Jones' is correct, but 'Thanks Captain Jones' is incorrect. And 'Thanks, Captain' is even more so." "Corporal to Field Officer." Internet Archive, last viewed on 6/16/2020. https://archive.org/details/ CorporalToFieldOfficer/page/n43 (Canadian, 1940, but following British traditions. See also French 128).

hand grenades, bayonet fighting, and sword drill. He would learn about trench mortars, machine guns and entrenching.

In August 1915, Tolkien began his odyssey through training camps but maintained as much of his personal and imaginative life as he could. He joined the 13th Battalion at Lichfield, Staffordshire, and was billeted at a camp outside the city, rewriting *Thoughts on Parade* (*C&G* 1.79-80). In the autumn of 1915, Tolkien and another officer bought an "ancient AJS motorcycle" (Morton and Hayes 48) which Tolkien used to visit Edith in Warwick (*Bio* 77), his brother Hilary at Phoenix Farm in Gedling before he shipped out in November 1915 (Morton and Hayes 48), and friends (*C&G* 1.80). Hilary would soon depart for the Front arriving in Boulogne, France with the 16th Royal Warwickshire Regiment on November 21, 1915 (*C&G* 1.82).

Tolkien then moved to Whittington Heath camp near Lichfield by September 12, 1915. Ronald was able to continue his writing with *A Song of Aryador* and *Dark are the Clouds Above the North* (*C&G* 1.80). On September 14, 1915, Edith wrote to Ronald: "'A Song of Aryador' is my favourite. How can you compose such dainty things while you're in that old camp?" (*LT1* 52-53, McIlwaine 160). With Whittington Heath being so close to Lichfield, Tolkien was present on September 25-26, 1915, when all of the TCBS met at Lichfield for the last time.

By October 15, 1915, Tolkien moved to Penkridge Bank Camp, an informally adopted name for that part of Rugeley Camp on Cannock Chase. On November 26, 1915, he sent Edith a copy of his poem, *Kortirion*, with a prologue which dedicated it to Warwick (*C&G* 1.81-3, *Letters* 8, *LT1* 16). By December 15, Tolkien transferred to Brocton Camp on Cannock Chase (*C&G* 1.83).

'Kortirion', later spelled 'Cortirion', is Ronald Tolkien's Elvish name for Warwick. Warwick with its elms, so common they were known as "Warwickshire weeds," and its castle with peacocks form the setting for the "holy fairies and the immortal elves/singing a song of faded longing" (*LT1* 26, 29). Elves and fairies were interchangeable terms for Tolkien at this time (Fimi 22-23, *B&L* 33). *Kortirion among the Trees*, the poem's later title, fits exactly with Ronald Tolkien's hope, expressed in a letter to Edith dated February 12, 1916, that he wanted "more than anything" for his writing "'to make England Catholic' again" so that "beauty, purity, and love" could return to England (McIlwaine 157).

In Tolkien's early stories, 'Kortirion', the ancient dwelling of the Fairies, came to be known in English as 'Warwick' (*LT2* 293).[10] In Tolkien's early mythology, Ingil, leader of the Elvish migration to Tol Eressëa and the son of Inwë, built the great tower which gave the town its name: 'Kortirion' (*LT1* 5). Men called it Ingil's Tirin, and it was so high the Moon had to climb far before "he thrust his face above it" (*LT2* 4; note the Moon is masculine in Elvish.). Ingil's Tirin was a copy of the tower in the Elvish city of Kôr in Valinor or Aman. In *The Silmarillion*, Kôr of Aman became Tirion upon Túna (Great Watch Tower upon the Hill of Túna) and its tower, 'Mindon Eldaliéva' or 'Lofty Tower of the Eldalië' ('Elven-folk', *S* 326), had a silver lamp which "shone far out into the mists of the sea" (*S* 62).

If Kortirion of Ingil is identified with Warwick, then Ingils's tower would have been built on the highest point to allow its beams to travel far. The highest point in Warwick is at the base of the steps of St. Mary's, an eighteenth-century construction built to replace the church burned in the 1694 Warwick fire. Tolkien would have been acutely aware that previously this Anglican church was the site of a Catholic church. The light from Tolkien's tower, built on that highest point by "holy fairies and the immortal elves" (*LT1* 26) could "'make England Catholic' again" so that "beauty, purity, and love" could return (McIlwaine 157).

In Tolkien's 1915 poem, Kortirion by the sea materializes when the Warwick elms become vessels "full sails on,/Like the clothéd masts of verdurous ships, /A fleet of galleons that proudly slips/Across long sunlit seas" (*LT1* 26). The trees of Kortirion are "Seen rising up through pallid mists and wan,/Like vessels floating vague and long afar/Down opal seas beyond the shadowy bar/Of cloudy ports forlorn" (*LT1* 28). The trees/ships "leave behind for ever havens" where "their crews a while held feasting long," and are now "wafted by slow airs to

---

10 Both the Qenya 'Kortirion' and the Gnomish 'Mindon-Gwar' names mean 'Tower of Kôr' (*LT2* 291). Tolkien's notes develop an etymology which equates the Welsh 'Caergwâr' ['caer' being the Welsh word for 'fort' or 'castle'] with the English 'Warwíc'. "Thus the element *War-* in *Warwick*, is derived from the same Elvish source as *Kor-* in *Kortirion* and *Gwar* in *Mindon-Gwar*" (*LT2* 292).

empty coasts" (*LT1* 28-29).[11] The ships and their crews are guided by the light streaming from the tower of Kortirion. Tolkien elaborates the 1915 verbal image of the tower of Kortirion in his 1917 drawing of what looks like a lighthouse in the Cortirion crest or coat-of-arms.[12] This crest is part of Tolkien's *i glin grandin a Dol Erethrin Airi* or *Three Designs Representing the Towns of Tavrobel [Great Haywood], Cortirion [Warwick], and Celbaros [Cheltenham]* (McIlwaine 213). A translation of Tolkien's Gnomish title, *i glin grandin a Dol Erethrin Airi* would be *The Fair (walled) Towns of (the) Holy/Sacred Tol Eressëa (the Lonely Isle)* (*PE*13 93). This translation will be used to refer to this drawing as McIlwaine's complete title is so long.

The drawing of *The Fair Towns of Holy Tol Eressëa* is composed as a triptych commemorating the towns which were important to Tolkien during his first years of marriage (McIlwaine 213). Tolkien's 1915 *Kortirion* poem should be considered in the context of his design for the Cortirion crest, which commands the center of the drawing. Cortirion's coat-of-arms, part of a set of city crests, was almost certainly done in late 1917 or after, as the symbolism of the Celbaros/Cheltenham design would have not been available until November 1917.

Cortirion's coat-of-arms contains emblems characteristic of Warwick. The peacock at the bottom of the Cortirion design comes from the Warwick Castle Italian or Peacock Garden where the birds paraded for the admiration of all. Peacocks, "majestic, sapphirine, and emerald," appear in Tolkien's 1915 *Kortirion* poem (*LT1* 26). The annotation, 'Miril i Durwin', could be read as an early spelling of the attested form 'Meril I Durwin', glossed as 'Queen of the Flowers'. The Queen of the Flowers, an epithet for the Rose, could refer to the Warwick Castle Peacock garden, with its roses and/or perhaps Edith.[13] Warwick Castle not only had roses in front of the conservatory which previ-

---

11 "The icy blue-tipped spears of winter" originate in Qenya 'Yelin' or 'winter', and this word is found in "the wintry spell of Yelin" written on an envelope (Great War 222, 354-5).

12 Unfortunately, since the 1915 poem is titled *Kortirion* and the drawing, as named by McIlwaine, uses the later spelling of 'Cortirion', both spellings are used in this text, though the two names refer to the same place.

13 The Gnomish lexicon glosses 'turwin' as 'queen' (*LT1* 260). Later additions to the Gnomish lexicon include 'Gwidhil-i-Durinthi = Meril-i-Turinqi' (as changed to D by lenition), glossed as 'Queen of Flowers', but with a note which glosses 'turinthi' as "princess, especially title of Gwidhil" (*LT1* 260). 'Miril i·durwin' is only translated as 'Meril the Queen' (*PE*13 95).'Miril' as 'jewel' is a weak possibility because it comes from a much later development found in "The Etymologies" of the 1930s (*Lost Road* 414-5).

ously housed the famous Warwick Vase, but also a separate, well-known Rose Garden.[14] The Peacock Garden, created in 1870, with its topiary trees and peacocks, was evidently a special place for this couple.

Above the peacock is a central tower with a topiary tree on each side. Topiary trees were found in the Warwick Castle Peacock garden, and these topiary trees should be interpreted as the "two fair trees" as found previously in Tolkien's poem of that name, standing for Edith Bratt and Ronald Tolkien. The Warwick coat-of-arms, reproduced below, whose two towers each have an identifying sun or moon, echo the theme of the Trees of the Sun and the Moon from either the *Kalevala* and/or Hindu legends (Hooker, *Tolkienotēca* 17-26). Warwick now is in

Warwick Castle's Peacock garden with topiary tree above the bird
(David Stowell: Warwick Castle – The Peacock Garden/CC BY-SA 2.0)

---

14 https://www.gardenvisit.com/gardens/warwick_castle, last viewed on 6/20/2020.
In Tolkien's drawing, the central tower looks very much like a generic lighthouse. Tolkien would have become familiar with a lighthouse at Withernsea quite close to where his wife Edith stayed in 1917. However, it is very doubtful if that particular lighthouse was a conscious model for the image in this drawing because during the war the military painted lighthouses with camouflage to minimize their use as navigational landmarks by enemy planes and ships. The military would also have extinguished the beacon during the war except for specific times to aid British convoys (Ridgway 11).

alignment with Tolkien's Faërie because the celestial bodies which appear in the Warwick coat of arms leave Warwick/Kortirion "East of the Sun and West of the Moon," as in the fairytale.

The central tower in Tolkien's drawing is labeled in Qenya 'Tirin (tower) na (of the) Silweth', with the last word unattested elsewhere. Tolkien's handwriting is hard to read, and the editors of *Parma Eldalamberon* read this word as 'Gilweth', which is the Gnomish name for Ingil, as opposed to 'Silweth'. The foot of the initial capital letter in the name of the tower curves back to the left, which is not a feature of Tolkien's 'G' as found in his alphabet (*A&I* 200, McIlwaine 187). In contrast, the foot of the capital G curves back to the right. 'Silweth' probably comes from the root 'SIL–' 'shine silver' as found in 'Silpion', tree of the moon, and 'Isil' meaning 'moon' plus '-weth' (abstract

Warwick coat of arms with the twin gate towers with sun and moon icons
from a 1908 postcard

noun suffix) (*Lost Road* 430, see also QL 'SILI-' 83).[15] Based on the tower's predecessor, 'Mindon Eldaliéva', with its silver light, the tower's name could

---

15 The only similar attested form is 'Tirin na Gilweth' from 'gil' meaning 'to gleam', 'to shine' and is translated as 'Gilweth' ('Region of the Stars') in later Elvish (*PE13* 95).

be glossed as 'Tower of Silver Sheen'. The smaller tree on the left probably represents Edith as she was smaller than Ronald, and she is associated with a mysterious post topped with a ball and a shining sun. The sun in Elvish is feminine so it accompanies Edith.

Ronald Tolkien could write about the "holy fairies and the immortal elves" as he now experienced his life hallowed in his betrothal and commitment to Edith and her reciprocal caring and empathy for his feelings. In Tolkien's early Gnomish lexicon from 1917, the entry 'elf' refers to 'feeling', 'heart only as seat of emotions and feelings', and this meaning was separate from the homonym, 'elf', meaning 'five' (GL 32). Tolkien was already using 'elf' with this meaning for his character, Elfriniel/Elfrith (Little Heart), in his story, *The Fall of Gondolin*, written around January 1917 (QL xv). Edith embodied the elvish virtue of "heart" as seen in her association with the Elvish sun and the city of Kortirion, part of Ronald's Middle-earth. Tolkien also experienced "heart" in the teachings of Catholicism such that Tolkien's early Qenya lexicon of this period contained words for 'saint', 'monastery', 'crucifixion', 'nun', and 'Christian missionary' (*Great War* 112). The home which Edith created in Warwick may have felt to Ronald Tolkien like a refuge and a promise of the future, like the land of Kôr which bordered on the land of the Valar or angelic beings (*Great War* 113).[16] With Edith, "holy fairies and the immortal elves" sing not only "a wistful song of things that were," but also of the future, a hopeful song of things that "could be yet" (*LT1* 27).

Tolkien did not attend a second meeting of the TCBS in London in late October 1915. Rather, in a letter of October 24, 1915, Tolkien was depressed partly because Edith was ill, and probably partly because he could not get leave to be with her (*C&G* 1.81). Members of the TCBS wrote Tolkien to keep him abreast of their latest thoughts. In a letter likewise dated October 24, 1915, G.B. Smith wrote Tolkien about the meeting's consensus that the purpose of the TCBS was to "reestablish sanity, cleanliness and the love of real and true beauty in

---

16 Lynn Forest-Hill proposes that Tolkien modeled two important settlements on Warwick: Edoras closely modeled on the early town and Minas Tirith more remotely on the Norman. Also, she notes aspects of the plot of *The Lord of the Rings* are parallel to the romance known as *Guy of Warwick*, part of the "Matter of Britain."

everybody's breast" (*C&G* 2.1285). Christopher Wiseman and Robert Gilson wrote similar letters reporting on the conference (*C&G* 2.1285).

While there is no doubt the TCBS was important to Tolkien's creativity, by 1915 the center of gravity in Tolkien's life seems to have shifted away from the clubby, all-male camaraderie of the TCBS to include the newly found future focus in Tolkien's life, a stable home with Edith, a place of the heart ('elf') in mythical Kortirion. Tolkien no longer seems to need the TCBS in the same way as he did before Edith became the anchor in his life. Tolkien's endorsement of the importance of the TCBS in a letter of August 12, 1916 to G.B. Smith should be viewed in its context: as a letter of support and encouragement to a dear friend, written when both young men were struggling to maintain their sanity in the midst of War World I's trench warfare. In the same letter, Tolkien wrote that after the TCBS's London meeting of December 1914 he found "a voice for all kinds of pent up things and a tremendous opening up of everything for me: – I have always laid that to the credit of the inspiration" of the TCBS (*Letters* 10).

Ronald Tolkien would have wanted Edith to be provided for if he did not return from the war. This required that Edith be officially listed as his wife and the probably postponed wedding must take place. Tolkien wrote, "I found the situation intolerable and married March 22, 1916" (*Letters* 53). In the context of a letter about Edith, "his lover," his "intolerable situation" might suggest a lack of physical consummation. However, it is as likely to reflect his irritation with the Army and his commanding officer: prior to World War I all ranks in the British military needed the permission of their commanding officer to marry. However, by October 1914, Prime Minister H. H. Asquith's (1852-1928) unilateral announcement to the House of Commons, that the traditional regimental marriage establishment was to be abolished forthwith and for the duration of hostilities, put a new arrangement into effect. This decree meant civilian volunteers, who were "enlisted men" or "other ranks" (OR), had their marriages recognized, and their families immediately began receiving payments as well as any death benefits.

This declaration did not extend to officers, like Tolkien, who had always been discouraged from marrying before the age of thirty in the traditional military

(French 128). The fact Tolkien was betrothed in the Catholic Church before he applied for a commission would have had little weight with the professional military, though with the casualties mounting in the war there was some softening of hard lines. Tolkien's OTC instructor was very unlikely to have mentioned any need to get permission to marry. However, when Tolkien accepted his commission at the end of June 1915, he had probably inquired about scheduling leave for his wedding. He would have, of course, been told this matter needed to await his first posting. In July, 1915, when Tolkien arrived at Bedford, he again probably sought an answer only to be told this concern was not within the purview of his present commander and must wait until he was actually deployed.

So when Tolkien arrived in August 1915 at Whitfield, he would have filled out an application beginning, "Sir, I have the honour to request permission to marry, etc. etc.," and ending "I have the honour to be, Sir, Your obedient servant" (French 128). This obligatory closing salutation underscored the fact Tolkien had no freedom of action in this matter. Ronald would have then handed the application to his Company Commander, a Major. The Company Commander would have had a chat with Tolkien, in order to establish that, although Tolkien was a mere 23-year old, second lieutenant, he had sufficient funds to support a wife and in due course, a family. This requirement meant Tolkien would have revealed his assets, "£20-40" annually (*Letters* 53) from what his father left him plus revealing something of Edith's assets. Tolkien may have regarded this interrogation as an intrusion of his privacy and none of their business.

Now, his request, along with the required documentation, must be relayed up the proper chain of command, all of whom were preoccupied with other priorities of an ongoing war. The Major would have made hand-written comments in the file, such as justifying an exception to the traditional policy of discouraging junior officers' marriage before the age of thirty, and passed the file to the Battalion Adjutant, a senior Major with responsibility for all administrative matters. When the Adjutant had the time, he would have formally interviewed Tolkien to determine his wife was the sort of proper person the military would approve of. Having ascertained that Tolkien's intended was an owner of property who had had a good education, the Adjutant would make his recommendations to the Battalion Commander, probably a Lieutenant Colonel, but perhaps a full Colonel, given the unusual size of the Battalion at 2000 men (*Great War* 93). However, there was the potential for the Adjutant to send the file back to the Major, if he felt, for example, there was not enough information concerning Edith's family. Then the file could have recycled ping-ponging between the two for weeks.[17] The traversal of the administrative labyrinth could then have continued with the Battalion's Commanding Officer himself interviewing Tolkien. Having given Tolkien the good news of permission to marry, the Commanding Officer would offer his congratulations. However, any scheduled leave for this ceremony would await the needs and priorities of the military. After the wedding, Tolkien would have provided the Regimental Pay Office with a copy of his marriage certificate.

Tolkien's outburst, in the context of his son's military induction, about "the most improper job of any man [...] is bossing other men" (*Letters* 64) and his own known dislike of being on the receiving end of "bossing about" (Morton and Hayes 51) seems to have had some deep roots. But, without suffering the vicissitudes of this bureaucratic procedure and obtaining the permission with the accompanying correct paperwork, Edith would not have been entitled to any benefits if Ronald were to be killed in action.

By late January 1916, Ronald and Edith had set a wedding date of March 22, 1916 (*C&G* 1.84). That date was in Lent and no wedding mass could be celebrated. Lent is a season of penitence for sin and of fasting in the Catholic Church so there would be no or few flowers on the altar and little or no music in keeping with the somber season. Marriage, as a sacrament, could not be withheld in Lent, but the wedding could not be solemnized, that is have a solemn blessing. Ronald's imminent departure to France and the need to compress graduation, wedding, and honeymoon into one period of leave may have all contributed to the choice of the date (*C&G* 1.84). Ronald and Edith picked a Wednesday for the wedding as that was the day of the week on which they had been reunited in 1913 (*Bio* 79). They knew Ronald would soon be sent overseas and might not return. This was a factor in their having separate formal portraits taken on February 3, 1916, presumably as keepsakes (McIlwaine 156, Priestman 52).

---

17 Personal email from a retired British staff officer.

Putting his affairs in order to leave Edith in the best possible position, Tolkien sold his share in the motorbike (*Bio* 78).

When Ronald Tolkien visited Father Francis Morgan to make financial arrangements before he left for the war, he failed to tell his former guardian about the wedding date (*Bio* 78). In explaining this lapse, Carpenter focuses on Tolkien remembering Father Francis Morgan's previous opposition. In reevaluating the evidence of the 1909/1910 separation, it seems more likely Ronald Tolkien may have been embarrassed and/or ashamed of how he had repeatedly deceived his kind and generous benefactor, who had only had Tolkien's best interests in mind. Tolkien finally wrote Father Francis Morgan on March 8, 1916. The completely forgiving Father Francis Morgan offered "every blessing and happiness" to the new couple and wanted to conduct the service himself (*Bio* 78).

Announcing his wedding date to his friends in the TCBS, Tolkien appears to have been uneasy at what he knew was his increasing distance from his friends. However, all three reassured him (*Great War* 129-30). Ronald Tolkien's friends, brought up as English gentlemen, may have been reluctant to stir up any divisions on the eve of their entry in World War I.

Following Tolkien's degree ceremony on March 16, 1916, Father Murphy married Edith and Ronald in the Roman Catholic Church of St. Mary Immaculate in Warwick with Jennie Grove and Anne M. Johnson as witnesses on March 22 (*C&G* 1.86).[18] After the ceremony, the need to write her father's name in the marriage register took Edith by surprise (*Bio* 79). She wrote the name, Frederick Bratt. If she had written any name without the surname of Bratt, Edith would have revealed her secret. Edith did have an uncle with this name (*Bio* 79), but she probably did not know this man as he was born prematurely in 1861 and did not survive (census 1861). She could not think of what profession or rank to add and left this blank. The church's usual procedure would have been for Edith to show a copy of her baptismal registration before they read the banns and permitted the marriage so her response had to be consistent with the baptismal register. Most likely she wrote what was on her baptismal register

---

18 http://www.elendilion.pl/2009/04/15/for-the-first-time-we-can-see-the-marriage-certificate-of-mr-and-mrs-tolkien/, last viewed on 11/10/2020.

(*C&G* 1.2) plus her last name Bratt, as that would be as truthful as she could be in the circumstances.

Edith finally told Ronald her secret: she was illegitimate. She then could celebrate her new name, Mrs. J.R.R. Tolkien (*Bio* 79). The hated name of Bratt, which announced her shameful past, was now concealed. Later, Ronald wrote, "I love you even more tenderly because of all that [...] and we must as far as possible forget it and entrust it to God" (*Bio* 79). Tolkien had known Edith for almost two years when he lived at the Faulkners' boarding house beginning in early 1908 and then saw and wrote her for another three years before the 1916 wedding (1913-1916). Somehow Edith never broached the topic of her dead father. To be willing to avoid what the other person was unwilling to bring up would be likely in someone who knew the importance of silence concerning family secrets. Carpenter implies Tolkien did have family secrets ("Learning about Ourselves" 270, 271).

Edith and Ronald Tolkien then had time for a brief honeymoon. They took a train to Clevedon in Somerset for a week and visited Cheddar Gorge and its caves (*Bio* 79, *C&G* 1.86). Clevedon was a fashionable spa and winter resort for invalids due to its mild climate, a result of being protected by the Mendip hills from the northern and easterly winds. The town was at the mouth of the Severn River overlooking the Bristol Channel and the islands of Steep Holme and Flat Holme with a view of the mountains of Glamorgan and Monmouth. Due to wartime constraints, the Tolkiens' best source of information on accommodations in Clevedon was likely to have been from 1914. While there were apartments for rent in town in 1914, the only hotel was the Walton Park offering four tennis courts, two croquet lawns, an eighteen-hole golf course, a motor garage, and a bus which met all trains, not to mention a commanding view of the coast (Kelly's directory). This establishment continues to operate today, and it was the Tolkiens' most likely destination.[19]

A trip to Cheddar Gorge is almost obligatory for a Clevedon visit. By train, one would go south four miles to Yatton and then change trains at Yatton for

---

19 An image of the substantial Walton Park Hotel circa 1900 is available at https://www.ebay.co.uk/itm/Somerset-CLEVEDON-Walton-Park-Hotel-used-c1900s-PPC-/161980690324, last viewed on 7/1/2020.

Cheddar Gorge
(Courtesy Tanya Dedyukhina, Wikipedia Commons)

Cheddar. Years later, Tolkien wrote that this and a later visit to the caves in Cheddar Gorge were the source of his "Glittering Caves of Aglarond" in Helm's Deep (*Letters* 407).[20]

---

20 These caves would have brought back memories of Tolkien's 1902 visit to Torquay's Kent's Cavern with his brother Hilary, his Incledon cousins, Marjorie and Mary, and his Aunt May Incledon (née Suffield; see Bunting and Hamill-Keays, "The Other Suffield Aunt Part IV"). On Scull and Hammond's online website, they reject as evidence the signature visual matches between the landscape of Torquay's Ore Stone and Thatcher's Rock from Meadfoot Beach and the view of Redgate Beach in Anstey's Cove with Tolkien's artwork, calling such an equation "conjecture", even though the visual verification of these landmarks is, if not more, distinctive than written documentation. Hammond and Scull previously stated the paintings were done on a seaside holiday in 1902 with a godfather (*A&I* 13). Simon Tolkien reports a letter from his grandfather, J.R.R. Tolkien, who wrote he visited Torquay at the age of ten, i.e. in 1902 ("My Grandfather – J.R.R. Tolkien." www. simontolkien.com/ author.html, last viewed on 11/12/2020).

Now that they had married, Ronald and Edith Tolkien agreed Edith would live in furnished rooms as near as possible to Ronald's camp (*Bio* 80). Neither had

Chris Allen: Reflections in Gough's Cave (in the Cheddar gorge)
(CC BY-SA 2.0. From geograph.org.uk)

any idea Edith would move twenty-two times during the war to follow Ronald (P. Tolkien 7). Edith would have only been able to keep this commitment to Ronald because Edith's independent income allowed her to handle the numerous early terminations on rental agreements due to Ronald's unpredictable reassignment orders. Their commitment to each other appears to have been what both of them wanted most, given the desperate uncertainty of the times. The non-professional troops in World War I did not just fight out of patriotism. The 1943 British movie, *The Life and Death of Colonel Blimp*, filmed during World War II, portrays the life of an honorable British officer who is somehow thinking of "the girl I left behind me." Frank Capra's World War II propaganda series, *Why We Fight*, focused on fears for the future of children under Nazism. In the trenches and heat of battle, men fought to protect their unit, but it was the family waiting for them at home which made it worthwhile.

Edith Bratt Tolkien Confronts the War, 1916

After waiting six years for her Ronald, Edith was finally married on March 22, 1916 and was officially known as Mrs. J.R.R. Tolkien. The unforeseeable cataclysm of the war placed all their plans in jeopardy. Edith could only wait again, hoping that, despite the terrible odds, Ronald, as a junior officer, would survive the Western Front and return. When Ronald returned home sick with trench fever in November 1916, a new chronicle of repeated moves followed. They had no idea of the unremitting interruptions this would create in Edith's life as Edith would move twenty-two times during the war to follow Ronald (P. Tolkien 7). Despite all these troubles, they supported each other as recorded by Ronald Tolkien in his art and poetry.

As a military wife, Edith could accompany her husband's moves from camp to camp. After their honeymoon in March, 1916, Tolkien went to a signals school in Yorkshire at Farnley Park, Otley. Tolkien's signaling scores with a lamp in 1916 were slow: six words per minute when the average was between seven and ten (*Great War* 134). However, speed of signaling was only a small part of Tolkien's training at Farnley, and he was competent on his written exam and with map-reading (*Great War* 134). Ronald Tolkien also would have had some mastery of electrical engineering matters as evidenced by a diagram from Farnley showing the wiring of the telephone exchanges he would have been expected to set up. Tolkien also would have had an understanding of how his work interfaced with the cables of the Royal Engineers. His certificate from Farnley was labeled "provisional" due to his lack of experience in actually instructing Army signalers in 1916. His training in all the responsibilities of a Signals officer was adequate to meet the requirements of the "Big Push" of 1916 before the Battle of the Somme.

On May 13, 1916, after passing his signaling exam, the military gave Ronald Tolkien only two days leave, and he returned to Warwick (*Great War* 134).

At Tolkien's next post, Cannock Chase, he quickly "found good lodging" for Edith at Mrs. Kendrick's near the Catholic Church of St. John the Baptist in Great Haywood by May 18, 1916 (*Bio* 80).[1] Edith closed her house and moved to Great Haywood, Staffordshire, arriving May 26, 1916.[2]

Ronald Tolkien had already arrived at Brocton Camp by May, 18, 1916, when he wrote Edith about her imminent arrival in Great Haywood to take up lodging at "Hazel Dene."[3] He mentioned Edith should remember the walk from Colwich, north of Cannock Chase on the River Trent to Great Haywood. She should also remember Mrs. Kendrick's property was just before she would get to Mrs. Asbury's. This letter indicates Edith must have visited Great Haywood before May 18 and after May 13 when Ronald was given leave from Farnley Park. The directions indicate she was familiar with the landmark of Mrs. Asbury's boarding house, suggesting she may have stayed there on her previous visit.

Mrs. Kendrick managed Hazel Dene in 1916.[4] Previously, in the census of 1911, 78 year-old William Asbury and 55 year-old Elizabeth Asbury lived in a large house with twelve rooms. William had "No occupation" and Elizabeth was a "Boarding House/Lodging House keeper" [*sic*] (1901 census). By following the path of the census enumerator, it is possible to map the Asbury residence opposite the vicarage. That means the Asbury residence would have been Hazel Dene. William Asbury died in 1915. Given that the Asburys were almost certainly tenants, the lease on Hazel Dene may have stipulated a married couple. If so, on William's death, Elizabeth would have surrendered the tenancy. That may explain why Elizabeth Asbury literally moved down the street to open another

---

1 The *Chronology*, under the heading, "April 1916," states "Edith gave up the house in Warwick she had been renting" (*C&G* 1.86). However, Garth states that on May 13, 1916 when given leave, Tolkien went to Warwick (*Great War* 134). This suggests Edith had not yet left Warwick or why else would Ronald Tolkien have gone there? Garth has a letter to establish the date of May 13, 1916 (*Great War* 337). This and the information from Whitehouse and Robbie indicate the date in the *Chronology* is inaccurate.

2 Personal email from local Staffordshire historians, Scott Whitehouse and David Robbie, based on information received from the Tolkien Estate.

3 Ibid. A photograph of Hazel Dene is available at "Tolkien Trail." Staffordshire County Council, last viewed on 6/16/2020. https://www.staffordshire.gov.uk/environment/RightsofWay/distancewalks/Staffordshire-Tolkien-Trail.aspx.

4 "Staffordshire Tolkien Trail," last viewed on 6/19/2020. https://www.staffordshire.gov.uk/environment/RightsofWay/distancewalks/Staffordshire-Tolkien-Trail.aspx. According to the local historians, David Robbie and Scott Whitehouse, Mrs. Kendrick is a puzzle. The 1911 census lists a Geary Kendrick. He was a thirty-eight-year-old grocer/baker in Leicestershire about 50 miles from Great Haywood and married to a thirty-five-year-old Elizabeth.

boarding house opposite the present Hazeldene Terrace and diagonally across from the Clifford Arms by 1916.

While Ronald Tolkien was arranging "good lodgings" for Edith in Great Haywood, he, as one of the hundreds of newly-commissioned officers involved in the preparations for "The Big Push," lived in the camps on Cannock Chase. These camps were known as Brocton and Rugeley, with Penkridge Camp built as part of Rugeley Camp on Penkridge Bank.[5] Lord Lichfield permitted the construction of these camps on his estate. The Earls of Lichfield lived near this area in their ancestral home, Shugborough Hall, and they owned the nearby impressive packhorse bridge which Tolkien included in his heraldic drawing of late 1917, *The Fair Towns of (the) Holy Tol Eressëa* (McIlwaine 213). The large area of beautiful woodland and heath with its wildlife at Cannock Chase earned the status as an area of Outstanding Natural Beauty in 1958.[6]

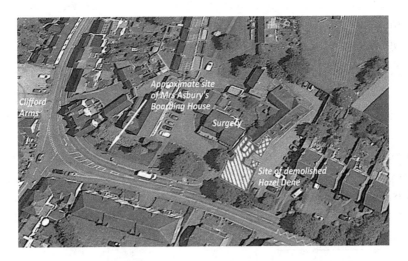

Aerial view of Great Haywood showing the previous location of Hazel Dene opposite the vicarage of the Anglican Church of St. Stephen with cross-hatching representing conservatories (SH-K) (Google Earth)

5 An informative photograph of "Penkridge Bank 'Camp' huts at Rugeley Camp" is available at Staffordshire Past Track. http://www.staffspasttrack.org.uk/, last viewed on 9/2019.
6 "Cannock Chase." Discover Britain, last viewed on 6/19/2020. https://www.discoverbritainmag.com/cannock-chase/.

Tolkien would continue to live at Brocton Camp after the arrival of Edith in Great Haywood (*C&G* 1.87). To live off camp would have required his Commanding Officer's permission, and that would not be forthcoming: to the British Army, wives of junior officers were extra baggage and a confounded nuisance (French 128).

The soldiers, in training on Cannock Chase, lived in prefabricated "huts." Constructed of wood with a door in each end and windows down the side, the huts had corrugated metal roofs.[7] The huts for officers contained only two cubicles, each with a coal stove for heating, and each cubicle held two officers.[8] For the enlisted men, or Tommies, or other ranks (OR), the first layout (known as A) for the huts accommodated thirty men each with four feet of wall space per bed. Two stoves, located in the middle, heated each hut. The tables for meals were also located in the middle of the hut. When the camp had a dining room, accommodations for more men replaced the space the tables previously occupied. The later redesigned hut (known as B) held twenty-two men each, but the fabrication of B huts only began later in the war. Generally, the military arranged sleeping huts in rows with washrooms and latrines in blocks between every pair of rows.

After obtaining his provisional instructor's certificate on May 16, 1916 (*Great War* 134), Tolkien's duties would have predominantly been concerned with signals matters and instructing Army signalers. Prior to his signals training at Farnley Park, Tolkien would have been responsible for the discipline and train-ing of newly enlisted infantrymen: route marching; parades; daily inspection of his men; bombing practice; musketry and bayonet practice; night exercises; platoon, company and battalion attacks; dawn stand-tos;[9] entrenching; and

---

7 Draper, K. L. (2018). Wartime Huts: The Development, Typology, and Identification of Temporary Military Buildings in Britain 1914-1945 (Doctoral thesis). https://doi.org/10.17863/CAM.17581 Apollo. University of Cambridge. https://www.repository.cam.ac.uk/handle/1810/270649, last viewed on 6/19/2020.

8 Personal email from local Staffordshire historians, Scott Whitehouse and David Robbie.

9 Stand-to or "Standing to Arms" was a routine military precaution taken because the dawn was often judged to be the most likely time for an enemy attack. The stand-to has a long history in the British Army. A battalion, about 800 men, comprising a number of companies, each commanded by a Major, would be roused from slumber and ordered to "Fix Bayonets!" an hour before dawn. They would stand down an hour after dawn. On the Western Front, the rising sun would be shining into the defenders' eyes as the line formed along the trench. Dawn was held to be the time one could see a gray horse at the distance of one mile (Bowyer).

Orderly Officer Duties and Orderly Room procedures, i.e. hearing charges against his soldiers. His attendance at the evening Officers' Mess was compulsory, even when not on duty. Any gaps in attendance or lapses in adhering to the Mess's strict social norms would have attracted unfavorable attention, from both his Regular Army superiors and his peers. Tolkien would have needed a pass to leave camp for any reason, a rule he would have been enforcing with his own troops (Lewis-Stempel 64). There were also Guard Commander and Church Parades' duties.

A Church Parade would normally be held at 10:15 am on Sunday with battalions, not on military training exercises, forming up and marching to church (Crang 93-94).[10] The formation of the parade would ensure different denominations went to the church of their faith, if sufficient in number. The Roman Catholic church, The Holy Child and St. Joseph, had just been completed in Bedford in 1913 so Tolkien may have attended it when he was in training in Bedford. Alternatively, there could be a drumhead service, i.e. one held in the open air with the altar composed of the drums of the battalion and draped with its colors conducted by the unit's Anglican chaplain.[11] The Anglican minister always said prayers during these services and on other more formal parades. At the drumhead service before the chaplain said prayers, an officer gave the order: "Jews, Roman Catholics, and Other Denominations, [i.e. Nonconformists or 'Dissenters' like Baptists, Methodists, Presbyterians, Unitarians, etc.] may fall out!" Any such would take a half-turn to the right and march smartly to the rear of their parade with their backs to it. Ronald Tolkien was one of these. As a result of such officially sanctioned, institutional Freedom of Religion, Tolkien would have been likely to seek out the local Catholic church in Great Haywood. Tolkien, as a former ward of a Catholic priest from the Birmingham Oratory, would probably have impressed the priest there. Father Augustine Emery would have been happy to have him as part of the congregation.

---

10 See also *The King's Regulations and Orders for the Army*. 1912. 266, 312. Hathi Trust Digital Library, last viewed on 6/20/2020. https://babel.hathitrust.org./cgi/pt?id=hvd.32044048604474&view=1up& seq=334&q1=church=https://*King's Regulations and Orders for the Army 1912*. Divine Service. 1332 *et seq.* HMSO London.

11 For a visual of a drumhead service see Pathé. "Drumhead Service 1919," last viewed on 6/20/2020. *YouTube*. Uploaded by British Pathé. https://www.youtube.com/watch?v=z0RRJF-uhtw.

Church of St John the Baptist, Great Haywood (CC BY-SA 2.0)
(Wikipedia Commons: Tim Heaton https://www.geograph.org.uk/photo/5200511[12])

There were lulls and free time in this intense activity. Just as Ronald Tolkien wrote to Edith about his everyday activities at Oxford (*TFA* 35), he would have been writing Edith all about his life in the camps (*Bio* 77-78). To visit Edith in Great Haywood, Tolkien could have planned to either walk or possibly borrow a bicycle as he regularly pedaled between camp and the Clarkes' residence in Gipsy Green where the Tolkien family lived in 1918 (McIlwaine 260-61).[13] Once Edith was in Great Haywood in late May 1916, Tolkien may have thought he could snatch maybe an hour or two in the afternoon to see her or just after Last Post (generally 22.00 hours or 10 pm followed by Lights Out) with his coming back early in the morning by 06.30 (6:30 am) when a

---

12 The nucleus of the Church of St John the Baptist had been the Clifford family's private chapel, built at Tixall in 1827. The Cliffords left the private chapel and land in Great Haywood to the "Catholic People" of the area. The local congregation moved the private chapel, stone by stone, to Great Haywood by 1845. The resulting church, somewhat modified from the original chapel, provides a lovely setting for worship.

13 Gipsy Green was the name of a small hamlet with four dwellings, not the name of a house (1911 census).

normal day in the Army commenced with Reveille and often a Color Hoisting Parade at 08.00 (8:00 am).[14]

1902 OS map (National Library of Scotland) annotated with
four mile route from Brocton Camp to Great Haywood or
4-5 miles from Rugeley Camp (SH-K)

For the weekend of May 27-28, 1916, when G.B. Smith of the TCBS visited, Ronald Tolkien was able to procure time, but the Army soon had other plans for Tolkien (*Great War* 135). Edith and Jennie had only arrived on May 26 and must have been hard-pressed as to how to entertain Ronald's friend the next day. On Friday, June 2, 1915, following Smith's visit, Tolkien received his embarkation orders with 48 hours of leave, with Edith indeed "scarcely" settled in Great Haywood (*Bio* 80). Edith and Ronald traveled to Birmingham

14 "Daily Duties." *The King's Regulations and Orders for the Army. 1912.* 207. Hathi Trust Digital
   Library, last viewed on 6/20/2020. https://babel.hathitrust.org/cgi/pt?id=hvd.32044048604474&view
   =1up&seq=276&q1=%22last%20post%22.

to say farewell to friends and family. On June 3, they stayed the night at the Plough and Harrow Hotel (*TFA* 39). On June 4 in the afternoon, Edith and Ronald said their goodbyes, presumably at the station, when Ronald took the train to London on the way to his embarkation port, Folkestone, Kent (*C&G* 1.88; Garth, *Worlds* 62). He sailed two days later arriving at Calais on June 6, 1916 (*TFA* 39).

1901 OS map of Great Haywood from National Library of Scotland with Hazel Dene marked by SH-K

On the eve of his departure for the battlefields of France, Tolkien said, "Parting from my wife then […] it was like a death" (qtd. in *Great War* 138). This was an understandable sentiment. Britain's casualties in 1915 were severe due to the military staff's continuing belief in the efficacy of "morale" even when faced with the machine guns' lethal efficiency. For example, at the "Second Battle of Ypres in April 1915, whole brigades were almost annihilated" and at the Battle of Loos in September 1915, in the first two hours the "British lost more men than were lost on the whole of D-Day 1945 by all three arms of the Services" (Ellis 93). The survival rate for junior officers on the front lines was abysmal: subalterns had an average life expectancy of 42 days on the Western Front (Lewis-Stempel 6).

Edith found herself in the new World War I role for a woman: the "heroine" behind the man on the front lines. In this role, she faced food shortages, re-mained optimistic in the face of uncertainty, provided comfort and courage by maintaining a home, writing letters, and visiting, though "worn by anxieties as to her absent husband or sons" (qtd. in Jensen 68). Edith kept a large map of France on the wall in Great Haywood, presumably still at Mrs. Kendrick's, where she tracked Ronald's military position. Before leaving, Ronald Tolkien had devised a system of dots so that Edith could know his location in France as the military censored the mail and offered uninformative official forms (*TFA* 39). Both Roland Leighton writing to his fiancée, Vera Brittain, and Ronald Tolkien, writing to Edith, put small pencil dots under certain letters (Lewis-Stempel 100). This strategy derives from a fourth century BC writer, Aeneas Tacitus, and presumably both men knew about this strategy because of their excellent classical educations (Hooker, "Private Code" 5). Relaying this information was, by the way, a breach of military regulations which could have put Tolkien in prison (Tucker 281-82). Edith's map was also technically a violation of military regulations.

Tolkien, as a junior officer, was responsible for the endless task of censoring and signing all the letters and postcards sent home by the enlisted men. If the base censors discovered a breach of security, they could identify the negligent party by his signature (Lewis-Stempel 98). Tolkien may have felt he had little to worry about. By a gentlemen's agreement, letters of junior officers went directly to the anonymous base censor (Lewis-Stempel 100).

Edith had made friends with Great Haywood's Catholic priest, Father Augustin Emery, who remained a family friend known as "Uncle Gus." He became the godfather of Edith and Ronald's second child, Michael, born in 1920 (P. Tolkien 5). In May 1916, Father Augustin Emery, knowing the Tolkiens had been unable to celebrate a "Solemn" Nuptial or Wedding Mass because their wedding had been in Lent, arranged a special Nuptial Blessing during the usual Sunday mass before the local congregation (P. Tolkien 5). This must have been on Sunday, May 27, as Edith only arrived in Great Haywood on May 26, and the Tolkiens left Great Haywood for Birmingham on Saturday, June 3, 1916. Edith was reportedly amused that many of the congregation seemed to think this blessing finalized their wedding and put an end to their living in sin (P. Tolkien 5).

Edith enjoyed playing the piano together with Father Emery on the violin (P. Tolkien 5). The piano may have been at the church, as opposed to Mrs.

Kendrick's house. Edith needed the comfort of music and the beauty of St John the Baptist chapel as an August 1916 photograph in Llandudno shows her forlorn, uncertain, and anxious (McIlwaine 13).

With Ronald in France, Edith and Jennie went to Llandudno on the Welsh sea coast from July 14 to September 26, 1916.[15] Llandudno is not far from Liverpool where Jennie Grove grew up. It was the largest seaside resort in Wales and hailed as "the Queen of the Welsh Watering Places," or what we would now call a "resort" as early as 1861.[16] It was famous for its Victorian architecture and stunning scenery as well as an electric tram line between Llandudno and Colwyn Bay. A wide curving Victorian promenade, known as The Parade, ran for most of the length of Llandudno's North Shore Beach. Llandudno provided entertainment and attractions to the well-heeled and well-to-do: pubs, cafes, amusement arcades, assorted shops and kiosks, and "The Happy Valley" with its gardens, a putting green, a popular open-air theater, and extensive lawns. For children, there were fairground rides, miniature golf, and Punch and Judy shows. The Prince's concert hall also presented a repertoire of plays and musicals. As seen in Edith's picture of August 1916 (McIlwaine 13), none of these distractions and amusements seemed to have lightened Edith's somber mood, evident in the tight mouth and dull eyes expressing her uncertainty and feelings of helplessness. She knew Ronald was at the Front in France, and she would have braced herself for a highly probable letter from the War Department announcing his death or serious injury. The Battle of the Somme began July 1, 1916 and various subsidiary battles of this offensive continued through November 1916, leading to horrifying reports of casualties.

Edith may or may not have been able to make arrangements to return to Mrs. Kendrick's in Great Haywood in late September. She may have needed to rent temporary rooms in September until she could get an October lease.

In France, Tolkien was sustained by his Catholicism which was tolerated by the British Army. He was able to attend mass on Sunday, July 2, 1916, ministered by the chaplain of the Royal Irish Rifles. His battalion's Anglican chaplain,

15 Personal email from local Staffordshire historians, Scott Whitehouse and David Robbie based on information received from the Tolkien Estate.
16 "The history of Llandudno." Information Britain, last viewed on 6/19/2020. http://www.informationbritain.co.uk/history/town/Llandudno68/.

Mervyn Evers, was known to be "averse to Roman Catholics" (*Great War* 157). Tolkien attended mass in Bertrancourt on August 6 (*Great War* 173, *C&G* 1.93) and in the Roman Catholic Church in Beauval, on September 10 (Great War 100, *C&G* 1.97). Because the mass was in Latin, Tolkien would have felt at home attending a mass even abroad in France.[17] At the Battle of the Somme, Evers, the Anglican chaplain, followed the stretcher-bearers to tend to some of the 117 wounded and found himself cheered by the battalion (*Great War* 197, 199-200). He won one Military Cross in 1916 and a second in 1917.[18]

Evers' bravery at the Front was not typical. Robert Graves, an Anglican, like Siegfried Sassoon and Guy Chapman, had sharp words about Anglican chaplains:

> For Anglican regimental chaplains we had little respect. If they had shown one-tenth the courage, endurance, and other human qualities that the regimental doctors showed, we agreed, the British Expeditionary Force might well have started a religious revival. But they had not, being under orders to avoid getting mixed up in the fighting and to stay behind with the transport. Soldiers could hardly respect a chaplain who obeyed these orders, and yet not one in fifty seemed sorry to obey them [...] [the chaplain] was always much to the fore in rest-billets. [When] summon[ed] to come up with the rations and bury the day's dead; he would arrive, speak his lines, and shoot off again [...] the Roman Catholic chaplains were not only permitted to visit posts of danger, but definitely enjoyed to be wherever fighting was, so that they could give extreme unction to the dying. And we had never heard of one who failed to do all that was expected of him and more. Jovial Father Gleeson of the [Royal] Munster [Fusiliers], when all the officers were killed or wounded at the first battle of Ypres, had stripped off his black badges and, taking command of the survivors, held the line. (197-98)

Later research has modified Graves' condemnation of the cowardice of Anglican clergy to a more balanced and nuanced view, but what is important is that during World War I and for years afterward, the Roman Catholic clergy was now seen

---

17 Ronald's mother did teach him French (*Bio* 22) and he had some classes when he first attended King Edward's (*C&G* 2.617). By 1913, "his French deserted him" when he needed to speak it (*Bio* 67). Tolkien's ability to read French was sufficient for him to review papers, written in French, for *The Year's Work in English Studies* in the 1920s.

18 The Military Cross was awarded for "an act or acts of exemplary gallantry during active operations against the enemy on land, to captains or officers of lower rank." For more see "The Gazette, The Official Public Record," https://www.thegazette.co.uk/awards-and-accreditation/content/100068, last viewed on 2/9/21.

in a much more respectful light.[19] This included an award of the Military Cross to another priest, a Jesuit, Father William Doyle for his part in the Wytschaete Ridge assault in June 1917.[20] Many believed his bravery under fire merited rather the Victoria Cross.[21]

Ronald Tolkien, faced with impending combat in France, appears to have turned to Edith as his anchor for a future, relegating the TCBS to a position of secondary importance. Preparing for the Battle of the Somme on July 6, 1916, Tolkien "re-read all of Edith's letters," but only "glanced once again at his collection of notes" from the TCBS members (*Bio* 83). He wrote a poem, *A Dream of Coming Home*, "a vision of Great Haywood in May" "dedicated to my wife, Bouzincourt, July 4-8, 1916" (*C&G* 1.90).

Tolkien would get his dream of coming home by contracting trench fever. From July 1, 1916 to October 31, 1916, during the Battle of the Somme, eight of the probably twenty-eight junior officers in Tolkien's 11th (Service) Battalion Lancashire Fusiliers were killed: Second Lieutenants J. Kay, S. Rowson, and S. Hetherington; Lieutenants F. Dunn and N. Holden; and Captains R. Ganly, P. Ward, and R. Mackinnon.[22] The *Field Service Manual, 1914* specified an Infantry Battalion had thirty officers including one Lieutenant Colonel, two Majors and a Captain in the Battalion Headquarters (see Section 2, pages 7-11 in the *Field Service Manual*). This total of thirty officers also included the one officer who was the head of each of the sixteen platoons plus the eight officers who were in command of each of four companies. By 1916, specialist officers had been added to the organization: two Signals Officers and a Trench Mortar Officer, although the Machine Gun Officer would have been transferred to the newly-formed Machine Gun Corps. That gives a nominal

---

19 Parker, Linda Mary. Shell-shocked Prophets: The influence of former Anglican army chaplains on the Church of England and British society in the inter-war years. University of Birmingham etheses, last viewed on 6/19/2020. https://etheses.bham.ac.uk/id/eprint/4495/1/ParkerL13PhD.pdf.
20 "How Irish priests brought comfort to the battlefield." *The Independent.* Ie. Dublin. June 21, 2020. https://www.independent.ie/life/world-war-1/how-irish-priests-brought-comfort-to-the-battlefield-30270519.html; last viewed on 6/20/2020.
21 The Victoria Cross is Britain's highest "military decoration, awarded for valour and devotion to duty in the face of the enemy to members of the armed forces, regardless of rank." For more see "The Gazette, The Official Public Record' https://www.thegazette.co.uk/awards-and-accreditation/content/100077, last viewed on 2/8/21.
22 "Commonwealth War Graves Commission," https://www.cwgc.org/, last viewed on 2/10/21.

establishment of thirty-two officers, twenty-eight of whom would be junior officers, i.e. having the rank of Captain and below.

Those who died from any cause and all wounded were counted as casualties by the military. For each officer killed in France throughout World War I, on average 2.4 (specifically 2.398) officers were wounded (*Statistics of the Military Effort* 238). Consequently, we can extrapolate and apply this known rate to Tolkien's unit during the Battle of the Somme's heavy fighting. With eight officers known dead in this unit, another nineteen were likely to have been wounded. The likely sum of dead and wounded would have been a total of twenty-seven casualties plus Tolkien, sick and unfit for combat, out of a twenty-eight junior officers, if the unit was at full strength. This would be a casualty rate of 96% for the group of officers in the unit when Tolkien joined it in France.

We do not know when Edith would have received word Ronald was sick in the Officers' Hospital in Gézaincourt. Documents place him there by October 28, 1917. Before entering the hospital, Tolkien would have been stripped for a delousing bath (Patch and van Emden 111-12, qtd. in Lewis and Currie, *Codemaker* 161). From Gézaincourt, Tolkien then transferred by train to No. 1 British Red Cross Hospital at Le Touquet where he stayed from October 29 to November 7, 1916. He then boarded the hospital ship, HMHS *Asturias*, November 8. She sailed at night on November 9, arriving at Southampton that same day because a night crossing of the channel minimized the danger of submarine attack. By November 10, Tolkien was in the 1st Southern General Hospital in Birmingham.

During World War I, the War Office requisitioned the Great Hall in the Aston Webb Building and nine other buildings at Birmingham University. This newly consolidated medical facility was named the 1st Southern General Hospital. The Royal Army Medical Corps used this facility to treat military casualties, and it held 520 beds and treated 125,000 injured servicemen. To meet its growing needs, the hospital's capacity increased to 800 beds by the end of 1914. The 2/1st Southern General established an expansion at Dudley Road Infirmary in May 1915, adding an extra 1,000 beds to the medical unit.

The nursing staff began with only sisters of religious orders and staff nurses of the Territorial Force Nursing Society. By May 1915, the Voluntary Aid

Detachment nurses (VADs) were supplementing the staff. In his article of 1915, Gilbert Barling, Surgeon to the General Hospital and the 1st Southern General, described how the hospital was, to a large extent, functioning as a clearing hospital sending many of the patients to smaller hospitals or convalescent homes.[23]

Edith presumably hurried to Birmingham and probably stayed with Ronald's aunt and uncle, the T.E. Mittons, in Moseley where she had visited in the summer of 1916. This was Ronald's address for his correspondence in November 1916. If Edith and Jennie Grove stayed there from early November to early December, she probably lost her lease in Great Haywood. The demands for rental rooms would have been high near the camp, with only a limited supply.

Visiting hours in hospitals were generally not yet regulated with visitors likely to arrive at all hours (Carden-Coyne 222, 228). Visitors, who were denied entry, were known to write and complain to the War Office. This created inconvenience and problems for the medical staff. There was an attempt to manage the traffic of well-intentioned visitors using passes signed by the MOs [Medical Officers] and restricted to two days per week, but these passes were often traded or passed on to other visitors (Carden-Coyne 222-23). Mothers, elderly ladies, and well-meaning young ladies came to see wounded heroes from the front, not just as a patriotic gesture but as a means of hearing the latest and most dramatic tales of the War (Carden-Coyne 222). The ringing of a bell or the blowing of a whistle would announce that visiting hours were coming to an end.

The hospitalized Ronald Tolkien was likely to have attracted little attention as he had not been wounded and was only sick (Carden-Coyne 235). He would have been placed in an "Officers Only" ward. Edith and the Mittons would have come to visit as would Father Francis Morgan. May Incledon (neé Suffield), his aunt and godmother, certainly would have come with Ronald's two cousins, Marjorie and Mary. Rob Gilson's sister, Molly, who was dressing wounds at the hospital, would probably have stopped to see him as she would have known Ronald from the TCBS (*Great War* 169). Tolkien saw his old teacher, R.W.

---

23 "Untold Stories: Birmingham's Wounded Soldiers from WW1." Voices of War and Peace, last viewed on 9/20/2020. http://peoplesheritagecoop.blogspot.com/p/untold-stories.html, last viewed on 6/20/2020. http://www.voicesofwarandpeace.org/wp-content/uploads/2016/10/untold-stories_learning-guide.pdf.

Reynolds, who had encouraged his writing (*C&G* 1.102). All Ronald's visitors would have been happy to see him in one piece and with a good prognosis as opposed to many others in the wards they would have passed.

Ronald Tolkien had time now for his writing. He made a new list of Qenya words, "The Poetic and Mythologic Words of Eldarissa" (QL). Tolkien also created a chart of names in Qenya, English and Gnomish or Goldogrin, with Qenya reflecting his predilection for Finnish and Gnomish displaying characteristics of Welsh (*Great War* 212, *C&G* 1.102). He rewrote the poem, *The Town of Dreams and the City of Present Sorrow* originally written in March 1916 at the time of his Oxford graduation ceremony.

While in the hospital in November 1916, Tolkien wrote an as yet unpublished poem, *The Lonely Harebell* (*C&G* 1.103). Because the poem is still unpublished, the contents are not available for analysis, but the title, and its subsequent revision to *Elf Alone*, are suggestive of Tolkien's concerns at the time. The *Oxford English Dictionary* notes that the name 'Harebell' (*campunula*) comes from this flower's tendency to grow where hares lived, and the hare has had a long association with magic and witches. Unsurprisingly, these flowers are also closely linked with fairy-lore.[24] Folklore said the ringing of the harebells (*Campunula rotundifolia*) or bluebells (*Hyacinthoides non-scripta*) summons the fairy folk to their gatherings. The associations to fairies are reinforced in the revised title, *Elf Alone*, as 'fairy' and 'elf' were interchangeable terms for Ronald Tolkien in his early writings. Harebells (*Campunula r.*), often called "bluebells," grow in a variety of habitats including woods, meadows, cliffs, and beaches, and it flowers in the summer and fall.[25] The most popular meaning for bluebells is humility or sometimes gratitude, but in Scotland harebells and bluebells are symbolic of constancy and everlasting love. They also have an association with death and grief. Consequently, plantings on or near graves often include harebells.

The poem *The Lonely Harebell* was inspired in 1914 (*C&G* 1.103), and for Tolkien's generation 1914 was defined by Britain's mid-August declaration

---

24 "Harebells and Bluebells: A Shakespearean Garden," last viewed on 6/20/2020. https://bardgarden. blogspot.com/2017/03/harebells-and-bluebells.html.

25 Tolkien was well acquainted with the confusion of the hyacinth and campanula with both being labeled 'bluebells' (*Letters* 106).

of war. Edith and Ronald already knew there would be a separation and the risk of death. While a network of family including Ronald's brother, his aunt and godmother May Incledon, and myriad other Tolkien and Suffield aunts, uncles, and cousins supported Ronald Tolkien, Edith had no family besides Jennie Grove. Edith was probably in contact with Mabel Sheaf from Dresden House, but, as mentioned previously, Edith was probably estranged from Molly Field after breaking her engagement with Molly's brother George. In June 1913, Edith had left behind the social network she had built up in Charlton Kings. If Ronald died, she would be virtually alone, perhaps like a lonely flower staying faithful to her Ronald. She was risking her future and seemingly almost everything which made her life meaningful. Would she, like the harebell, be left remembering by Ronald's grave? By 1914, Edith had already waited four years, and now they faced another obstacle and more delay and distressing uncertainty.

Tolkien's annotations of *The Lonely Harebell* specify he drew inspiration from a 1914 visit to Cromer and wrote part of the poem when he was camped near Lichfield in September, 1915 (*C&G* 1.103).

Cromer is a coastal town on the north coast of the English county of Norfolk. It became a resort for the wealthy in the nineteenth century, known for its gardens, ornate Victorian houses and hotels, and the late-Victorian Cromer Pier, home to the Pavilion Theater. Tolkien wrote his Aunt May Incledon on August 23, 1914 from Warwick where he had been seeing Edith (*C&G* 1.61). World War I had just started, and his Aunt May, his godmother, would be eager to see her nephew and find out his plans in response to the declaration of war. The *Chronology* has a noticeable gap in September before Tolkien's Michaelmas term at Oxford began on October 11, 1914. A visit to Cromer could easily fit there. Cromer was the type of fashionable resort the Incledons would favor, and September would have been an optimal time at the seashore where Tolkien would have seen the well-known harebells (campanula) of Cromer blooming (Pigott 71). Tolkien's likely 1914 visit with the Incledons separated him from

Edith, foreshadowing their future parting which must be overcome by their constancy and everlasting love, symbolized in *The Lonely Harebell*.[26]

Lichfield, in August 1915, was Tolkien's first experience of camp life in huts, or even under canvas, after having accommodations in town during his training at Bedford. Here, again, the separation from Edith would have loomed large, and the harebell with its fairy associations would beckon toward a hopeful future with its bells summoning the fairy folk, "holy fairies and the immortal elves" of Kortirion/Warwick, about whom Tolkien wrote in late November 1915 (*C&G* 1.82). In November 1916, safe in England and reunited with Edith, Ronald Tolkien could write *The Lonely Harebell* as they had survived farewells in the shadow of death.

Ronald Tolkien's final reworking of *The Lonely Harebell* into *Elf Alone* appears to be the result of the couple's separation from August to November, 1917 before their son John's birth. If *The Lonely Harebell* was based on Tolkien's reflections about previous partings, as discussed above, then the new version of the poem continues that pattern. It was written in early 1918 at a farmhouse in Easington, Yorkshire, where the Tolkien family settled after John's birth (*C&G* 1.111, Great War 243). The new title, *Elf Alone*, like the harebell of the previous title, could easily refer to Edith, as an 'elf' was someone with a heart (GL 32).

In the Qenya lexicon of 1916, Tolkien places Erinti among the Valar as "the Vali of love, music, beauty and purity" (QL 36). This lexicon organized the vocabulary of Tolkien's invented Elvish language which he had been accumulating since 1915 as seen in various poems (QL xiii-xiv). Erinti's attributes would all fit Edith, and Erinti is a calque of Tolkien's favorite name for Edith,

---

26 John Garth states, Tolkien "was reunited with Edith" in April, 1918, implying they had been separated (*Great War* 245). If so, one would expect a possible rewrite of *The Lonely Harebell/The Elf Alone* due to this separation. I have copies of all of Tolkien's World War I medical records from the Archives, and there are no hospital records between February and April, 1918. The evaluations at Easington on Humber for January 10 and February 19, 1918 both state under "What treatment is the officer receiving and where and from whom?" "Reqd Mo" (Requested Medical Officer). The next line is "Is the officer in need of special medical treatment of any kind, and, if so, what nature?" The blank has only "No." Garth does not report any changes from the service record that would result in a separation. Consequently, the "reunion" after a separation from Edith is puzzling and did not occasion further revision of *The Elf Alone* which other separations had elicited.

"little one" (*Bio* 67).[27] Another entry in the Qenya lexicon states 'Akairis' means 'wife, bride, name of Erinti' [who] "was in love with and to marry –" (QL 30), but the discreet Ronald does not name himself or his Vala avatar, Noldorin (QL 36).

Ronald Tolkien also specifies Erinti/Edith "= 'helinyetille'" with 'helin' meaning 'pansy' (QL 39). Tolkien, as a good Victorian steeped in the "language of flowers" and a good hobbit (*Letters* 228-29), gave flower names with meaningful associations to various female characters, including ones from his own life. His Aunt Jane Neave (née Suffield), his mother's sister, is likely to be linked to the lobelia flower which is also known as puke weed (Bunting, "Again, Lobelia"). His own mother, Mabel Suffield Tolkien has a name connected both to the poisonous and beautiful belladonna (Bunting, Fairies, "Fairy Queens, and the Character of Guinevere in Tolkien's *The Fall of Arthur*" 173-74) and probably also to the Lalia, or rather 'lælia' named for one of the vestal virgins of ancient Rome (Bunting, "Finding Hilary, Part II" 5). Tolkien not only saw Edith in terms of the harebell, but also in relation to the rich lore of pansies.

'Helinyetille' is also glossed as 'Eyes of Heartsease' (QL 39). 'Heartsease' was a "common name for pansy," and 'pansy' is "a corruption of *pensée*, the French word for 'thought'" (Wright 270). *Pensée* may have originally referred to "the flower of one's thoughts, for *la dame de ses pensées*, or one's lady-love" (Wright 270). Edith certainly filled that role when Ronald was composing his Elvish vocabulary. She was in his thoughts by at least 1913, if not 1910, when Ronald Tolkien rededicated himself to her and his Catholic faith with his marriage proposal. The pansy, also known as "Love-in-idleness," is where "the bolt of Cupid fell" in Act II, scene 1 of Shakespeare's *Midsummer Night's Dream*. In the same play in Act IV, scene 1, the pansy is "Cupid's flower." Tolkien's definition of 'Helin' or 'pansy' in his lexicon emphasizes this is a blue violet pansy (QL 39). While pansies come in many colors, including

27 The name 'Erinti' can be parsed in Qenya as: 'Er(e) ('one') + in(ya) ('tiny') + '-t' (noun suffix) + '-i' (feminine suffix) (QL 36, 42; GL 18; *WJ* 392, 396) creating the meaning 'Little One.' Tolkien calqued his own name in Gothic as 'Dwalakoneis' (*Letters* 357) and as 'Rashbold' in "The Notion Papers Club" (*Sauron Defeated* 151). Even as a teenager at King Edward's High School, Ronald played with his name, Tolkien, as 'toll keen,' naming himself in Latin as 'Vectigalius Acer', 'Portorius Acer Germanicus' as well as 'Eisphorides Acribus Polyglotteus' (*Great War* 19). The first may be translated as 'toll' (as in 'tax, money to pay') + 'keen' ('sharp, fierce'); the second as 'toll' (as in 'tax') + 'keen' + 'the German'; and the last as Ancient Greek 'special toll' + 'keen' + 'the polyglot'.

red, white, orange, and yellow, it is also one of the rare blue flowers. Blue is traditionally associated with calmness and trustworthiness.[28] Consequently, the 'Eyes of Heartsease' gloss may refer to Edith's peaceful and tranquil presence, perhaps particularly communicated by her loving gaze, as well as the fact her eyes were "bright blue.[29]

As one of the many victims of trench fever, Tolkien was sent home to recuperate. That was the "standard" treatment the medical profession had to offer at the time. Trench fever, in World War I, was a new disease, having been first reported in mid-1915. Within a few months, hundreds of cases had been identified clinically. Trench fever was a severe logistic problem for the armies which fought on both sides of the Western Front in World War I because it reached epidemic proportions and the infected soldiers were too sick to fight. There was no effective treatment of trench fever in World War I, though doctors tried every promising pharmaceutical without a positive result, including quinine, Salvarsan (arsphenamine), etc.[30] 80% of infected men remained unfit for duty for up to three months.[31]

The typical three-month clinical course of trench fever was already well known in late 1916. This is probably why Tolkien's medical follow-up appointment was scheduled on January 23, 1917. That date was just around three months after Tolkien's initial October 27, 1916 diagnosis. Based on experience, the doctors would be expecting improvement by that time. Tolkien's case, however, fell in the 20% of soldiers with trench fever who did not recover in three months.

The April 21, 1917 letter from the Commanding Officer of the Lancashire Fusiliers, confirming Tolkien had finally joined the unit, validates this timeline. In that letter, the Commander refers to a letter of December 18, 1916 which indicated Tolkien should be coming soon (Mathison 57), i.e. in late January, 1917, three months after the onset of Tolkien's symptoms.

---

28 "The Pansy Flower: its Meaning and Symbolism," last viewed on 6/29/20. https://www.flowermeaning.com/pansy-flower-meaning/.

29 Martsch, 9.

30 "Trench Fever in the First World War." Medicine in the First World War. University of Kansas Medical Center, last viewed on 4/11/2020. http://www.kumc.edu/wwi/index-of-essays/trench-fever.html.

31 "Of Lice and Men, Trench Fever and Trench Life in the AIF" by Dr. M. G. Miller, last viewed on 4/11//2020. Great War Primary Documents Archive. http://www.gwpda.org/medical/liceand.htm.

Edith, the war bride, had survived the terrible uncertainty of Ronald's fate in the trenches of 1916. Now she faced a new ordeal of following Ronald through a series of unpredictable assignments and temporary placements throughout 1917.

Edith Bratt Tolkien's Wanderings, 1917

In 1916, the expected length of disability for Tolkien was three months.[1] He was to be reevaluated by doctors early in 1917 because they expected him to be much improved by then. The unforeseen, lengthy convalescence that Tolkien needed to recuperate from trench fever set the stage for repeated moves and changes for Edith throughout 1917.

The next move for Edith followed the December 2, 1916 Medical Board's examiners' decision that, although Tolkien's temperature had now been normal for a week, he was weak and unfit for service. They granted him leave from December 9 to January 12, 1917. With this news, Edith would have made arrangements to secure lodging in Great Haywood where the support of Father Augustin Emery awaited them at St John the Baptist. This would be at least her fifth move, counting the summer stay in Wales and probably her sixth if she had to stay in temporary rooms in Great Haywood before securing an October lease. Given the sudden news of Ronald's release in early December, the couple may have stayed at the presbytery of St John or even the Clifford Arms, but there is no documentation of this. They may have then moved to what is now known as the "Rock Cottage" with its three chimneys and yew hedge opposite, but again there is no independent, confirming documentation of this.

The couple's first Christmas, together as a married couple, in December 1916, would have held a gamut of emotions. The news of the death of G.B. Smith, one of the members of the TCBS, dampened their joy. Tolkien wrote a commemorative poem, *GBS* (*C&G* 1.104), and inscribed on the diary he kept in France, "Diary of brief time in France and of the last seven times I saw G.B.S" (*C&G* 1.86). Nevertheless, Tolkien wrote a draft of *The Fall of Gondolin* which was "almost fully formed" (*Letters* 215). This first story, full of images reflecting

---

1 "Of Lice and Men, Trench Fever and Trench Life in the AIF" by Dr. M. G. Miller, last accessed 4/11//2020. Great War Primary Documents Archive. http://www.gwpda.org/medical/liceand.htm.

Tolkien's war experiences and his reading of the classics (see Bruce; Keaton; and Lewis and Currie, *Forsaken Realm*), demonstrates how fairy-stories, awakened by philology and nurtured by being with Edith in Kortirion/Warwick, were "quickened to full life by war" (OFS 135). He appears to have started *The Cottage of Lost Play* next, urged on by Christopher Wiseman's letter of January 18, 1917: "You ought to start the epic" (*Great War* 224).

Tolkien's *The Fall of Gondolin* and *The Cottage of Lost Play*, which followed, are both prose works. There has been some discussion of why Tolkien, who had been writing poetry mainly for the consumption of the TCBS, now wrote in prose. C.S. Lewis, Tolkien, and the TCBS were of the generation which believed poetry – narrative, epic, or tragic – was the epitome of great writing (Jacobs 28). Novelists were a lesser breed, mere entertainers. Tolkien may have now begun writing in prose partly because he was no longer reaching to impress his peers with what they expected, i.e. poetry, but also because his mythology that he started in 1910, probably based on the invented "private language" Gautisk, was likely to be in prose. Tolkien, who recycled and reused names and themes throughout his legendarium, may have started to pick up and consolidate his mythology, begun in 1910, in his new work (McIlwaine 204).

Edith's sixth, or possibly her eighth, move would have been to Birmingham by January 12, 1917, when Ronald Tolkien reported to 1st Southern General Hospital.[2] Tolkien listed his residence as 185 Monument Road, Edgbaston, Birmingham. Edith and Jennie Grove are likely to have moved with Ronald as they did not know how long he would be there. Dr. J.A.H. White owned the properties at 185 and 186 Monument Road where the Tolkiens resided (1911 census). The 1910 *Annual Report for the Birmingham Royal Institution for the Blind* listed him, and he also appeared in the *British Medical Journal* as a doctor at Birmingham Central Hospital in 1915 and 1920. Tolkien's contact with Birmingham hospital staff may have led him to Dr. White's property as a temporary lodging while at the hospital.

---

2 There would be seven previous moves if Edith had had to obtain temporary rooms in September in Great Haywood and temporary rooms again in Great Haywood in December before obtaining a January lease.

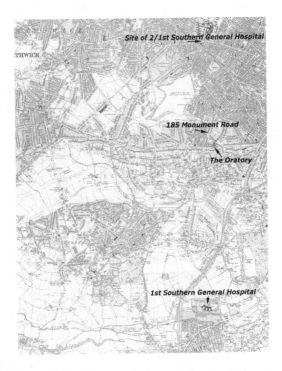

An annotated 1908 OS Map (National Library of Scotland) showing the relationship of 185 Monument St. to Dudley & 1st Southern General Hospitals (SH-K)

The map above shows 185 Monument Road is less than 1½ miles from the 2/1st Southern General Hospital on Dudley Road (Birmingham) in Ladywood with easy transportation connections down Monument Road and up Spring Hall and Dudley Road. This location strongly suggests Tolkien went to the Dudley Road facility as opposed to the hospital created at Birmingham University, which was being used as a clearing house. Dudley Road, or Birmingham Union Infirmary, was built as a single, quarter-of-a-mile corridor with nine, radiating Nightingale wardblocks. When the doctors evaluated Tolkien on January 23, 1917, they extended his leave until February 22, 1917.

After two weeks in Birmingham, the Tolkiens returned to Great Haywood. Their place of residence is unknown. It is likely an arrival in Great Haywood in late January left them with a choice of only temporary accommodations until they could secure a rental agreement in February. February was a happy period with Edith playing the piano and Ronald drawing and reciting his poetry (*Bio* 95).[3] This was a special time for the couple as Edith became pregnant (*Bio* 95), and Tolkien would commemorate this event, probably in late 1917, in the Great Haywood portion of his drawing, the triptych *The Fair Towns of Holy Tol Eressëa*. By February 22, Edith had created a fair, handwritten copy of *The Cottage of Lost Play* from *The Book of Lost Tales* (McIlwaine 208-09).

Edith's next move, at least the eighth, and possibly the eleventh, was precipitated on February 27, 1917 when the doctors examined Ronald at the Military Hospital in Lichfield, only twelve miles from Great Haywood.[4] They found Tolkien improved but unfit for service (*C&G* 1.106). The military ordered him to an officers' convalescent hospital, Furness Auxiliary Hospital in Harrogate, Yorkshire, for one month. The treatment record specified "Indoor hospital treatment," as this option was standard in the medical records of all soldiers (Archives, *C&G* 1.106). In modern terminology, the ill person was an "in-patient" as opposed to an "out-patient." Ronald Tolkien would have had daily supervised treatment while staying in a hospital.

The Furness Auxiliary Hospital was named for Marmaduke Furness, First Baron Furness. His first wife Ada or "Daisy" was very active in the Red Cross during the Great War. Red Cross nurses and Voluntary Aid Detachments (VADs), ladies who wished to help with the treatment of ill and wounded soldiers, staffed this Auxiliary Hospital, one of many hundreds. Many VADs served at the Front.

---

3 Carpenter writes that Tolkien made sketches of Edith at this time in Great Haywood (*Bio* 95). Tolkien may have made some unpublished drawings of Edith in Great Haywood in 1917, but these have neither been cataloged nor acknowledged. No complete catalog of Tolkien's artwork presently exists. It is possible that Carpenter confused the sketches of Edith from 1917 with the drawing known as *High Life at Gipsy Green* done in 1918 (McIlwaine 261). Carpenter states, after the move from Yorkshire in 1918, Edith "settled at Penkridge" and not the more definite destination of Gipsy Green (*Bio* 98). There may be some confusion here.

4 If Edith had to get temporary rooms while waiting for rental agreements for October 1916, January 1917, and February 1917.

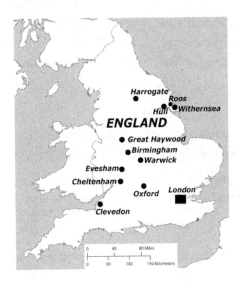

Map of important locations for Edith and Ronald Tolkien in
1916-1917 (SH-K)

The Furness Auxiliary Hospital, now Windsor House (Google Earth)[5]

---

5 The builders of Harrogate used mainly sandstone from the surrounding area, which gives the town
   its characteristic look. These stones vary in color from gray to brown, and many look darker than the
   southern limestones typical of places like Bath. Consequently, the color in the photograph is not the
   result of industrial grime or soot. The stone is also often finished less smoothly – sometimes rock-
   faced, sometimes with a flat face – but with the chisel's tool marks left very much visible. This finish is
   evident in the photograph of Furness Auxiliary Hospital.

The Furness Auxiliary Hospital was actually a relabeled Grand Hotel Harrogate, set conveniently close to the many spa and bathing facilities which Harrogate, a spa town, was known for.[6] The most likely reason the military sent Tolkien to Harrogate for treatment was because there he could have possibly daily treatment bathing in spa water, under medical supervision, to ease trench fever pains.

The referral to Harrogate's Furness Auxiliary Hospital may have also reflected a new policy implemented by the War Office. As Robert Graves reported:

> The War Office now stopped the privilege that officers enjoyed, after leaving the hospital, of going to their own homes for convalescence. It had been noticed that many of them took no trouble to get well and return to duty; they kept late hours, drank, and overtaxed their strength. (261)

Tolkien's placement at Furness Auxiliary Hospital was likely to be part of the new policy which Graves reports. In light of this report, during Tolkien's second trip to the Birmingham hospital on January 12 to 23, 1917, he may have stayed at Monument Drive with Edith and Jennie.

However, Tolkien was one of the "walking wounded," and it was not necessary for him to occupy a bed in a hospital ward which would be needed for a more seriously ill officer. Ronald Tolkien was unlikely to perish from trench fever. His Harrogate address, 95 Valley Drive, was quite close to The Grand Hotel, or Furness Auxiliary Hospital. After an initial examination and the establishment of a treatment regime, while temporarily residing in the hospital, Ronald Tolkien may have transferred to the nearby accommodation at 95 Valley Drive where Edith and Jennie were staying.

Two pieces of information support this move. One clue is from a review of the 1911 census for Valley Drive showing more than half of the approximately sixty-six properties (odd numbers only) were boarding houses, including No. 95. The 1911 census shows fifteen rooms at 95 Valley Drive. The Army probably booked many of these rooms on a long-term basis. It is extremely unlikely in a town filled with recuperating soldiers, Edith and Jennie could have secured such a prime location, near numerous spas, on their own, especially as they moved by early March 1917, a very short period of time (*Great War* 232). With

---

6 "Wednesday Gossip." *Harrogate Herald.* Wednesday, August 8, 1917. page 3.

the military designating Tolkien as the tenant plus the payment of an additional amount, the landlord would have been willing for Edith, and possibly Jennie, to move in. This would have been permissible as long as there was no expense to the public purse.

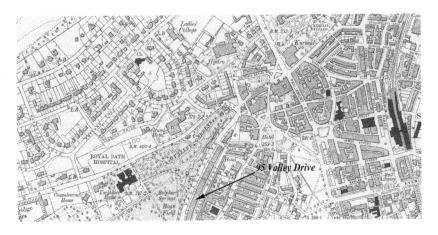

An annotated 1910 OS Map of Harrogate (National Library of Scotland)
showing many spa or bath facilities (SH-K)

Secondly, Christopher Wiseman, the only other surviving member of the TCBS, addressed his letters to Tolkien at the 95 Valley Drive suggesting Tolkien was residing there (*C&G* 1.107). Tolkien had written to G.B. Smith's mother at the beginning of March. This letter was evidently written from Furness Auxiliary Hospital as Mrs. Smith replied to Tolkien on March 6, 1917 at that address (*C&G* 1.106, 107). Tolkien's use of the hospital address in early March would be consistent with his early residence there for the initial evaluation and establishment of the treatment regime proposed above.

The month in Harrogate gave Edith and Ronald more time together. Edith knew "[e]very day in bed means another day in England" and away from the deadly trenches of World War I (*Bio* 95). After one month, the medical board declared Tolkien fit for light duty and gave him a little less than two weeks' leave from April 7 to 18, 1917. Christopher Wiseman was able to stop and see Ronald and Edith Tolkien and Jennie on April 18 (*C&G* 1.107).

Map of part of the East Riding (or administrative district) of
Yorkshire with Tolkien's deployments (SH-K)

Edith and Jennie's ninth, or possibly twelfth, move would have been by May 5,
1917, to 1 Bank Terrace, Hornsea, close to the Hornsea Bridge railway station
(*C&G* 1.107, Mathison 33). They stayed in the seaside town of Hornsea until
June 1, 1917.[7] Edith and Jennie followed Ronald Tolkien, who was posted to
the 3rd (Reserve) Battalion of the Lancashire Fusiliers under the command of
the Humber Garrison on April 19, 1917 (*C&G* 1.107).

Hornsea Musketry Camp was Tolkien's next posting (Mathison 33), but he
was soon at the main camp of the Battalion which was at Thirtle Bridge, near
Withernsea, a seaside town on the Holderness Peninsula in the East Riding of
Yorkshire. It is believed the headquarters of the 3rd (Reserve) Battalion of the
Lancashire Fusiliers was, at this time, at Tunstall Hall, a couple of miles to
the north (Mathison 68, 57; cf. *C&G* 1.107). As a battle-experienced Signals
Officer and a qualified instructor, Tolkien would have been a valuable and

---

7 The residence was owned by the Shepherd family (Mathison 24).

sought-after asset for the training staff at Thirtle Bridge. The letter of April 21, 1917 to the War Office confirming Tolkien had joined the Lancashire Fusiliers, noted Tolkien had been expected for several months (Mathison 57). The delay in his arrival was the result of his continuing convalescence.

The Thirtle Bridge camp housed 1600 men (*C&G* 1.107, Mathison 61). The photograph of Tolkien in his Thirtle Bridge cubicle may have been taken at this time as Tolkien wrote on the back of the photograph: "Self in Hux's and my cubicle, Withernsea [Thirtle Bridge] 1917" (Flowers 135, *TFA* 38). A photograph of Tolkien and Edith has written on the back "Withernsea/July (?) /1917/ taken by L.R. Huxtable" (Flowers 141). L.R. Huxtable should be Leslie Risdon Huxtable, another signaling officer, with whom Tolkien had shared quarters in Cannock Chase and in France (*Great War* 190). At Withernsea/Thirtle Bridge Camp during his free time, Tolkien started compiling his Gnomish or Goldogrin lexicon, *i·Lam na·Ngoldathon*, dated between May and August 1917 (*C&G* 1.108, *Great War* 236).

After being declared fit for service on June 1, 1917, Tolkien was put in charge of an outpost. This was in Roos, as Tolkien wrote: "Roos in Yorkshire (where I was for a brief time in command of an outpost of the Humber Garrison in 1917)" (*Letters* 420). Roos would be a logical place for an outpost as it occupies a strategic rise above the surrounding flat territory almost equal to the level of Waxholme Hill, 2 ½ miles southeast of Thirtle Bridge Camp. Waxholme Hill's mill was used as a watchtower to secure the nearby beach and it was protected by a nearby, prominent roadblock (Flowers 137-8). The Lancashire Fusiliers' headquarters in nearby Tunstall Hall was also situated above the flood plain (Mathison 57, 68). Both Carpenter and Garth agree that after the birth of John Tolkien in November, 1917, Edith, Jennie and John moved "back to Yorkshire [...] at Roos" to be with Ronald, again indicating Roos was a military post (*Bio* 97, *Great War* 242-43).

While Tolkien had happily escaped the slaughter of the trenches in France and Belgium due to his recurrent case of trench fever, his posting to the Humber estuary was not a guarantee of peaceful convalescence in a "rear area" in World War I. The June 1915 Zeppelin attacks on Hull precipitated a reconfiguration of military thinking and positions from a singular focus designed to oppose

1 Bank Terrace, Withernsea
(Photograph courtesy of Michael Flowers, http://eybirdwatching.blogspot.
com/2015/07/tolkiens-hemlock-glade-part-4.html, last viewed on 6/21/2020)

landings by the German army backed up by the Imperial High Seas Fleet. The
new conception established a second concentration on a front line of air defense
against the dreaded night-time bombing runs by Zeppelins.[8] Unfortunately,
the popular imagination, especially for Americans, often limits the British front
line of World War I to the trenches and maybe Gallipolli. In contrast, the reality was the whole coast of England, especially the east coast, was vulnerable.
In response to this new threat, cooperation and coordination were established
among the units of the Army's Humber Garrison, the Royal Flying Corps, and
the Royal Navy warships in the area so that on-shore batteries with searchlights
countered these Zeppelin incursions. The defense was a collective effort depend-
ing on good communications between units and was carried out by using a

---

8   See Hamill-Keays for further detail.

combination of WT (wireless telegraphy), and wired telephony and telegraphy. This communication network carried the latest intelligence on the airships' night-time movements which were tracked overland by their bomb drops and by their engine noise.[9] Cordons of observers, connected by the telephone network, relayed this information to Home Defence Headquarters in London. After the ships lifted off from Germany, they were tracked by Marconi direction finders that picked up their WT exchanges with their bases.

Tolkien wrote he was "in command of an outpost of the Humber Garrison" (*Letters* 340), as opposed to identifying it as an outpost of his Lancaster Fusiliers' Battalion. Tolkien's phrasing here comes from standard military parlance which indicates the outpost was under the direct command of the Headquarters of the Humber Garrison in Hull. The Humber Garrison was the equivalent of a Division in the Order of Battle, being commanded by a Major General (Jones 178). Its units included the Royal Garrison Artillery; East Riding (Fortress) Royal Engineers; other units of the Royal Engineers; a Territorial Force Cyclist Battalion of the East Yorkshire Regiment at Roos; and 3rd (Reserve) Battalions of the East Yorkshire Regiment at Withernsea, of the Leicestershire Regiment at Partington, and of the Lancashire Fusilier Regiment at Thirtle Bridge.[10] 3rd Battalions were always Reserve units, dedicated to training, and they included men, who had returned to England invalided, but capable of being retrained. The 9th Battalion of the Royal Defence Regiment was located at Easington, and Tolkien was later attached to that unit (Mathison 87). The 20th Reserve Brigade, consisting of another four infantry battalions, was positioned around Hornsea.[11]

---

9   An acoustic mirror, a device which could detect the engine noise of an approaching Zeppelin, was in place near Easington where Tolkien was later stationed. It served as an aid for the aiming of searchlights, by tracking the approaches of Zeppelins. They were introduced in mid-1916 probably to provide early detection of *die Höhenkletterer*, Height Climbers, that approached the coast at 20,000 feet where their engine noise could not be heard by the human ear (Robinson 131).

10 3rd (Reserve) Battalion Lancashire Fusiliers. "Army: Regiments and Corps: the British infantry Regiments of 1914-1918: The Line Regiments." The Long, Long Trail, last viewed on 6/23/2020. https://www.longlongtrail.co.uk/army/regiments-and-corps/thebritish-infantry-regiments-of-1914-1918/lancashire-fusiliers/.
     3rd (Reserve) Battalion East Yorkshire Regiment. *Ibid.*

11 20th Reserve Brigade. (consisting of 3 Reserve Battalions of Northumberland Fusiliers and one Reserve Battalion of the Durham Light Infantry). "Army: Regiments and Corps: the British infantry Regiments of 1914-1918: The Line Regiments." The Long, Long Trail, last viewed on 6/23/2020. https://www.longlongtrail.co.uk/army/regiments-and-corps/the-british-infantry-regiments-of-1914-1918/northumberland-fusiliers/. For a complete list see also "British Army First World War reserve brigades." wikipedia.

In addition, other forces were present on the Holderness peninsula and coordinated with the Humber Garrison. The Royal Flying Corps, some months after the first Zeppelin bombing of Hull on June 6, 1915, moved fighter aircraft into Holderness at Beverley and further to the west at Bramham Moor. These aircraft included Flights of the 33 Squadron, which possibly used the emergency landing ground at Owthorne next to Withernsea. The Royal Naval Air Service established a sea-plane base at Hornsea (Jackson 20). There was a substantial military presence in the area.

During World War I, the War Office took over the GPO (General Post Office) telephone and telegraphy network. This would include the post office in Roos. Under the 1915 planned response to German operations, the Signalers of the Royal Engineers Signal Service of the Humber Garrison were to take over the telegraph station in the Post Office in Roos after any Zeppelin attacks as Roos was less than 4 miles from the coast.[12] This was because all "signals" matters, above the battalion level, were the province of the Royal Engineers as the Royal Corps of Signals did not exist before 1920. The military preferred telegraphy to telephony for military messages because a telegraphy message could have multiple addressees encoded in one transmission. Consequently, with telegraphy the Signalers only needed to encipher the message one time.

The Roos Post Office on Roos' main road housed the telegraph station. Hull had a telephone exchange installed in 1907, and the lines had been extended to Roos and other villages in Holderness before the outbreak of the war (*GPO Post Office Guide* 1917 HMSO [His Majesty's Stationery Office]). The telephone line terminated at a switchboard in the Roos Post Office's manual exchange.[13] The Post Office in Roos is clearly marked on the 1910 and 1927 maps as being in the same place, namely the corner of Hodgson Lane and Main Road (sometimes labeled Coltman). That is where it would have been in 1917 when Tolkien was there.

---

12 "Fighting talk: First World War Telecommunications: Home Front." The National Archives Map (Cat ref:MUN 4/5355), last viewed on 6/23/2020. https://www.nationalarchives.gov.uk/first-world-war/telecommunications-in-war/.

13 Communication. "Telephone exchanges: A look inside British manual exchanges." Everyday Life in the early-mid 20th century by people who were there, last viewed on 6/21/2020. https://www.1900s.org.uk/1940s50s-telephone-exchange.htm and Communication: "Wind-up telephones," last viewed on 6/21/2020. https://www.1900s.org.uk/1920s60s-windup-phones.htm#early-exchanges.

1920 Roos Post Office with a man in front of the post office door
and another apartment next door (Courtesy of Willis Ainley, Roos)

Given the military situation in the immediate area of Roos, it would be very
unlikely for a private individual to secure accommodation next to the only
telegraph station for miles around. It logically follows that the War Office
rented the space next to the Post Office for the Royal Engineer military
operators, who were in charge of "signals" and worked around the clock in
shifts decoding telegraph messages and at times using the phone lines. They
would need to stay next to the Post Office. The 1911 census indicates the
residence directly north of the Post Office (and within the same building)
had four rooms occupied by a jobbing gardener. The War Office could have
requisitioned this small space with living quarters upstairs and space for
equipment and records downstairs. Only messages requiring less security
would have used a telephone.[14]

---

14 Mathison is quite doubtful of the 1968 "schoolboy" report that Tolkien was living next to the Post
Office in Roos (48). However, what the young man was likely to have heard was the report of lots of
military personnel coming and going from the residence next to the Post Office, and this is exactly
what the military situation would require.

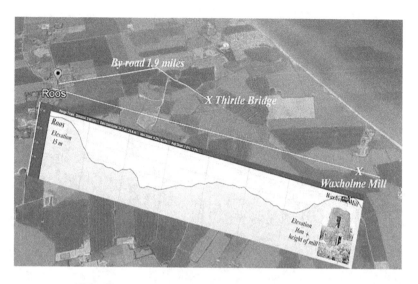

1.5 miles (as the crow flies) from Roos to Head Quarters at Tunstall
Hall at Thirtle Bridge Camp (SH-K)

Previously, Tolkien, carrying out the mission of the 3rd (Reserve) Battalion Lancashire Fusiliers, trained or retrained men to operate a Signals Section in an infantry company with the rehearsals made more realistic by the ongoing threat of German attacks. This would be in line with the battalion's mission to train recruits for the front and to guard against any assault from the sea (*C&G* 1.107). When the Humber Garrison detached Tolkien from his battalion and placed him "in command of an outpost of the Humber Garrison," Tolkien would then have followed a different Operation Order or Standing Orders for the Officer Commanding [OC] from Garrison Headquarters, aimed at addressing his local situation as the Signals Officer in command.

If the house next to the Post Office was "a working communication center," the military would not have their OC [Officer Commanding], Tolkien, live there in close domestic proximity to Other Ranks. This would be contrary to the British military's tradition of substantially better housing for officers and separation of officers from the other ranks. Another local tradition identifies the Rectory as Tolkien's residence (Mathison 47). Tolkien wrote he lived "in a lonely house near Roos" (*Shaping of Middle-earth* 215). The map on page 183

The Rectory at Roos, sitting back from the road at the edge of Roos
(cc by sa/2.0 by Paul Glazzard geography.org.ukp268547)

shows the Rectory standing on its own grounds away from the village, which certainly qualifies the house as "lonely."

In 1911, the Anglican Rector of All Saints church in Roos was Edward Milsom, aged 59 and single. Milsom had studied at and been ordained in Cuddesdon College, Oxford, a college noted for its Anglo-Catholicism with some of its students remaining celibate (Brown and Woodhead 18, *Crockford's Clerical Directory* 1908). However, the February 20, 1914 edition of the *Hull Daily Mail* announced Rev. Milsom's marriage.

Edith's tenth, or possibly thirteenth, move was probably to the Old Rectory after Ronald Tolkien's posting to Roos in June, 1917 (*Bio* 97, *Letters* 420). The Rectory had fourteen rooms, not including ancillary rooms or bathrooms (1911 census). The War Office could have hired rooms and billeted Tolkien there, as one of a series of officers. The report Tolkien was "given quarters" there indicates this likely situation (*C&G* 1.107). An Anglican rectory might have felt particularly "lonely" for a Roman Catholic, like Tolkien, who saw the Church of England as "a pathetic and shadowy medley of half-remembered traditions and mutilated beliefs" (*Bio* 65). The Anglican Milsom may also have found this situation awkward as previously he was likely to dine with and welcome officers and their wives into his congregation.[15]

The position of the Rectory was suitable for the military as the Post Office was 650 yards from the Rectory. As a result of this close proximity, a signaler could bring any urgent or high-security messages quickly to Tolkien. On the other hand, the War Office could have used its powers to install a phone in the Rectory as the introduction of an air raid warning organization needed a great expansion of the telephone network (Jones 174 et seq).

While at the Rectory, Tolkien continued his work on the Gnomish lexicon, and in June or July, he rewrote *Sea Song of an Eldar Day* (*Great War* 236, *C&G* 1.108).[16] Ronald and Edith found time to go for walks in a nearby wood. The wood has been identified in local lore as Dent's Garth, north of the church (*Bio* 97).[17] Also in June 1917, the couple knew Edith was pregnant, filled with new life despite the death and destruction of the war around them. The two homeless orphans would have a family.

---

15 Flowers suggests the Old Rectory, known as the Hall, which burned down on September 8, 1937 may have been the "lonely" house where Tolkien resided in Roos. "Tolkien's Residence in Roos," last viewed on 7/1/2020. http://eybirdwatching.blogspot.com/2020/02/tolkiens-residence-in-roos.html. In a 7/1/2020 personal email from Willis Ainley, a previous editor of the *Roos Roster*, Mr. Ainley reports "George William Wilbraham (1886-1973) was [...] a historian by training and produced quite an extensive [unpublished] history of Roos." In this history, it states: "In 1901 on the retirement of Canon Machell, the Rectory was sold at the request of the new incumbent, Rev. E. Milsom. It was bought by Mr. & Mrs. W. Dickinson (the latter was the daughter of the former rector) and they took up their residence on January 1ˢᵗ 1892 and renamed it 'The Hall'. After the death of Mr. Dickinson, his widow and children went away and the Hall stood empty. During the Great War, it was used as a billet."
While this information establishes that "The Hall" next to Dent's Garth was used to billet troops, a Territorial Force Cyclist Battalion of the East Yorkshire Regiment, as well as other units in the area, were stationed at Roos. Some of their troops could have been billeted at The Hall. Just as an Officer Commanding was unlikely to be residing next to the Post Office due to the separation of officers and other ranks, it is unlikely Tolkien as OC would be billeted at The Hall with a number of enlisted men.
16 Garth presents the fact Tolkien was writing about Ulmo at Roos as evidence that the seaside setting of the Humber Garrison was the basis for this character and Tolkien's interest in him without any other corroborating or supporting evidence (*Great War* 237). In his latest book, *The Worlds of J.R.R. Tolkien*, Garth acknowledges numerous earlier influences. These include Tolkien being impressed by dramatic seascapes as in his drawing, *Cove near The Lizard August 12, 1914* (McIlwaine 172), and *Water, Wind & Sand* in 1915, labeled as an "Illustration of *Sea-Chant of an Eldar Day*," based on his 1912 poem, *The Grimness of the Sea* (McIlwaine 172). *Sea-Chant of an Eldar Day* was the basis for *The Horns of Ulmo*.
17 *The Rooster, The Roos Village Newsletter*, May 2001, No. 75.

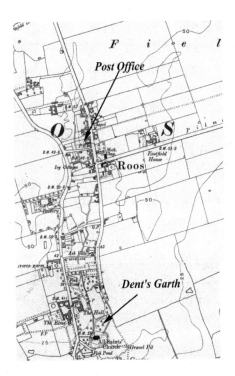

An annotated 6-inch 1908 OS Map of Roos (National Library of Scotland)
showing Dent's Garth in relation to the Post Office and Rectory (SH-K)

A 'dent' is a depression or hollow. The 1908 Ordnance Survey 25- inch map (not shown), identifies Dent's Garth as a dell by marking a surrounding hummock, an indicator of a drop in elevation. Dent's Garth is "a piece of rough ground with a stream running through it."[18] This sunken area would have been similar

18 This book uses the spelling 'Dent's Garth' as that spelling follows the use found in the local *The Rooster, Roos Village Newsletter,* May 2001, No. 75 and the Roos Parish Council archives, dated 1985, mentioning a Mr. Dent and referring to Dent's Garth as "a small plot of enclosed land." Previously, following Garth, the accepted orthography had been 'Dents Garth'. Mr. Garth, in a personal email of 1/14/2020, stated he took that spelling from an Ordnance Survey 1:25,000 map. However, what appears on the Ordnance map as 'Dents Garth' is a lane or a small road. The Ordnance map does not label the "enclosed land" containing the woods and stream of Dent's Garth. This is why the authors inserted a label on the map in this text. Garth apparently misunderstood what 'Dents Garth' identified on the map. To confuse matters further, there is a building in Roos known as 'Dent's Garth' which appears to have been the home of Mr. Dent.

In his email, Mr. Garth added, "In my experience, apostrophes are often included or omitted in place-names unpredictably. For example, places in Tolkien's childhood area near Birmingham appear as both Kings and King's Norton; Kings and King's Heath. What appears in a local newsletter may not be authoritative; on the other hand, what appears on an Ordnance Survey map may not reflect local usage."

to the garden behind Dresden House in Evesham which was likely to recall positive memories for Edith. It also seems like the dell which Hilary recalled as being a special retreat for the Tolkien brothers in Sarehole (H. Tolkien 4, 8). The Sarehole dell may reappear in the dell of the Ent moot (Bunting, "Finding Hilary, Part II" 3), and there is another special dell, a "little sheltered hollow hidden from view" in "Leaf by Niggle" (158). A secluded arena with flowering hemlocks set the stage for Edith's dance which became the germ of the story of Beren and Lúthien in *The Silmarillion*.

The idyll appears to have ended when Tolkien was sent to the Royal Engineers Signal Depot at Dunstable, Bedfordshire for training from approximately July 20 to 25, 1917 (Mathison 37; see C&G 1.108: July 14 to 21).[19] Following Tolkien's course of training at the Depot, he took a signals test and evidently failed (*Bio* 96). If Tolkien had passed, he had the prospect of a likely appointment as a Signals Officer in Yorkshire, a post which would have kept him from the trenches (*Bio* 96). Instead Ronald returned to Thirtle Bridge by July 25 (Mathison 73).

Tolkien's poor test scores in 1917 have not had a good explanation except for an appeal to his possible poor health. The explanation may be in the new demands being placed on the Royal Engineers Signals Depot in 1917.

In 1917, The High Command was demanding greater speed and accuracy in messaging. Robert Graves reports an error in Morse code allegedly sent his unit, the 3rd (Garrison) Battalion Royal Welch Fusiliers, to Cork (Ireland) instead of York (England) (281). Also in 1917, wireless telegraphy (WT) was supplanting the vulnerable telephone and telegraph lines. Continuous Wave (CW) transmission resulted in improved clarity for messages, especially when compared to the transmission by spark-gap radios, i.e. British Field (B.F.) Radio (Hall 290, Leggett 332). Training for officers in managing the new, up-to-date equipment was the function of the Signal Service Depot of the Royal Engineers at Dunstable. The length and the dates of Tolkien's course suggest training on new equipment, like CW radio, or on new encryption systems. At Dunstable,

---

19 The dating hinges on the date of a letter Edith wrote to Ronald at Dunstable dated July 14 (Mathison 72). Tolkien's promotion on 11/24/1917 from 2nd Lieutenant to Lieutenant was backdated to July 1, 1917 (Mathison 108, *Bio* 97). Both of Tolkien's ranks are considered subaltern. The British Army has no rank of 1st Lieutenant.

Tolkien may have been overwhelmed by a manual, similar to the 1918 *Manual of Signalling Procedures*, listing a formidable amount of new technical details and a mass of new procedures which Ronald must memorize. In addition, he may have needed to learn how to handle the new equipment, which had its own separate manual. Mastery of all this material was required within a very short period of time and with rapid execution when Tolkien's health was still not optimal.

Edith and Jennie packed their bags once more for their eleventh, or possibly fourteenth, move, arriving by July 12, 1917 at 76 Queen Street, Withernsea, owned by the Bishop family (Mathison 71-72). Edith's move suggests Tolkien had either received his orders to go to Dunstable for training and/or he had been replaced as Officer Commanding. Sometime in July 1917, the Tolkiens had a picture taken with Ronald looking thin (*TFA* 41).[20]

Edith and Ronald experienced a setback about August 13, 1917, when Ronald was admitted to the Brooklands Officers' Hospital with what was an expectable relapse of trench fever. The *Hull Daily Mail* of August 1, 1917 reported this

76 Queen's Street, Withernsea on left. Courtesy of Michael Flowers,
last viewed on 6/21/2020 (http://eybirdwatching.blogspot.com/2015/07/
tolkiens-hemlock-glade-part-3.html)

20 Dating from display in Staffordshire. See Flowers: "A Weekend in Tolkien's Staffordshire." Birding with Flowers, last viewed on 6/21/2020. http://eybirdwatching.blogspot.com/2016/07/a-weekend-in-tolkiens-staffordshire.html.

new hospital opened on July 24, 1917 and had seventeen beds. Edith wrote a letter to Ronald there dated August 14 (Mathison 72).

Tolkien stayed there until October 16, 1917 when the Humber Garrison Medical Board stated, "He has been in Brooklands Officers' Hospital for past 9 weeks. It is now 3 weeks since his temperature reached normal" (Mathison 21).[21] The doctors assessed him at 30% disabled and sent him to rejoin the 3rd (Reserve) Battalion of Lancashire Fusiliers at Thirtle Bridge.

While Tolkien was in the hospital, Zeppelin L.41 attacked Hull on the night of September 24/25, 1917 with sixteen bombs. Bombs fell less than two miles from Brooklands Hospital.[22] Fort Paull's searchlights illuminated the craft and then a fighter chased it until it was out of range of the lights.[23]

Tolkien had one more stay at Brooklands, returning on July 12, 1918 from Cannock Chase in Staffordshire and staying through September 11, 1918 due to a case of gastritis which caused a 28 lb. weight loss (*C&G* 1.112-13). There is no reason to believe Tolkien's gastritis was a sequel to trench fever, except in the general sense that Tolkien's immune system was probably still not as strong as it was previously. Tolkien's health problems would have been compounded by the poor diet available in 1917/1918 due to the German blockade. The most common cause of gastritis was, and still is, poor food handling. That could easily occur in the Mess or elsewhere. In September 1918, the military transferred Tolkien to Savoy Convalescent Hospital in Blackpool on the west coast of England where he was at the end of the war when the Armistice was signed November 11, 1918 (*C&G* 1.113).

Brooklands Officers' Hospital was a creation of World War I. Before the war, the building housing the Brooklands Officers' Hospital, had been the home of Robert Foster (Mathison 17). During the war, the hospital was run by The East Riding Branch of the Red Cross Society under the command of Mrs.

---

21 "Tolkien's temperature ran high for the first six weeks" (*Great War* 239) is not in agreement with the medical record cited above and is in error. A high fever would have interfered with Tolkien's ability to concentrate and maintain clear thinking while writing. A low temperature would reflect Tolkien's chronic illness and contribute to low energy, but it would not interfere with focusing on writing.
22 Hamill-Keays, 19.
23 "Social history: Hull in the First World War." Paul Gibson's Hull and East Yorkshire History, last viewed on 6/21/2020. https://www.paul-gibson.com/social-history/hull-in-the-first-world-war.php.

A recent photograph of Brooklands Officers' Hospital, now part of Dennison Centre of Hull University. Brooklands on the right and the Cedars on the left were semi-detached buildings. (Google Earth)

Strickland-Constable (1873-1961). Mrs. Strickland-Constable's husband, Lieutenant Colonel Frederick Charles Constable, helped set up one of the Red Cross units in the hospital and held the family estate, Old Hall, in Hornsea.

Mrs. Strickland-Constable was the only child of Rear-Admiral Honorable Thomas Alexander Pakenham and Sophia Frances Pakenham (née Sykes). The Strickland-Constable couple married in 1898 and had three children. Lieutenant Colonel Frederick Charles Constable committed suicide in 1917 at the age of 57 after a "nervous breakdown" in 1916, probably a casualty of what we would now call Post-Traumatic Stress Disorder (PTSD). Mrs. Strickland-Constable would have been a person of interest to Tolkien at Brooklands Hospital as she spoke Swedish, Norwegian, German, French and Danish.[24] She traveled fifteen miles from Hornsea to come to the hospital, though she was not there daily.[25]

---

24 https://www.dailymail.co.uk/news/article-3602387/On-market-fascinating-home-woman-saved-Lord-Rings.html 21 May 2016, last viewed on 6/21/2020. Garth gives her name as "Strickland Constable" instead of the correct hyphenated spelling, Strickland-Constable (*Great War* 239).

25 Margaret Strickland-Constable's diaries reveal she did not visit Brooklands every day. She was nominally in charge, but she seems to have left the day-to-day running of the hospital to her deputy. Flowers assumes this to be a Mrs. B. Hyde. (Personal email Michael Flowers 11/13/19).

Margaret Strickland-Constable

Numerous groups coordinated to operate and maintain military hospitals. These included: the Royal Army Medical Corps, Queen Alexandra's Imperial Military Nursing Service, and voluntary workers from organizations like the Voluntary Aid Detachments, the Red Cross, St. John's Ambulance, and YMCA.[26]

Ronald Tolkien's move to Brooklands Hospital created an unmanageable crisis in the series of temporary housing which Edith had used. With Ronald now in Hull in the hospital and Edith in Withernsea, visits were difficult. Edith would have caught the train to Hull and then would have taken a bus or walked the two miles to Brooklands (Mathison 20). She had entered her last exhausting trimester of pregnancy. Her lodgings in Withernsea were unsatisfactory. There was no piano at the boarding house, and the German blockade limited food (*Bio* 96). This was because in April 1917 mines or submarines destroyed a quarter of all ships leaving English ports, and voluntary rationing began in England in February 1917 (*Great War* 233). Ronald's worry about

---

26 "Hull's WWI Hospitals. Brooklands Officers' Hospital," last viewed on 6/21/2020. Kingston upon Hull War Memorial 1914-1918. https://www.ww1hull.com/hospitals/.

Edith during this time survives in his recalling 1917 as the "starvation year'"
(*Letters* 53). In addition, the Catholic church in Withernsea was a make-shift
affair set up in a cinema.

The rear view of Brooklands Officers' Hospital and the Cheddars with its lovely lawn[27]
(Courtesy of Michael Flowers; http://eybirdwatching.blogspot.com
/2015/07/tolkiens-hemlock-glade-part-4.html, last viewed on 6/23/2020)

To resolve this situation, Edith "decided to go back to Cheltenham." It seems
very unlikely this was because Cheltenham "was the only town she really
liked" (*Bio* 96). Three years of kowtowing to "Uncle" Jessop's tantrums and
being so bored Edith spent time copying music, when she could well afford
to buy printed, does not add up to nostalgia. It is more likely the pregnancy
had aggravated Edith's back problems which had developed when she lived in
Charlton Kings. Edith knew the doctor who had treated her in Cheltenham,

---

27 Flowers proposes Tolkien's two stays at Brooklands with its distinctive lawn became the basis of the
description of the Houses of Healing in Minas Tirith: "about them was a garden and greensward with
trees, the only such place in the City. There dwelt the few women that had been permitted to remain
in Minas Tirith, since they were skilled in healing or in the service of the healers" (*RK* V 7 131-32);
"Then when Merry became weary, they went and sat upon the greensward of the Houses of Healing"
(*RK* V 9 149); and "Faramir and Éowyn walked on the grass and sat under a green tree together"
(*RK* VI 5 239). This would fit well with Hilary Longstreet's contention that Merry represents several
aspects of J.R.R. Tolkien's experience, especially being sick while his comrades continue to risk their
lives in the war. See also Bunting's discussion of how other aspects of Tolkien fit Merry (Finding
Hilary, Part 1, 3). A whiff of the linguistically capable Mrs. Strickland-Constable may be found in the
character, the Master of the Houses of Healing, who was in charge of the women and who could name
herbs in a number of languages. http://eybirdwatching.blogspot.com/2015/07/tolkiens-hemlock-
glade-part-4.html, last viewed on 6/23/20.

and he could probably arrange appropriate care. It would make sense to return to a physician Edith trusted. Edith last wrote to Ronald from Withernsea on August 21, 1917, and she probably stopped in Hull at the hospital to see Ronald on her way south (Mathison 20). By August 24, Edith wrote to Ronald from 37 Montpellier Villas, Cheltenham where she stayed through September 11, 1917 (*C&G* 1.109).

This house was obviously a great change from where Edith had been living in Yorkshire. This villa would have been at least the twelfth, or possibly the fifteenth, residence for Edith since her marriage. Built around 1824-1828, it was three-story with a basement and two (British) first-floor (or second-floor for an American) windows. It is built with stucco over brick, a slate roof, and iron porch railings and window box. The plan is double-depth with entrance and stairwell to the right. The entrance has a 6-fielded-panel door in fluted

37 Montpellier Villas (Google Earth)

jambs. The interior still has two marble fireplaces (on the ground and British first floors) with roundels to corners, paneled shutters, 6-panel doors, and a dogleg staircase with stick balusters.[28]

Edith's next move was to the nursing home at 6 Royal Well Terrace, Cheltenham on September 11, 1917.[29] Malnutrition is a risk factor for both mother and child during pregnancy, and Edith's doctor may have been able to obtain better meals for Edith at the nursing home. Also, one of the most common "treatments" for a difficult pregnancy was bed rest. As the graph at the beginning of Chapter Two (p. 16) indicates, maternal death in childbirth was still high and stayed high until the improvement of prenatal nutrition and the use of antibiotics for infections brought the rates down in the late 1930s and 1940s. Edith and Ronald's son John was born on November 16, 1917 after a difficult birth. Edith's life was seen to be at risk during childbirth (*Bio* 97). Tolkien was not able to obtain leave until about November 22. Ronald's aunt and godmother, May Incledon, who was there, wrote to Ronald to reassure him about the condition of Edith and the baby (Priestman 36).

After leaving the nursing home where she delivered John, Edith moved to 2 Trinity Terrace, Cheltenham (Mathison 108). Since beginning her odyssey in May 1916, this was at least her fourteenth or possibly seventeenth, address. Edith would return to stay at 2 Trinity Terrace by August 10, 1918, after refusing to move north again to Hull when Ronald was again sent to Brooklands Officers' Hospital on July 12, 1918. She was tired of a "miserable wandering homeless sort of life" (*Bio* 98), especially now with a baby to care for and continued problems with pain. Repeatedly picking up eight-month-old John may have been aggravating her back. She stayed at Trinity Terrace until at least November 19, 1918 (*C&G* 1.113). In contrast to her needing to take care of her son, she wrote Ronald, "I should think you ought never to feel tired again [...] for the amount of Bed you have had since you came back from France nearly two years ago is enormous" (*Bio* 98). Writing "I'll never go round with you again" (*Bio* 98), she ended her two and a half years of gypsy life following Ronald from Army camp

---

28   "37, Montpellier Villas" Historic England, last viewed on 6/21/2020. https://historicengland.org.uk/listing/the-list/list-entry/1387358 .

29   6 Royal Well Terrace was a long-established Nursing Home in 1917. A note in the Cheltenham historical society indicates the 6 Royal Well Nursing Home was still operating in 1937. No further information could be found on this facility at this time.

to another military placement for twenty-two moves. The war ended November 11, 1918, and Ronald Tolkien was out of danger from combat.

However, on November 22, 1917, the present for Edith and Ronald was the baptism of their son, John Francis Reuel Tolkien, by Father Francis Morgan, one of his namesakes, who came down from Birmingham (*Bio* 97). Ronald's brother, Hilary, and his cousin, Mary Incledon, were the godparents.[30]

Enduring a vagabond life as a war bride in order to comfort and support Ronald Tolkien, Edith found herself a mother in November 1917. In August through October 1917, Ronald Tolkien had time to write at Brooklands, anticipated

A number '2' marks the house where Edith lived in this building at
Trinity Terrace. (SH-K, Google Earth)

---

30 In December 1917, Tolkien received several letters from Christopher Wiseman. Garth dates their falling out from this time due to disagreements over literary matters. However, Wiseman, whatever his intentions, wrote, "When your kiddie comes to take his place with the rest of us who have spent their lives fighting God's enemies, perhaps he will find I can teach him to use his sword" and then added, "I insist on the appointment of uncle" (qtd. in *Great War* 242). The implication that Tolkien did not do his duty "fighting God's enemies" due to his repeated bouts of ill health presumably rankled Tolkien as he was acutely aware of his friends dying on the front line while he was stuck in bed. Further, Wiseman seems to allege Tolkien may not do his duty to teach his son to fight God's enemies, and Wiseman can do that. Wiseman may have known and/or suspected something about Tolkien's personal reservations about war and the use of force. While Tolkien had been in the trenches, Wiseman, while involved in at least the naval battle of Jutland, may have escaped exposure to the kind of carnage and mayhem which Tolkien survived. At this point, the two men may have had philosophical differences. Be that as it may, this seems to be an inappropriate, if not an impertinent, comment to a first-time father. Tolkien may not have taken these remarks well. Wiseman's needling suggests there are some differences which are more than literary.

being a father, and realized how precious Edith was to him because of her risk from pregnancy. All this together inspired Ronald to create a story to commemorate his "gallant" Edith. But first, he had to find a name.

Edith: Creation, Subcreation, and Tinúviel/Lúthien

Edith departed from Withernsea to go to Cheltenham by August 23, 1917. Ronald Tolkien remained at the congenial, seventeen-bed Brooklands Officers' Hospital which he had entered around August 14. Edith was in the last stage of her first pregnancy and facing her first childbirth, which still held numerous risks for women. Also, both Edith and Ronald must have been aware of the danger of the air raids on eastern England. The Tolkiens would have been relieved Edith was in Cheltenham after bombs fell the night of August 21/22 during one of the six Zeppelin raids on Hull.

Tolkien's comfort with Brooklands may have been partly due to the fact that many of the staff and the Commandant, Mrs. Strickland-Constable, were Roman Catholics (Flowers 139, 125). Sister Mary Michael visited Ronlad Tolkien in Brooklands Hospital from Endsleigh House, which was about three-quarters of a mile away (Mathison 23). Her friendship was important enough to Tolkien that Sister Mary Michael became the godmother of Ronald and Edith's son Michael in 1920. There was a small group of officers as the hospital had only opened in July 1917 (Flowers 139). A friend of Tolkien's from the Lancashire Fusiliers happened to be there (*Bio* 96).

Tolkien began to write; his stories, artwork and poetry now revolved around Edith. He revised two poems of his legendarium (*C&G* 1.109), but he was thinking of Edith. He wrote the six stanza poem, *The Grey Bridge of Tavrobel* dated "Sept or Aug 1917" in Brooklands Hospital (*C&G* 1.109). The four middle stanzas of this poem are available in Garth's *Tolkien and the Great War*, and Garth states the first stanza sets the scene with "two rivers running fleetly," namely the Trent and Sow, and with a reference to the Essex packhorse bridge (*Great War* 207-08).[1] The final stanza laments "lost days of sunlight" (208). This poem is

---

1 This poem was originally published in *Inter-University Magazine*, Oxford, May 1927, page 82 (*Great War* 352). The University Catholic Societies' Federation of Great Britain published the *Inter-University Magazine* (*C&G* 2.47).

Essex packhorse bridge
(Wikipedia Commons: Greg Pearce on 9 April 2007)

patently about Ronald and Edith's reunion in Great Haywood after Tolkien's return from France in November, 1916. Edith has "waited, waited, wearily" and "things go but ill,/And my little garden withers" as Ronald is away and in danger. Ronald Tolkien, on his part, has been, "Dreaming always of the day,/Of my returning hither." Indeed, Tolkien had written, *A Dream of Coming Home*, "a vision of Great Haywood in May" "dedicated to my wife, Bouzincourt, July 4-8, 1916" (*C&G* 1.90). Tolkien would return to the image of *The Grey Bridge of Tavrobel* late in 1917 when he created the heraldry of *The Fair Towns of Holy Tol Eressëa*. Edith and Tolkien are now denizens of Middle-earth.

Tolkien's creation, Middle-earth, was filled with the author's own life. Tolkien confessed, "Edith *Lúthien* [...] was the source of the story that in time became the chief part of the *Silmarillion*. It was conceived in a small woodland glade filled with hemlocks at Roos [...] In those days her hair was raven, her skin clear, her eyes brighter than you have seen them, and she could sing – and dance" (*Letters* 420). After his wife's death, Tolkien wrote, "I met the Lúthien Tinúviel [Edith Tolkien] of my own personal 'romance' with her long dark hair, fair face and starry eyes, and beautiful voice [...] But she has now gone before Beren [i.e. Tolkien]" (*Letters* 417). Tolkien acknowledged his identification with Beren and his wife with Lúthien by having those names carved on their headstone, hers in 1972, and his after his death in 1973.

Tolkien had a name and began writing "The Tale of Tinúviel." "In writing I always begin with a name. Give me a name and I'll produce a story - not the

Tolkien headstone Wolvercote Cemetery
(Wikipedia Commons: 1 June 2013 Twooars)

other way about" (26). In the early version of "The Tale of Tinúviel," Thingol, an elf, (originally called Tinwë Linto or Tinwelint) was Tinúviel/Lúthien's father, and Melian, Tinúviel's mother, (originally called Gwendeling) was "a fay, a daughter of the Gods" (LT2 8). Melian was "a sprite" who had escaped from Lórien's gardens, and nightingales sang about her as she went (LT2 41). Thingol and Melian's daughter's name Tinúviel was glossed as Nightingale (LT2 8). Tinúviel, meaning literally 'daughter of twilight', was a kenning for nightingale so the daughter and mother were both associated with nightingales (Lost Road 440). Tinúviel (later Lúthien) was half-elven from her father and half-fay from her mother. Tinúviel fell in love with Beren, a man, though Beren's human mortality was erased in the original tale and only reintroduced in 1925/1926 (LT2 51). Beren came upon Tinúviel dancing "On a time in June" with "white umbels of hemlocks" (LT2 8-9) in the moonlight, just as

Ronald and Edith Tolkien wandered in June 1917 into Dent's Garth with its hemlocks, and Edith began to dance when the moon was full (*C&G* 1.108).

In visualizing this formative scene in Roos in June 1917, it should be remembered that Edith's education, as a proficient Edwardian young lady, would have included learning to dance: waltz, polka, schottische, and quadrille. A solitary figure waltzing could have been sufficient for the image Ronald cherished. Tolkien's later descriptions and elaborations of Lúthien's dancing in the *Lay of Leithian* echo the popular imagery of the alluring dances created by Loie Fuller (1862-1928), a celebrity pioneer of modern dance (Lewis and Currie, *The Epic Realm of Tolkien* 148-56). But we have no evidence Edith had that kind of training. Edith certainly would have danced with her fiancé, George Field.

Tolkien's writing appears to recreate a scene in Dent's Garth from June, 1917.[2] People dance to music and either Edith was singing or there were possibly

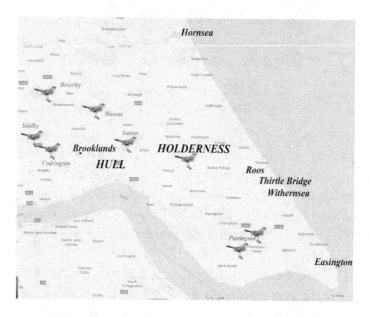

Likely distribution of nightingales in Yorkshire's East Riding
around 1917 (SH-K)

---

2 Consulting the map of Roos in Chapter 9, Dent's Garth is between All Saints Church and "The Hall," which prior to Rev. Milsom's time as rector, had been the Rectory. There were troops staying at The Hall (Ainley from Wilbraham's unpublished "A History of Roos") so it is likely Tolkien was familiar with the area from his duties.

nightingales with their astonishing, melodious songs in the grove. Nightingales were breeding at Brough and Patrington, either side of Hull, in the late 1870s, and these songsters were also reported near Beverley around that time. Sporadic breeding seems to have been occurring in woods and copses throughout East Yorkshire and south Holderness, from the Wolds to the coast (Nelson, Clark, and Boyes). While nightingales are famous for singing on moonlit nights, they begin singing soon after daybreak until about an hour before noon, and then after a silence during the hottest hours, again through the afternoon into the darkness (Aflalo 140). They begin singing in the spring. When Edith and Ronald were in Roos in possibly late May through June, the birds should have been in full song. These birds are generally easy to distinguish from other nocturnal singers including blackbirds, robins and song thrushes.[3] On June 2, 1917, the moon was 90% full; on June 3, 95% full; on June 4, 99% full; on June 5, full; and 99% full on June 6, optimal conditions for nightingales. Ronald Tolkien may have heard nightingales elsewhere when training in the Hull area, and he is likely to have heard them in the woods around Sarehole in his boyhood. These are birds of the countryside. Tolkien would not have heard them in the urban area of Birmingham. The likelihood there were nightingales in the wooded Dent's Garth, a congenial habitat on a moonlit night at the height of song season, strongly suggests a tie between Edith's dance and nightingales.

Edith was fond of birds. By the time the Tolkiens lived in Oxford on Northmoor Road, Edith had an aviary of canaries and budgerigars (*Bio* 118). The birds certainly would have surrounded and followed her as she was the one who fed them. One does not start with an aviary; one starts with owning one bird, so we can assume Edith had had birds for a while before the aviary in the 1920s Oxford. She is not likely to have had a canary or budgerigar at the Faulkners' or even "Uncle" Jessop's. In March 1915, Ronald Tolkien wrote a poem for Edith, *Sparrow-song* ('bilink' from 'blinic' GL 22-23), indicating he associated Edith with singing birds and suggesting Edith might have such a pet. Edith may have heard nightingales at Dresden House in the Evesham area as Hilary Tolkien reports he could hear them on his farm near Evesham

---

3 "Where can I go to hear nightingales singing?" Royal Society for the Protection of Birds, last viewed on 6/23/2020. https://ww2.rspb.org.uk/birds-and-wildlife/bird-and-wildlife-guides/ask-an-expert/previous//nightingalesong.aspx.

Nightingale
(Courtesy of Michael Flowers, http://eybirdwatching.blogspot.com/2015/04/
next-term-11-nightingale.html, last viewed on 9/2020)

until World War II (H. Tolkien 42). Edith would have been likely to have known of many famous musical pieces which imitate birds, like the cuckoo and the nightingale.

So, Edith and Ronald could have enjoyed an evening lit by the full moon in June. The brightness of a full moon would have acted almost like a street lamp to illuminate the country darkness of Roos. The sweetness of this moment with its romantic moonlight, music from Edith's singing or the evening birds, and her "enchanting" dancing (*LT2* 9) stayed with Ronald Tolkien.

> It was a lover and his lass,
> With a hey, and a ho, and a hey nonino,
> That o'er the green cornfield did pass.
> In the spring-time, the only pretty ring-time
> When birds do sing, hey ding a ding, ding.
> Sweet lovers love the spring. (*As You Like It* V.3)

By August 1925, in *The Lay of Leithian*, Tolkien changed the name of Tinúviel, Thingol's daughter, to Lúthien (*The Lays of Beleriand* 154).[4] The original gloss in *The Etymologies* for Lúthien was 'Enchantress', from the root 'LUK-' 'magic, enchantment' (*PE17* 15; *Lost Road* 412). 'Enchantress' fits because when Beren first sees Tinúviel dancing "the enchantment made him faint" (*LT2* 9). Beren then catches "a sparkle afar off" revealing Tinúviel's dancing, and the root 'TIN-', found in Tinúviel, is glossed 'glints' and 'sparkle' (*Lost Road* 440).[5]

Tolkien, the scholar and philologist, probably knew a Hindu legend about a beautiful, young girl, who is faithful and pledged to a man who forgets about her for years, somewhat like the way Tolkien had to "forget" about Edith and focus on his studies for three years from 1910 to 1913. In the story, the girl is eventually happily reunited with the hero. This girl, like Edith, was illegitimate, and her name referred to the fact that after being abandoned by her parents, she was cared for "by birds," recalling Tinúviel whose name means nightingale. The story was in Sanskrit.

Tolkien likely had training in Sanskrit. He obtained a pure alpha on his paper on "Comparative Philology as applied to Greek and Latin, with a special knowledge of Greek philology" (*C&G* 1.44, 1.823). In 1969, Tolkien recalled his grade as alpha+ in "G[reek] Philol[ogy]" (*Letters* 397). However, to apply comparative philology to Greek and Latin means one needs to use the bedrock of nineteenth-century philology, Sanskrit. A mastery of Sanskrit would have strongly contributed to an alpha. Tolkien described himself as "principally a philologist" or a "pure philologist" (*Letters* 247, 264). In his 1968 BBC Interview,

---

4 Beginning in August 1925, Tolkien wrote *The Lay of Leithian* as "Release from Bondage," "but never explained the title" (*B&L* 88). Given the importance of the collapse of Tevildo's/Thû's/Sauron's fortress, the immediate reference for "Release from Bondage" in *Beren and Lúthien* appears to be Lúthien's liberation of Beren from chains and imminent death, healing "his sorrow and the wasting of his imprisonment," following the destruction of the fortress (135). C. Tolkien presents the confused and conflicting relationships among 'Leithian' ('set free' 'release'), 'Leithien' ('England'), 'Lúthien' (referring to both 'England' and at the same time Tinúviel, Thingol's daughter), and 'Leithien', a later spelling of Lúthien, in *The Lays of Beleriand* (154). The 1926 "Sketch of the Mythology" also gives Tinúviel as Beren's name for Lúthien (*B&L* 90).
5 Like Lúthien, first called Tinúviel, the nightingale, Melian, her mother, causes "an enchantment to fall upon" Elwë (Thingol) when he entered the wood of Nan Elmoth alone and "heard the song of nightingales," which followed Melian (*S* 57).
See Hooker's *Tolkienothēca*. and see Appendix Tolkien and Sanskrit for problems with Goering's critique of Hooker.

Tolkien, casually and matter-of-factly, mentions sound differences between Sanskrit and other languages, indicating this knowledge was easily called up and well-known (Lee 138). In 1912 in his first year at Oxford, Tolkien began to have tutorials with Joseph Wright (*Bio* 56) who would have demanded Tolkien master Sanskrit as Wright's textbook expected the student to acquire "elements of the Comparative Grammar of the Sanskrit, Latin, and Germanic languages" (qtd. in *Tolkienothēca* 6). Wright "helped him [Tolkien] develop a firm foundation in the principles of philology" (Grotta-Kurska 38). Wright "imparted to his student [Tolkien] the methods by which a language with consistent roots, sound laws, and inflection [...] developed" (Grotta-Kurska 38). This pattern would almost certainly demonstrate a knowledge of Sanskrit, the bread and butter of comparative philology.[6] Wright did not teach Sanskrit, but he was familiar enough with Sanskrit literature, including the *Mahābhārata*, to quote it spontaneously (Hooker, *Tolkienothēca* 6).

For whatever reason, Tolkien was reticent about his knowledge and use of Sanskrit. In a reply to a letter printed in a January 1938 issue of *The Observer*, Tolkien was forthright about his source for the names of the dwarves and the dragon Smaug in *The Hobbit*, but he did some uncharacteristic waffling about the names 'hobbit' and 'Bilbo Baggins' (*Letters* 30). When asked, Tolkien responded: "I do not remember anything about the name and inception of the hero. I could guess, of course, but the guesses would have no more authority than those of future researchers, and I leave the game to them" (*Letters* 30). Tolkien contradicts this assertion with, among other statements: 'Baggins' was "intended to recall 'bag' and meant to be associated (by hobbits) with Bag End. [...] (It was the local name for my aunt's farm in Worcestershire, which was at the end of a lane leading to it and no further)" (Hammond and Scull, *Reader's Companion* 753). Alternatively, in a 1955 letter to W.H. Auden, Tolkien wrote, "All I can remember [...] is sitting correcting School Certificate papers

---

6 Tolkien owned a collection of standard works on Indo-European languages or 'Indogermanische' as his German references labeled it. German texts were the leading edge of comparative philological studies in Tolkien's day. He owned an annotated edition of *Der Indogermanische Ablaut vornehmlich in seinem Verhältnis zur Betonung* (1900) and seven volumes of *Indogermanische Grammatik*, published 1927 through 1934, demonstrating Tolkien's continued interest and expertise in this area (Cilli 122-23). The translated titles are *The Indo-European* (literally: *Indo-Germanic*) *Vowel Change Especially in its Relationship to Accent* (1900) and *Indo-Germanic Grammar*. Tolkien bought a copy of *Chamber's Etymological Dictionary* in 1903, and it defines words in terms of their Sanskrit origins (Hooker, *Tolkienothēca*; *T&S* 1).

[...] On a blank leaf I scrawled: 'In a hole in the ground there lived a hobbit'" (*Letters* 215; see also Lee 142). When *The Hobbit* was published in 1937, one of Tolkien's colleagues at Leeds University, G.H. Cowling, wanted Tolkien to "speak learnedly of hobbits, and say whether they derived their name from 'hobs' or 'rabbits'" (Anderson 18-19). But Tolkien did not give a philological reply until the publication of the appendices in *The Return of the King* where he created a post-facto etymology to explain the name 'hobbit', out of a concocted derivation from 'holbytla' or 'hole-builder' (Appendix F 408).[7] The name 'Bilbo' can be derived from Sanskrit meaning 'Hole-Dweller' (*T&S* 119, 120).

Omitting his Sanskrit source could serve several purposes for Tolkien. First, he was modest, and he would never have thought to broadcast or proclaim his knowledge of Sanskrit, an unstated requirement for serious philology at the time. Also, Tolkien was "not inclined to admit to the influence on him of any other writers at all," i.e. he did not want to reveal his sources (Anonymous, "Dialogue" 21; see Long; Hooker, *Tolkienothēca* vi-vii). Tolkien valued the appearance of originality. Further, he was a private person, and the use of a Sanskrit legend would almost guarantee no one would recognize the source or the implications of the names and the story. With a Sanskrit tale, Tolkien could tell the intimate story of himself and Edith in a disguise which would safeguard their history. The story also gave Ronald an after-the-fact justification for his headstrong and impassioned behavior of 1909/10. As Carpenter, who had unlimited access to all of Tolkien's papers, diaries, and letters, wrote at the end of *J.R.R. Tolkien. A Biography*, "Tolkien's real biography is *The Hobbit*, *The Lord of the Rings*, and *The Silmarillion*; for the truth about him lies within their pages" (*Bio* 260) as has been shown in recent studies.[8]

Tolkien may have been familiar with the widely popular adaptations of this story (*Tolkienothēca* 94) about the beautiful, young, faithful and illegitimate girl, Sakuntalā, or have learned about it from his studies. Tolkien would not have thought about its applicability to himself until after his wedding in March 1916 when he learned Edith was illegitimate. At the very least, Tolkien prob-

---

7 John Rateliff does not assuage or resolve this question with his comment: "'Bilbo' is both a short, simple made-up name appropriate for the hero of a children's book [...] Bilbo is almost certainly Tolkien's own coinage" (47-48). See Seth "Tudor, Elizabethan and Jacobean Connections" for a catalog of Tolkien's evasions and inconsistencies with the names, 'Bilbo' and 'hobbit'.
8 See Bunting and Hamill-Keays' "Edith Mary, the Other Suffield Aunt, Parts I-IV."

ably knew this Sanskrit story from his Middle English studies of Chaucer. In Tolkien's lecture, "The Pardoner's Tale: The Story and its Form," Tolkien referred students to *Originals and Analogues of Some of Chaucer's Canterbury Tales* (Furnivall, Brock, and Clouston).[9] Furnivall et al.'s discussion of Chaucer's "The Patient Griselda" (i.e. "The Clerk's Tale") states:

> And in the tale of Dushmanta and Sakuntala, [...] (another episode in the *Mahábhárata*), we are told that 'she is a true wife whose heart is devoted to her lord'. The wife is man's half. The wife is the first of friends. They that have wives have the means of being cheerful. They that have wives can achieve good fortune. Sweet-speeched wives are as friends on occasions of joy. They are as mothers in hours of sickness and woe. (540)

In Sanskrit, the story of the illegitimate enchantress is known as *Sakuntalā*, after the name of the heroine, an "honest country girl full of the dignity of moral greatness" (Chintaman 108).[10] Sakuntalā was an illegitimate child whose parents did not want her. The mother of Shakuntalā, Menaka, was an *apsara*. In Hindu mythology, the *apsara* are the nymphs of Swerga, the celestial Court of Indra, celestial dancers, celebrated for their beauty. Apsara are sometimes described as celestial nymphs because of their many associations with water and the lotus, a flower which is a Hindu symbol of beauty. The father of Sakuntalā was a mortal man, Vishvamitra, a revered sage of ancient India. The god Indra sent the apsara Menaka from heaven to earth to seduce Vishvamitra and divert his concentration from his meditations as Vishvamitra was becoming too powerful by means of his austerities. Menaka was successful in her task, as her heavenly beauty overwhelmed the pious Vishvamitra. The result was the birth of Sakuntalā. Sakuntalā was, thus, half-celestial nymph and half-human. She was given the name 'Sakuntalā' because after her mother Menaka abandoned her on the mountainside, Sakuntalā was cared for by birds [Sanskrit: Sakunta (birds)] until found by the sage Kanva, who brought her up in his hermitage as his daughter (see Hooker, *Tolkienothēca* 94-96 for more detail).

---

9 Bowers 258, note 103. Tolkien referred to the Mahābhārata in class (Benedikz, 12). See Appendix Tolkien and Sanskrit for more.

10 English versions call the tale of Sakuntalā "The Fatal Ring" or "The Lost Ring." A version of the tale of Sakuntalā appears in the *Mahābhārata* (8th or 9th century B.C.), which Tolkien had probably read as a student of Sanskrit. This story does not appear under the name of "The Lost Ring" or "The Fatal Ring" in any of the Andrew Lang Fairy books with which Tolkien was familiar as seen in his research for "On Fairy-stories."

Neither Vishvamitra nor Alfred Warrillow could withstand Menaka/
Fannie Bratt's celestial *apsara* beauty and charms.
(Wikimedia Commons. Dancing Apsara. Photo by Ms. Sarah Welch.)

Like Menaka, the mother of Sakuntalā, Edith's mother, Fannie Bratt, seems
to be imagined to be so beautiful her charms seduced the responsible, hard-
working, Victorian Alfred Warrillow.[11] Like Sakuntalā, half-celestial nymph
and half-human, Tinúviel/Edith is the daughter of Maia and an elf. Like her
mother, Menaka, Sakuntalā and Tinúviel/Edith are divine dancers.

In the story, the valiant Raja Dushyanta was hunting in the forest. When
he saw the beautiful Sakuntalā, he persuaded her to become his wife by a
Gandharva marriage. A "Gandharva marriage" means a marriage based on
a simple declaration of mutual acceptance "as a marriage proceeding entirely
from love or the mutual inclination of a youth and maiden without ceremonies
and without consulting relatives" (Monier-Williams 282). This declaration of

---

11 There are no published pictures of Fannie Bratt.

mutual acceptance recalls the "declarations and promises" made by Ronald Tolkien to Edith Bratt when they lived at the Faulkners' in 1909/1910 (*Bio* 61). The Raja Dushyanta then gave Sakuntalā his ring with his royal seal as a pledge and returned to his city, leaving Sakuntalā behind. Sakuntalā was then placed under a curse: that she should be forgotten by the man she loved, but the curse should be removed as soon as her beloved Dushyanta saw his ring.[12] Indeed, when Dushyanta saw the ring again, he remembered the beautiful Sakuntalā, whom he had married. The Raja then went into the jungle and was reunited with his wife and child.[13]

Tolkien can be seen to weave a network of images using the Hindu myth and the fairy-tale aspects of Middle-earth. Edith and Tinúviel are both associated with birds. Tinúviel's name means nightingale, the birds which are associated with her mother, Melian. Edith was fond of birds and there probably were nightingales at Dent's Garth in Roos in 1917. Sakuntalā is also associated with birds because her name is based on the Sanskrit word for bird. Like Sakuntalā, the illegitimate daughter of a celestial dancer, the illegitimate Edith dances in the clearing in Roos. Like Dushyanta hunting in the forest, Beren [Ronald Tolkien] looks "down into the little [woodland] glade where [Tinúviel/Edith] was dancing" (*Letters* 420, *LT2* 9). This melding of scraps of ancient sources and fairy tales is the result of Tolkien's ambitious goal of making his Secondary World's invented legends the origin and explanation of myths and tales in the actual Primary World (Hiley 851, 852). Analogously, to be consistent with its "concomitant" world and mythology ("Secret Vice" 207), Tolkien's "private" language, Elvish, would be the progenitor of Indo-European (Menn 143; Hooker, *Tolkienothēca* viii).

Tolkien will elaborate this story of Edith/Tinúviel, who is resourceful, fearless, and "gallant," as Tolkien himself called her (*Letters* 404). Lúthien repeatedly rescues Beren from various dangers. Entering the world of fantasy, which aspires

---

12 Sakuntalā, realizing she is pregnant, journeys to her husband's palace, but on her way she bathes in a sacred pool. The ring with the royal seal slips from her finger. When Sakuntalā reaches the palace of the Raja, Dushyanta does not remember her. Sakuntalā then returns to the jungle, where she gives birth to a son, Bhárata, the namesake of the *Mahābhārata*. Dushyanta's ring is found in the belly of the fish. When Dushyanta sees the royal ring, he remembers the beautiful Sakuntalā, his wife. Needless to say, a ring found in a fish has similarities to Tolkien's story of Déagol and Sméagol and the Ring.

13 See Hooker's *Tolkienothēca* for a more detailed presentation and analysis of this story (94-96).

to the enchantment of Faërie (OFS 122, 143), Tolkien becomes a subcreator apparently recreating his own story in a time and a place of wonder. Lúthien's liberation of Beren may parallel Edith's ability to comfort and reassure Ronald Tolkien who had wrestled with bouts of depression since his mother's death (*Bio* 31), the "chaos" from his "youth and early manhood" (McIlwaine 170). Edith/Lúthien was Ronald's anchor and lodestar, or North star, keeping Ronald on course in his Oxford studies after two years of dithering. This image of the guiding star reoccurs with Arwen, the Evening Star, another Tinúviel. Arwen inspires Aragorn to persist through his trials, just as Edith was Tolkien's reason to endure and succeed.

Creation

Tolkien was not only writing about Edith; he may have also enshrined her as a central, but hidden, element in his drawing, *The Fair Towns of Holy Tol Eressëa*. Given some of the imagery in this drawing, Tolkien can only have created this drawing after his visit to Cheltenham for his new son's baptism in late November 1917.[14] This drawing is comprised of three sections, or panels, recalling the well-known triptych pattern of Christian religious art which began in the Middle Ages.

The central panel of the triptych represents Warwick or Kortirion. Warwick's emblems, probably holding a special meaning for Edith and Ronald, are displayed. These include the peacock and topiary trees recalling the Warwick Castle Peacock garden which probably held fond memories for Ronald and Edith from their time there in 1913-1916. On either side of the peacock, there are two six-pointed stars with a dot in the middle. These are not the seven-pointed stars known as Faery Stars which became popular in the 1980s. Rather these are most likely the Hindu symbol called 'Shatkona'. The Shatkona is the union of an upward and downward triangle with a dot ('bindu' in Sanskrit) in the center. The Shatkona represents the union of both

---

14 The *Chronology*'s statement, "It is perhaps during the time of convalescence at Great Haywood [December 1916 to February 1917] that Tolkien draws heraldic devices for three places in England" (*C&G* 1.105) is not accurate. These dates are too early as the drawing has imagery from the Cheltenham visit of November 1917 as discussed below.

the male and female form.[15] Bindu can represent the union of sperm and ova, and it is considered the point at which creation begins and may become unity (Ranganathananda 21). It is described as "the sacred symbol of the cosmos in its unmanifested state," a symbol of cosmic mysteries and creative powers (Ranganathananda 21).

It is hard to imagine Tolkien would have had familiarity with this symbolism and its meaning except through his Sanskrit studies (Hooker, *Tolkienothēca* vi-vii; *T&S* "Addendum").

In contrast to the Hindu acceptance and celebration of sexual creation, the Judeo-Christian religious tradition has a paucity of literature acclaiming the interpenetration of spiritual and physical creation. In the Old Testament, "The Song of Songs" or "The Song of Solomon" is unique for rejoicing in sexual love: offering the voices of two lovers, who praise each other and yearn for each other, proffer invitations to enjoy, each desiring the other and rejoicing in sexual intimacy. Christianity, minimizing and obscuring the book's honoring of sexuality, has traditionally read this book as an allegory of Christ and "his bride," the Church. Even though marriage became a sacrament, the early Church fathers took a rather dim view of marriage, much less sexual pleasure, siding with St. Paul's reluctant acquiescence: "It is better to marry than to burn" (1 Corinthians 7:9).[16]

What the two dotted stars suggest is Tolkien's discreet tribute to the pleasure of full physical consummation now blessed by the Catholic Church in his marriage on March 22, 1916 in Warwick. For him, the waiting may have become "intolerable" for more than one reason (*Letters* 53). When Tolkien wrote of the wedding of Aragorn and Arwen, "together they went up into the High City, and all the stars flowered in the sky," these could be Shatkona stars (*RK* VI 5 251).

---

15 In Hinduism, the Shatkona traditionally represents the union of Shiva (male) and Shakti (female), Brahman (male) and Maya (female), Purusha (male) and Prakriti (female), etc. ("Six Pointed Star," last viewed on 6/29/20. https://www.sivasakti.com/tantra/introduction-to-yantra/).
The Shatkona has the same form as the Hebrew Star of David, except the Hebrew symbol does not have a central dot and is often blue as opposed to the red used for Shatkona.
16 St. Augustine (AD 354-430) authored the dogma of original sin based on sexual desire. St. Augustine's conflicted and ambivalent feelings about this subject are shown in his revealing and famously prayed, "Lord, make me chaste, but not yet."

Tolkien seems to not only celebrate his union with Edith, but also elevate her as Erinti or Lotisse, the Vali of love, beauty, and music, which are all characteristics of Edith, and also the Vali of purity (QL 36). This indicates Edith had decided that whatever their previous physical relationship in 1909 she would not repeat her mother's life.[17] Ronald was free to marry Edith, and she had an engagement ring and a Catholic betrothal. Edith had been a student of the Bible at Dresden House as noted in Chapter Three, and when faced with the catastrophe of her separation from Ronald in 1910, she went to the cathedral to pray (*Bio* 43). The Vali of purity became 'Akairis', the 'bride' (QL 36). The designation of purity may also indicate that not only has Edith, in her role as the Vali of purity, kept herself from sin, but she is without sin, i.e. immaculate, just as the Virgin Mary's conception by her parents was kept immaculate.[18]

Reading closely the context and meaning of the central Warwick panel of *The Fair Towns of Holy Tol Eressëa* shows how Tolkien's artwork, stories, and invented languages are all of one piece. Examining any one aspect creates a new appreciation of the nuances and implications for other parts. Garth argues that Tolkien's invented languages reflect his preoccupations: Qenya words for 'saint', 'monastery', 'crucifixion', 'nun', 'gospel', 'Christian missionary' for his religious focus (*Great War* 112), and words for trench warfare including: 'boom, bang', 'invalid', 'choking smoke, fog', 'device, machine, engine', 'gas-bag, balloon', 'noise of drums (or guns)', and 'Germans' (*Great War* 128).[19]

Using Garth's reasoning, Tolkien's Elvish vocabulary should reflect the themes of sacred physical and spiritual creation found in *The Fair Towns of Holy Tol Eressëa*. Tolkien's vocabulary in sexual matters is fairly complete, if discreet: '*cunnus*', '*coitus*', '*membrum virile*' in Latin, or '*teors*' in Old

---

17 Edith's epithets include 'Erinti'/'Little One' and 'Lotisse' (QL 36). The last is from Quenya 'lóte' 'large single flower' + '-isse' > '-esse' (abstract noun suffix) (*Lost Road* 412, 421); see Hooker, *Tolkienothéca* for 'Lotesse' (217).

18 The reader should not confuse the Catholic doctrine of the Immaculate Conception of Mary with the Catholic views on the Virgin Birth or the conception of Jesus. Non-Catholics often fail to distinguish the two doctrines. The Immaculate Conception of Mary is a special case in doctrine, making her free from original sin. Standard Catholic teaching saw illegitimacy as a civil concept, not a theological or moral one. Tolkien would not have suggested his wife was born without Original Sin in the theological sense, but her mythical avatar might have this distinction.

19 Garth skips some other words which seem likely to have been a function of Tolkien's war time experiences including: 'drunken' 'balfaug' (Gnomish/Noldorin) (*PE*13 138); 'vomit': 'to vomit' 'hich-' (G = Gnomish) (*PE*13 163), 'qama-' (Q = Qenya) (QL 76); 'feces' 'muk' (Q) (QL 63), 'gorn' (G) (GL 41), 'urine' 'mis' (Q) (QL 62), 'piglin' (G) (GL 64); and of course 'louse' 'gwef' (G) (GL 45).

English. One commentator notes, "all of the 'personal' words can be found in *PE*13."[20]

Tolkien's invented language reflects an acceptance and comfort with sexuality as an integral part of life in Middle-earth. In the undated "Laws and Customs of the Eldar," Tolkien expressed his views on the sexual relations among the Eldar or Elves. The statements in "Laws and Customs" are very likely to reflect Tolkien's own views on sex, as one would hardly expect a Victorian and very discreet Tolkien to be comparing experiences with others. First, Elves enjoy sex: "The union of love is indeed to them great delight and joy, and the 'days of [begetting] children' [...] remain in their memory as the most merry in life" (*Peoples* 213). Attractiveness is addressed in: "All the Eldar had beautiful hair (and were especially attracted by hair of exceptional loveliness)" (*War of the Ring* 340). Edith/Lúthien embodied this attribute because she had "long dark hair, fair face and starry eyes, and beautiful voice" (*Letters* 417) and "her hair was raven, her skin clear, her eyes brighter than you have seen them, and she could sing – and dance" (*Letters* 420). During the years 1909-1910 when Ronald and Edith's romance began, Edith had long hair (*TFA* 28, McIlwaine 147). She continued to wear it long as seen in the photograph of her with the Jessops (1910-1913) (*TFA* 29). It is not until the photograph of February 1916 that we can see Edith is now wearing a fashionable "bob" (*Bio*, Priestman 28). Lúthien, in some ways, embodies the Edith of their courtship, as opposed to the Edith of 1917.

Tolkien wrote, "Marriage is chiefly of the body, for it is achieved by bodily union, and its first operation is the begetting of the bodies of children, even though it endures beyond this and has other operations" (*Peoples* 212). The Shatkona symbol in the central Warwick panel in Tolkien's *The Fair Towns of Holy Tol Eressëa* represents the union of both the male and female form combined in the act of sacred sex. The Shatkona symbol functions as a celebration of a sacred physical merger. Further, among the Elves, "It was the act of bodily

---

20 Tolkien's vocabulary extends to semen, baby, marry, breast, to give suck, naked, buttocks, bed-mate, and sexual desires. See "What Tolkien Officially Said About Elf Sex." Ansereg, last viewed on 7/1/2020. http://ansereg.com/what_tolkien_officially_said_abo.htm . Also, "Linguistic Foolery: Twenty-Two Words You Never Thought Tolkien Would Provide." The Silmarillion Writers' Guild, last viewed on 7/1/12020. http://www.silmarillionwritersguild.org/reference/linguistic_foolery/22_words.php.

union that achieved marriage [and] [...] it was at all times lawful for any of the Eldar, both being unwed, to marry thus of free consent one to the other without ceremony or witness (save blessings exchanged and the naming of the Name) and the union so joined was indissolvable [...] in flight and exile and wandering, such marriages were often made" (*Peoples* 212). Tolkien specifically added, "Thus Beren and Tinúviel could lawfully have wedded, but for Beren's oath to Thingol" (*Peoples* 228). Ronald's "declarations and promises" to Edith, with Ronald [Beren] being prevented from marrying Edith [Tinúviel] in 1910 by Father Francis Morgan [Thingol], were like the verbal "Gandharva marriage" of Sakuntalā and Dushyanta (*Bio* 61). Elves "are seldom swayed by the desires of the body only, but are by nature continent and steadfast" (*Peoples* 211). This commitment seems true for Beren and Lúthien and, having kept their 1909/1910 commitment through unanticipated trials and delays and the doubts of guardians and family, for Ronald and Edith Tolkien. Edith was Ronald Tolkien's first – and only – love (Grotta-Kurska 23), and as C.S. Lewis noted with disapproval, Tolkien was "the most married man he knew" (Sayer 14).

Instead of potentially celebrating their date of birth, Elves celebrate the day their parents conceived them which, for Elves, is approximately one year earlier (*Peoples* 212). As a Roman Catholic, Tolkien would have routinely celebrated the Holy Days of Obligation for the conception of Christ on Lady Day (March 25) and the Immaculate Conception of Mary (December 8), though both of these feasts use the human nine-month gestation period.[21] This focus on conception would fit with Tolkien celebrating his son's conception in Tavrobel or Great Haywood in the top panel of *The Fair Towns of Holy Tol Eressëa* triptych.

The upper panel of the triptych could show Tavrobel or Great Haywood with the packhorse bridge, *The Grey Bridge of Tavrobel* of Tolkien's poem of September, 1917 (seen in the photograph above on page 196), with its grey stone hidden under a white blanket of snow and labeled in Elvish 'Tram Nybol' or 'Snowy Bridge' (*PE*13 94).[22] The weather report for December 1916 shows

---

21 More than twenty years later, Tolkien will carefully place the defeat of Sauron on March 25, Lady Day, a day marking the beginning of new hope.

22 The editors of *PE*13 seem puzzled at the use of 'snowy', but that is because they are making a purely linguistic analysis without reference to the real-world context Tolkien uses in this drawing (*PE*13 94).

no snow in the Cannock Chase/Great Hayward area. The February report finds the snow staying on the ground for six to twelve days due to earlier snow in late January with 8-10 cm (almost 4 inches) of snow.[23] Consequently, this panel appears to be commemorating the sexual conception of John, who was born on November 22, 1917. Assuming a normal gestational period of forty weeks, his conception would have been during this time in February, dated by the emblem of the snow-covered bridge (*Bio* 95). The Catholic Tolkien, like the Elves, might celebrate conception. The three trees above the bridge could highlight the spiritual aspect of this sacred physical moment. The motif of three trees, where Tolkien presents himself and Edith as two trees around the central tree/cross of Christ, is found in the 1914 paintings, *Beyond*, *Here*, and *The Land of Pohja*.

The lower panel of the triptych represents Cheltenham or 'Celbaros'. Ronald Tolkien arrived in the town of Cheltenham around November 22, 1917 to see Edith and their new son and to attend the baptism, which signaled his son's acceptance into the Catholic Church (*C&G* 1.110). The baptism would have been at the very beautiful St. Gregory's Church. Tolkien continues his pattern of using local landmarks to commemorate each of the three places in his triptych and to evoke meaningful memories linked to each location. The Celbaros ensemble of spire, fountain, and willow tree are iconic for Tolkien's Cheltenham. The Celbaros panel of *The Fair Towns of Holy Tol Eressëa* triptych suggests that during their stay together in Cheltenham, Ronald and Edith Tolkien visited the town's well-known Neptune fountain when the moon was full or near full. The weather for the month was generally dry with above-average temperatures.[24] By the Neptune fountain was a historic willow tree, and Edith and Ronald could observe the moon over the spire of St. Gregory.

The tall, pointed tower on the left side of Tolkien's drawing for Cheltenham/Celbaros appears to represent St. Gregory's spire. The 208 foot west tower

---

23 "Monthly Weather Report 1916." Met Office Digital Library and Archive, last viewed on 6/29/2020. https://digital.nmla.metoffice.gov.uk/SO_7498a04d-6a40-4207-a27f-772663ffd2fc/.

24 "Monthly Weather Report 1917." Met Office Digital Library and Archive, last viewed on 6/29/2020. https://digital.nmla.metoffice.gov.uk/SO_7498a04d-6a40-4207-a27f-772663ffd2fc/.

with spire, finished in 1876, provides a prominent local landmark rising 41 feet above the church.[25]

St. Gregory Roman Catholic Church
(Andrew Kerr, Wikipedia Commons)

Written on the left of Tolkien's drawing is 'Ranon'. This might be parsed as 'rána' ('moon') + '-on' (adjectival suffix in Gnomish) meaning here 'of the moon', as in 'fountain of the moon' or perhaps poetically 'moon-lit' in this

---

25 The Anglican church, St. Mary's, is also in the general area and has a very similar spire which is not quite as tall as St. Gregory's. Tolkien possibly took St. Mary's as his model, but he is more likely to have used the spire of the Roman Catholic St. Gregory, where his son was just baptized.

context.[26] When Tolkien arrived in Cheltenham by November 22, 1917, the moon was in its first quarter. November 27 and 28, 1917 featured a full moon and on November 26, it was 96% full.[27] In the 1915 watercolor, *The Shores of Faery*, the moon appears on the left with its rays forming the same corona or starburst pattern as it does in Tolkien's 1917 drawing of the moon over Celbaros (McIlwaine 202).[28]

On the other side of the drawing is a willow tree. It seems to be a reference to the well-known willow which grew next to the Neptune fountain on the Cheltenham promenade. Local lore rumored that the willow, planted around 1860, had grown from a cutting of the famous weeping willow by Napoleon's tomb on St. Helena (Burrow 23, 32). The tree died in the mid-1930s (Elder).

Tolkien associated willows with the beautiful and enchanting Land of Willows in "The Fall of Gondolin" which he had recently written (*LT2* 155-56). Whatever associations willows might have with the menacing Old Man Willow and the Withywindle's valley twenty-five years later in *The Lord of the Rings*, only happy memories and enjoyment of beauty seem to have marked this willow.

---

26 Alternatively, this word could be parsed as 'rána' (moon) + -on (agent suffix in Gnomish). Literally, 'the wanderer'; as the root ran- means 'wander, stray', as well as 'the Moon'. But the context suggests the other gloss (*S* 455).

27 The editors of *Parma Eldalamberon* posit a "vague phonological resemblance" between 'Ranon' and 'Ecthelin' and the names 'Ronald' and 'Edith', respectively. The identification of such an equivalence obviates a translation from Elvish (*PE*13 96). This assertion of this equivalence seems weak and is inconsistent with Tolkien's usual approach to creating a language. Carpenter states Tolkien's work in language was "painstaking" due to a "concern for accuracy" based on the "scrupulous standards of comparative philology" he was taught (*Bio* 135). Some authors used their initials in their work, e.g. Charles Dickens in *David Copperfield*, but I do not know of any documented examples in Tolkien. Each of the three panels is labeled in Elvish. It is not clear why the third should be an exception. Without knowledge of the historical context of the full moon and Tolkien's repeated use of local landmarks as emblems of the heraldry of each town in his drawing, *The Fair Towns of Holy Tol Eressëa*, the editors of *Parma Eldalamberon* state the object on the left is a mountain surmounted by the sun (*PE*13 96). Tolkien does have towers, e.g. Kôr in the May 1915 watercolor, *The Shores of Faery* (McIlwaine 203) and in the 1916 *Tanaqui* (McIlwaine 206) drawn in this manner, but not mountains. Further, there are no mountains near Cheltenham. There is Cleeve Hill or Cleeve Cloud at 1,082 feet a few miles away with a view of the Cotswolds. There is no documentation Tolkien went to Cleeve Hill or was interested in it. Tolkien came to Cheltenham for the occasion of his son's baptism at St. Gregory, whose spike-like spire is a good match for the object in Tolkien's drawing. St. Gregory was a place of personal importance in Tolkien's life. The presence of an aureole is not conclusive evidence the orb in this drawing is the sun because Tolkien previously used a similar aureole in the 1915 *The Shores of Faery* around his moon (McIlwaine 202).

28 Tolkien reused, reworked and recycled images and stories. He has the moon appear on the left in the 1915 watercolor, *The Shores of Faery*, and the moon appears on the left in this drawing. The tower image here recalls Tolkien's statement about Ingil's Tirin: the tower was so high "the moon climbed far or ever he thrust his face above it" (*LT2* 4).

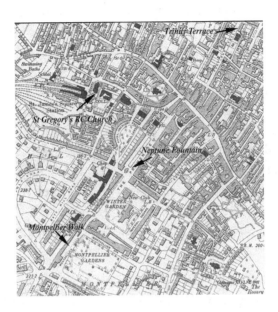

Annotated 1908 OS Cheltenham map (National Library of Scotland)
showing Neptune Fountain site on Montpellier Walk with St. Gregory's
Roman Catholic Church (SH-K)

In the center of the Cheltenham/Celbaros panel is a stylized, simple fountain. On the right side toward the top, the word 'Ecthelin' or 'fountain' appears. Given the symbolism of St. Gregory's spire, the fountain could be a baptismal font full of the "waters of life".[29] Within Tolkien's legendarium, the fountain recalls "a little running water" in the garden of Meril-i-Turinqi, "the Lady of the Isle" whose house was at the foot of the great tower of Kortirion (*LT1* 101-02). Meril-i-Turinqi replaced Erinti, an avatar of Edith Tolkien, the Vali of love, music, beauty, and purity (QL 36). Meril-i-Turinqi means "Queen of Flowers" recalling the meaning of Lúthien as "Daughter of Flowers" (GL 46).

---

29 Although the Tolkiens could have been at the 1893 Neptune Fountain on the Promenade next to the historic willow tree, the fountain in the drawing does not have any obvious resemblance to the Neptune Fountain or any other of the then existing fountains in Cheltenham, a spa town, known for its waters. This includes: the 1914 King Edward VII Fountain (Drew Fountain) on the Montpellier Walk and the Napoleon or Imperial Fountain, displayed from 1902 until 1926 in the Town Hall after being repaired. Another well-known fountain in Cheltenham, the Unwin Fountain in Sanford Park was not erected until 1927. Tolkien's drawing does not resemble the ornately carved stone panels on marble stands of St. Gregory's font.

Echoes of Meril-i-Turinqi, "the Lady of the Isle," reoccur with the Lady of the Galadrim, Galadriel, who also lives in a city of trees, is wise in ancient lore, and is the source of the almost Eucharistic lembas, recalling Meril's 'limpe' (*Great War* 228). Assuming Meril-i-Turinqi is a foremother of Galadriel, then the drawing's fountain is the "fountain shimmering" in "a wide lawn" whose waters "fell into a basin of silver, from which a white stream spilled," like Meril-i-Turinqi's "little running water" (*FR* II 7 369). The "white stream," now called a "silver stream," is by "a basin of silver, wide and shallow," the Mirror of Galadriel (*FR* II 7 376). Silver is the color of the moon and moon-light as is indicated by 'Ranon' at the top of the panel. At the bottom, the name 'Celbaros' could be read as 'Stream Town' from 'cel' ('stream, flow') + 'baros' ('hamlet') a good fit for the meaning of the name 'Cheltenham' as Cheltenham was a place of streams.[30]

The caption, 'bod'ominthadriel,' means 'coming together again, reunion' (*PE*13 96). The caption surrounds what are almost certainly two wedding rings, each with a central bindu dot. This design cannot be a memento of the engagement in 1913 as that was in Charlton Kings, which was separate from Cheltenham at the time. Further, there are two rings featured here, not one engagement ring. Instead, the coming together might be the spiritual and physical union in marriage on March 22, 1916, indicated by the bindu dots. This union is consummated in a new life which has been consecrated in the Church. With Edith, Ronald Tolkien could become not just a subcreator of story, but of life. The Catholic Church today uses the image of interlocked rings with a cross replacing the bindu dots, as an icon for weddings, the reading of the banns, and the "Marriage Encounter" program. This imagery of reunion recalls Tolkien's 1916 poem, written in France, *A Dream of Coming Home*, longing for the reunion with Edith and "Dreaming always of the day,/Of my returning hither" in the poem of August 1917, *The Grey Bridge of Tavrobel* (*C&G* 1.90).

The Fair Towns of Holy Tol Eressëa appears to commemorate this couple's triumph of creating a life both for themselves and their son: their seizing a

---

30 Alternatively, 'Celbaros' might also come from 'celeb' for 'silver' and 'ros' for 'rain' and refer to the silver rain of spray falling down from the upward jet of the fountain in the drawing (QL 96). However, if one glosses this word as 'Celeb' 'silver', which could go to 'Celb', the form 'celba' is genitive, which should make it a second, not a first element in a compound. If one used 'Celb', the second element would have to be 'aros', which does exist as Dorathrian in the sense of a red river, but that does not fit here.

slice of happiness and lusty pleasure in the shadow of World War I's misery, uncertainty, terror, and death.

Carpenter's faltering at Roos

Carpenter did not have Tolkien's military records when he wrote the biography. He mainly depended on letters, especially Edith's, to track the vagaries of Tolkien's military deployments. This method appears to be the basis of Carpenter's mistaken report Tolkien was "posted temporarily to Yorkshire," with Edith and Jennie moving to Hornsea, but then being sent to the Harrogate (*Bio* 95, *C&G* 1.835).

However, Carpenter has a strange, egregious error after the birth of John, when Edith, Jennie, and John move "back to Yorkshire [...] at Roos" to be with Ronald: namely the dating of Edith's dance in Roos' wooded Dent's Garth after November 1917 (97). Garth agrees the family moved back to Yorkshire at Roos, but then moved to Easington (*Great War* 242-43). This move is probably clear from Christopher Wiseman's letters of December 1917 which were available to both Carpenter and Garth (*C&G* 1.112). The lack of "surviving letters" between Ronald and Edith from November 1917 to July 1918 suggests strongly they were living together (Mathison 91, compare *C&G* 1.837 that shows no letters until May). Instead of the correct early June date for Edith's dance, Carpenter places the seminal scene sometime after November 1917. As Scull and Hammond remark, "One may question, however, if Edith would have danced on the windy coast of England in the middle of winter 1917/1918, while still recovering from a difficult birth" (*C&G* 1.836). Carpenter also pushed back the writing of "The Tale of Tinúviel" to 1918 after the writing of "The Tale of Turambar."

Carpenter had to include the dance in Roos because of its critical place in the legendarium. By placing the pivotal moment in Ronald and Edith's romance after John's birth, Carpenter obscured the celebration of the creation of life which Edith's conception may have represented to Ronald Tolkien as seen in *The Fair Towns of Holy Tol Eressëa*. Tolkien's further honoring of Edith's spiritual and physical vitality in "The Tale of Tinúviel" based on Edith's dance in Dent's Garth, in her creation of a family, and in her steadfast support of Ronald

Tolkien, loses its meaning by being stripped of its proper context. In keeping with Carpenter's task as required by Christopher Tolkien ("Learning" 270, Unwin 249), this alteration of chronology functions to mask the importance of the passion between Ronald and Edith. This change, consciously or unconsciously, operates to erase as far as possible this couple's physical dynamics. Carpenter's date for Tolkien's writing of "The Tale of Tinúviel" deletes the meaningful frame of reference and the important connections of this tale to Ronald's anxiously awaiting the birth of their first child and fearing for Edith's well-being while he was at Brooklands Officers' Hospital. The compelling subtext of Edith and Ronald Tolkien's loving relationship disappears.

Conclusion

Uncovering the life of Edith Bratt Tolkien exposes new aspects and meanings in Ronald Tolkien's life and writings. The official biography and those writers who follow its presentation have minimized, discounted, and effaced Edith's role and person. Seeking to protect Edith's reputation, threatened by the revelation of her illegitimacy throughout her life, Ronald Tolkien and his heirs sought not only to shield her but also to bury Ronald Tolkien's rash, and at the time, scandalous passion for Edith (*Letters* 420). Consequently, the reader is given only a "biographical legend," a distorted image of Tolkien's biography, controlled by his literary executor and used as the basis of literary criticism (Fimi 7). This redacted "biographical legend" allows only passing glimpses of Edith and only in relation to the famous author of the 1960s, J.R.R. Tolkien. The official biography's expunging of the importance of Edith in Ronald's life leads to gaps in our understanding of his writing and to a tendency to misread other texts due to our incomplete knowledge of Ronald Tolkien's context.[31]

By examining more of Edith's life, the reader can come to understand the many facets which led Tolkien to call her "gallant" (*Letters* 404). The *OED* derives 'gallant' from Old French 'galer' 'to make merry, make a show' and explains that "the early senses of the adjective in French are: 'dashing, spirited, bold' (obsolete in French, but the source of the prevailing sense in modern English); 'gay in appearance, handsome, gaily attired'; and 'fitted for the pleasures of society, attractive in manners, courteous, polished'." Meaning A1a is "gorgeous or showy in appearance, finely-dressed, smart (archaic)," and the girl who won prizes for her sowing at Dresden House as a teenager was always seen smartly and tastefully attired. B1b is "*Of a woman*: A fashionably attired beauty (obsolete)." Meaning A2 is "*Of women*: Fine-looking, handsome (obsolete)" (emphasis added in the previous two sentences). These definitions certainly could reflect Tolkien's attitude toward Edith. Meaning A3, "Suited to fashionable society; indulging in social gaiety or display; attractive in manners, polished, courtier-like (obsolete)," recalls Edith's "starry eyes, and beautiful voice" (*Letters* 404), her impeccable manners from being raised by a governess, and her enjoyment of gay music (*TFA* 30). Meaning A4 is "a general epithet of admiration or praise: 'Excellent', 'splendid', 'fine', 'grand'." This description could express Tolkien's

---

31 Holly Ordway is critical of Humphrey Carpenter, blaming him for shortcomings in the biography and letters (e.g. 14, 262). She notes he was "not carefully chosen and qualified researcher that might reasonably be expected by his readers" (276). However, her view ignores Rayner Unwin, Tolkien's publisher's testimony that Tolkien's and his publishers' first priority was control of the biography (17). It can be argued that opposed to Carpenter somehow imposing himself on the Tolkien family, they got exactly what they wanted: a bright "young man in a hurry," who was so pleased at his good fortune to be working on a Tolkien biography that the neophyte did not read the contract properly, leaving them in control of the biographical material. Not realizing he did not have control over the final result led to Carpenter's "castrat[ing] the book, cut[ting] out everything which was likely to be contentious. [So that] I've therefore always been displeased with it ever since" ("Learning About Ourselves" 270). We can infer that it is not Carpenter who made the final decision on what went into the biography. Nor is it believable that his employer, Christopher Tolkien, who "assisted" with the selection of letters, did not make the final editorial decisions with the employee, Carpenter, agreeing "on the final procedure" (*Letters* 3).

Another plausible example of exclusion from the official biography is the omission of the Incledon family. Tolkien's visit to Torquay in 1902 was very likely to have been with the Incledons (Bunting and Hamill-Keays, "The Other Suffield Aunt, Part IV"). The Inclendons were likely to have included Ronald Tolkien in their family summer art tours in 1910 and 1912 (Chapter 5), and Aunt May Inclendon was likely to have subsidized Tolkien's lavish lifestyle and dinners in 1913 and 1914 (Chapter 6). Tolkien's 1914 visit to Cromer was likely to have been to meet with the Incledons (Chapter 8). The Incledon family were likely to have repeatedly provided unacknowledged important relationships and experiences which affected and influenced Tolkien's life and writing.

estimate and view of Edith. Meaning A5a, "Chivalrously brave, full of noble daring," describes Edith's plighting her troth on Ronald's return in 1913 when he made good on his "promises and declarations" of 1909/1910, her throwing over the respectable George Field in 1913 to embrace the adventure and promise of life with Ronald Tolkien, and then when faced with the unknown challenges of war, committing to following Ronald wherever he was sent. Meaning A7, "(Usually gállant.) Of or pertaining to (sexual) love, amorous, amatory. Now somewhat rare," summons up the clandestine relationship of 1909/1910, their times of pleasure perhaps exemplified in Edith's spontaneous dance in the woods of Roos in 1917, and their strong physical relationship lasting certainly until the late 1920s if Tolkien's comments in "Laws and Customs of the Eldar" derive from his own experience. Ronald Tolkien would also have known the name 'Bratt' comes from the Danish meaning 'brave, valiant, courageous' (William 78).

Humphrey Carpenter was known for "revealing" biographies (Unwin 250). In compliance with the mandate to "cut out everything which was likely to be contentious," however, he deleted or minimized unwanted facts ("Learning" 270). The purged material included "the things that records do not record: the dreadful sufferings of our childhoods" (*Letters* 421) which brought Edith and Ronald together. As a result, the specifics are missing for what caused Tolkien to suffer "a terrible chaos which darkened my youth and early manhood" (McIlwaine 170, see Bunting, "Spiders, Parts I and II") or periods of depression (*Bio* 31). For Edith, Carpenter wrote the misleading statement that "Edith's childhood had been moderately happy" (*Bio* 39). This statement is true only when compared to the likely hunger, neglect, and ostracism she had suffered as a child at the Cliffords.

In addition, Carpenter cut and/or downplayed important financial information about both Edith and Ronald Tolkien. Edith's wealth is dismissed with his remarks that she "had inherited a small amount of land [...] and this produced just enough income to keep her" (*Bio* 39). In contrast, Edith was "the lost heiress" of Tolkien's December 1912 play, *The Bloodhound, the Chef, and the Suffragette* (*Bio* 59). The recognition of Edith's financial security and independence, which Carpenter tried to withhold, completely changes the dynamic between this couple. The reality is Edith provided the home and stability which, after "something of a wanderer's life" (qtd. in *Great War* 130), meant so much to Ronald Tolkien. Tolkien wrote on January 6, 1914, he and Edith were "two homeless children and had found one another after long waiting" (McIlwaine 148). To cover Edith's affluent financial status, Carpenter made repeated statements about Edith's plans for an unneeded music career. Further, without the context of Edith's vulnerability as a potential target of unscrupulous opportunists, the meaning of Gateley's protectiveness toward Edith in 1909/1910 becomes unclear. Carpenter also minimized the extent of Tolkien's extravagant living during Oxford with its expensive dinner parties and probably the fees for King Edward's Horse which almost certainly some unnamed benefactor, other than Father Francis Morgan, was paying.

By obscuring the physical and socially unacceptable level of Edith and Ronald's teenage intimacy in 1909/1910, "a Gandharva marriage," based on Ronald's declaration of acceptance and commitment (*Bio* 61) between the "lovers" (*Letters* 53), the essential impact of the loss of contact with Edith on Ronald's life and writing from 1910 to 1913 evaporates. Instead, to justify Ronald Tolkien's defiance and dishonesty with Father Francis Morgan in 1909/1910, Carpenter resorted to making the kind Father Francis Morgan, who wanted Ronald's long term welfare and happiness within the reality of the constraints and the expectations of Edwardian society, into a petty tyrant who was only focused on Ronald's future academic success (*Bio* 43). Carpenter elides the fact it was Edith who was the spur to Ronald Tolkien's immersing himself in his own world of escape through fantasy. In this legendary and poetic space, Tolkien could have total control over his "private lang," and its "concomitant" mythological world. Carpenter then suppressed any reference to Tolkien's legendarium before 1914. There is no acknowledgment of the polished manuscript Tolkien submitted to his publisher, "The Fall of the Númenóreans and the Change of the World," which may have grown from an earlier mythology.

Carpenter then continued to minimize the centrality and importance of Edith and Ronald's relationship. Carpenter repeatedly depreciates the level of Edith's education and how little of Ronald's "bookish" interests she was able to share and nurture (*Bio* 67). Carpenter conceals Ronald and Edith's pivotal, passionate relationship by moving the crucial dance in Dent's Garth to after the birth of their son John in November 1917 and by placing the writing of "The

Tale of Tinúviel " in 1918 instead of during the August to October 1917 stay at Brooklands Officers' Hospital. The intentional shrinking of Edith's significance may also include not publishing poetry like *The Lonely Harebell*, written at points of separation between the couple, and whose imagery of the solitary flower which grows by graves and calls the fairies, matches Edith's vulnerability when World War I threatened her future and all her years of waiting.

What Carpenter's bloodless recitation leaches out of the official narrative is Tolkien's deep and constant love as a teenage schoolboy, as an Oxford undergraduate, and as an officer in the Great War for his Lúthien Tinúviel. Who would have guessed at the drama of the slightly built, impecunious Ronald Tolkien, with a great sense of humor and a big imagination, subject to nightmares and a chaos of dark thoughts and emotions, full of dreams of going to Oxford, who found someone, a beautiful independently wealthy someone, his "lover," who accepted him and believed in him and his seemingly extravagant promises of true love and commitment? As their letters show, Edith's education and difficult childhood led to their being able to share openly their emotional lives which had been burdened by suffering. Like the *Kalevala*'s Maid of the North, the beautiful and well-to-do Edith ditched her more conventionally promising suitor when Ronald hastened to be a Ring-bearer. Somewhat to Ronald's amazement, Edith chose the Oxford student, with seemingly so little to offer. Edith was faithful and stood by him: reciprocating Ronald's passion after their enforced three-year separation and bravely facing the roulette risks of the War. She followed Ronald's military peregrinations as an officer invalided home from the Front and was his comfort and hope for stability and a new life. Knowing Edith was there for him allowed Tolkien to produce artwork, languages, poetry, and stories, when the TCBS no longer existed. The famous episode in the small woodland of Roos in the spring of 1917 and their creation of a family may have validated for Ronald and Edith their faith in each other and God.

Only a ghost of the "gallant" Edith is left in the official Tolkien biography. Tolkien's readers are consequently left with an impoverished understanding of the man and his works based on "biographical legend." Edith Bratt triumphed over her background, snatched love and happiness from the iron jaws of rigid class consciousness and social strictures in a life with Ronald Tolkien, and created the security and stability which Ronald Tolkien needed to write: a very Victorian story of "luck and pluck." Her vitality and her co-creation with Ronald Tolkien has been kept so secret that her reputed transformation into the brave and gay Lúthien seems baseless and puzzling. Edith was the spark which ignited Ronald's passion as seen in *The Fair Towns of Holy Tol Eressëa* triptych and Tolkien's Elvish vocabulary. Without the proper historical context and background, that compelling context sinks into shadow. When "the Bodleian [...] open[s] its Tolkien coffers fully," to disclose Carpenter's promised "magnificent new biography" (Carpenter "Review"), the muse, anchor, wife, and keeper of Ronald's heart will step forward and will take her central place: Edith Bratt.

Epilogue

H ugh Brogan, an early and a long-time Tolkien reader, fan and critic, wrote,

> Justifiably to discuss Tolkien's works in terms of their biographical purport, the critic must be able to show that some larger meaning, or pattern, may be discovered thereby. The works, not the author, must seem to be more truly known and understood by the demonstration. (354-55)

This was a response to Tolkien's repeated staunch rejection throughout the 1950s and 1960s of the importance of biography in appreciating his writings. For example in 1957, Tolkien wrote, "I doubt its relevance to criticism. Certainly in any form less than a complete biography, interior and exterior, which I alone could write, and which I do not intend to write" (*Letters* 257). Further,

> I do not like giving 'facts' about myself other than 'dry' ones (which anyway are quite as relevant to my books as any other more juicy details). Not simply for personal reasons; but also because I object to the contemporary trend in criticism, with it excessive interest in the details of the lives of authors and artists. They only distract attention from an author's works (if the works are in fact worthy of attention), and end, as one now often sees, in becoming the main interest. But only one's Guardian Angel, or indeed God Himself, could unravel the real relationship between personal facts and an author's works. Not the author himself (though he knows more than any investigator), and certainly not so-called 'psychologists'.

> But, of course, there is a scale of significance in 'facts' of this sort. There are insignificant facts (those particularly dear to analysts and writers about writers): such as drunkenness, wife-beating, and suchlike disorders. I do not happen to be guilty of these particular sins. But if I were, I should not suppose that artistic work proceeded from the weaknesses that produced them, but from other and still uncorrupted regions of my being [...] Then there are more significant facts, which have some relation to an author's works; though knowledge of them does not really explain the works, even if examined at length. (*Letters* 288)

Tolkien discouraged W.H. Auden in 1966 from writing a biography (*Letters* 367), but allowed William Ready, the former Director of Libraries at Marquette

University, to which Tolkien had sold some of his papers in 1968, to publish some biographical remarks. Tolkien then disparaged Ready's book publicly (*C&G* 1.757). Tolkien's publishers engaged Daniel Grotta-Kurska, a journalist, to write a biography in 1966, but this attempt appears to have been abruptly scuttled. Grotta-Kurska published *J.R.R. Tolkien. Architect of Middle-earth*, derived from his notes and newspaper articles, after Tolkien's death.

Tolkien's prestige as the Oxford professor, holding first the Rawlinson and Bosworth chair of Anglo-Saxon and then the Merton Professorship of English Literature, intimidated many and kept them from questioning his stance. The fact writers typically draw on their own experiences and relationships is widely documented, as in Amos' *The Originals. Who's Really Who in Fiction*, and would seem to contradict Tolkien's absolute assertion. The Tolkien fans, who anointed Tolkien a "Great Author," would not question the genius' dictum.

Because of Tolkien's claim that his personal life was irrelevant to his works, a very tight focus on Tolkien's academic involvement in philology and literature, mainly medieval, has formed the foundation of acceptable sources for Tolkien scholarship.[1] This separation between Tolkien's private life and his works appears to have been a guideline for Humphrey Carpenter's selection, under the supervision of Christopher Tolkien, of Tolkien's letters for publication. Of the thousands of letters Tolkien wrote, one volume of letters was published, as opposed to three volumes for C.S. Lewis and seven for Winston Churchill.

Tolkien's carefully and artfully argued conceit about biography having no significance in the understanding of his oeuvre collapsed, however, when he had the names Lúthien and Beren from his legendarium carved on his and his wife's headstone. Humphrey Carpenter was then allowed to reveal: "The personal element is far more revealing" and drew a parallel between Belladonna Took and Tolkien's mother, Mabel Tolkien (*Bio* 175). Carpenter could also disclose Tolkien's "real biography" was found in *The Hobbit*, *The Lord of the Rings*, and *The Silmarillion*, "for the truth about him lies within their pages" (*Bio* 260, see also *Peoples* x).

---

1 See Holly Ordway's *Tolkien's Modern Reading* (2021) for a welcome addition to the canon of studies investigating Tolkien's involvement in literature.

The more we know about Ronald Tolkien and the more closely we examine his writings, invented languages, artwork, and life, the more intimately they seem intertwined. The truth about the relationship between Tolkien's personal life and his creative works appears to be much more closely connected, possibly even the opposite, of what he strenuously averred.

This should not be surprising as *The Silmarillion*, with its numerous revisions and reformulations, along with the invented languages which were its foundation, was seemingly a private hobby, rarely shared with others.[2] *The Hobbit* also was not originally written with publication in mind, rather his children were the intended audience. Even *The Lord of the Rings* was written "as a personal satisfaction [...] I was not thinking much of the profit or delight of others" (*Letters* 211; see also 412).

Rateliff notes, "the totality of [Tolkien's] work has a unity unusual in any author. His mythology filled his mind to the extent that it is no surprise to find him borrowing names, ideas, and themes from it in a new work" (16). This continuity of the mythology appears to be a function of Tolkien's own history in "mythical and legendary dress" (*Letters* 211). Tolkien wrote, "[my nature] expresses itself about things deepest felt in tales and myths" (*Letters* 420-21). It seems "Legend and History have met and fused" in the transformation of Tolkien's own history in the legends of Middle-earth (OFS 156). Tolkien said "I hold the key" to any research which might be done on his books (Resnick 38). Tolkien's statement applies not only to his beloved invented languages (Fimi 7). We cannot fully assess the complexity of Tolkien's secondary reality if we do not know the primary reality on which it was based because "fantasy is made out of the Primary World" (OFS 147).

This study of Edith Bratt demonstrates the importance and usefulness of a long overdue examination of Tolkien's non-academic biography for a full appreciation

---

2 Tolkien's wife, Edith, copied out *The Cottage of Lost Play* in 1917 (*Bio* 95). On November 27, 1914, Tolkien read the poem, *Voyage of Earendel*, at the Oxford University's Essay Club (*C&G* 1.64). He did a reading of *The Fall of Gondolin*, one of the main stories in *The Silmarillion*, in March 10, 1920 for the Exeter Club (*C&G* 1.10). In 1926, Tolkien shared the unfinished *Lay of Leithian* and part of *The Children of Hurin* from the stories of *The Silmarillion* along with a *Sketch of the Mythology*, with his former teacher, R. W. Reynolds of King Edward's School (*C&G* 1.144.). Tolkien had previously shared some earlier poems in 1915/16 with this former teacher (*C&G* 2.1091). Tolkien shared *The Gest of Beren and Lúthien* with C.S. Lewis near the end of 1929 (*Bio* 145, *C&G* 1.161).

of his works, just in the way Brogan espoused and Fimi advocated. Understanding Tolkien's legendarium requires a thorough and complete knowledge of all of Tolkien's history and context, not just his academic interests and accomplishments. The reevaluation of Edith Bratt presented here draws on Carpenter's "official" biography which has been supplemented with a widely divergent array of materials, ranging from newspaper reports and legal documents, to the early lexicons, to Tolkien's probable views on sexuality found in "Laws and Customs of the Eldar," to an annotation on the back of a drawing from *Artist and Illustrator*. The relationship between Edith and Ronald illuminates his poetry and painting as reflected in Tolkien's development of the imagery of the *"Two Fair Trees,"* the elaboration of the story of Lúthien and Beren from a probable Sanskrit source, the reconstructed substance of the unpublished poems, *Sparrow-song* and *The Lonely Harebell/The Elf Alone* based on context, and the likely personal story telling function of *The Fair Towns of Holy Tol Eressëa*. Edith and Ronald's separation in 1910 appears to have set the stage for Tolkien's pattern of developing a private language, with a "concomitant" mythology, perhaps including the unpublished "The Fall of the Númenóreans and the Change of the World," (McIlwaine 218) and visual imagery, as reported by himself and others, and in the official biography.

Michael White, in his independent biography of Tolkien, *The Life and Work of J.R.R. Tolkien*, for the Critical Lives series, called himself a "long-standing fan" of Tolkien. He was "dismayed by the overprotective stance of 'official' or 'authorized' material about Professor Tolkien" (xvii). White notes how the

> published letters relate almost nothing of his [Tolkien's] private life. Veils of mystery are spread over anything personal, such as his true relationship with his wife, Edith, [...] No authorized description ever questions Tolkien's inner drives [...] Worse still, the accepted wisdom concerning Tolkien's emotions, his motivations, and his opinions are rarely investigated. (xvii)

The generally understood reason for the exclusion of Tolkien's private life and emotions, as reported by White, has been that these topics are irrelevant to the study of Tolkien, the writer and artist. White states he has dealt with the result of this kind of omission and "deifying" before when writing his biographies of Isaac Newton and Stephen Hawking. "In both cases, a search beneath the surface revealed for me a world of color and vitality" (xvii).

What White notices is how the access to the archives and the *a priori* restricted mind-set of researchers has continued to confirm and maintain the limited view of Tolkien's life available in the official biography, the "biographical legend." The results of this investigation of Edith Bratt show this is not an acceptable approach if, as the present study indicates, Tolkien's life and invented languages, writings and artworks are intimately connected. The present, apparently narrow use of primary sources in the Tolkien archives has not given the reader the richer understanding of Tolkien's works and imaginative creativity which a knowledge of the author's life and context makes possible as demonstrated in this life of Edith Bratt.

Concerning Tolkien and Sanskrit

The following is an addendum to the argument presented on pages 201-206 about Tolkien's knowledge of Sanskrit and its literature, and takes up some issues raised by Goering's review "*Tolkien and Sanskrit* (2016) by Mark T. Hooker," published in *Journal of Tolkien Research* 3 (2016), Article 6. It is useful to read Goering's text with a critical eye.

Goering dismisses as 'misremembered' an accepted source (Benedikz, *C&G* 2.965), documenting that a student recalled Tolkien's telling the class to compare the topic being discussed with the *Mahābhārata* (9). Goering's assumption and consequent denial of Benedikz's disconfirming evidence is untenable given that Tolkien's familiarity with the *Mahābhārata* is corroborated in John Bowers' *Tolkien's Lost Chaucer* (258).

Goering concedes that Tolkien was familiar with Sanskrit, if only from "the philological scholarship and popular imagination of Tolkien's day" (9). He adds, "There is probably a good case to be made that Tolkien's creative mind did draw on Sanskrit, both for philological facts of a fairly general sort, and for inspiration from the romanticized image of Sanskrit in the European imagination around the turn of the previous century" (9-10). Goering agrees with Scull and Hammond's statement that there is no evidence "Tolkien was an expert in Sanskrit" (9). This seems to be equivalent to Goering's statement that there is "no evidence Tolkien engaged with the Pāli original in any deep way" (9) and there is no evidence Tolkien "read stretches of the Ṛgveda or the *Mahābhārata*" (9) (cited in summary *C&G* 2.625). That would have been the job of Oxford University's Boden Professor of Sanskrit. However, Tolkien, like any competent professor, would not be recommending the *Mahābhārata* to his students if he had not read it, either in the original or in translation.

Consequently, this level of proof of expertise demanded by Goering appears to be a straw man and beside the point. It does not seem credible that Tolkien, who described himself as "principally a philologist" or a "*pure* philologist" (*Letters* 247, 264, italics in original), an Oxford University professor in the 1920s and 1930s when philology still had a strong presence at the university level, who would have been the authority for philology in his department, could be incompetent in Sanskrit, the foundation of philology. Tolkien's edition of *Der Indogermanische Ablaut vornehmlich in seinem Verhältnis zur Betonung* (1900) ('Indogermanisch' was the German term for Indo-European) with his annotations and seven volumes of *Indogermanische Grammatik*, published 1927 through 1934, also testify to his competence, if perhaps not to the lofty level of "expertise" in Sanskrit that Goering seems to demand which would be suitable for a different Oxford chair (Cilli 122-123).

Goering chides Hooker's methodology, like the use of *théos/deus* cognates, previously employed as a standard example of Grimm's Law, instead of a view of philology that has been updated in the twenty-first century which now rejects these previously accepted cognates (6-7). However, Hooker, who is presenting Tolkien's viewpoint, is correctly working with the philology available to Tolkien at the turn of the twentieth century when standard texts like Chambers accepted these words as cognates. Goering's criticism here turns on an anachronistic view of Tolkien/Hooker's exposition of Tolkien and consequently cannot be valid. It is Goering's methodology that is awry.

Goering criticizes Hooker's explication of maps and asserts his view that "The geographical correspondence is, at first glance, not very precise" (3), but later states the modeling of the Seven Rivers of Ossiriand on "Vedic [or perhaps rather Indian] geography" is "potentially plausible, though hardly proven" (6). Goering's position assumes that Tolkien would have intended a close correspondence between the Silmarillion map and the map of India.

This assumption does not fit with what we know about Tolkien's evolving use of maps. Tolkien repeatedly stated the importance of maps as the basis of *The Lord of the Rings* (e.g. *Letters* 168, 177), and he labeled the earliest map of Buckland, which has a striking and close resemblance to the 1905 OS (Ordnance Survey) map of Breconshire Buckland (Wales) in its shape, scale and distances around the river along with other riverside landmarks (Hamill-Keays and Bunting). This was a change from his earlier maps in *The Hobbit* and *The Silmarillion* which do not function at that level of precision and are much more conceptual. This lack of precision was part of the reason a new narrative for *The Hobbit* could not be smoothly worked into the geography of the now published *The Lord of the Rings*.

Goering states that *Gelion* meaning 'runner, running water', as Hooker claims, is not a strong link to identifying it with the river Indus because "Indus is a proper noun and 'running water' is not a generic word for 'river' being applied as a proper name" (4). Any reader of *The Hobbit* knows Tolkien commonly used generics as names for rivers, e.g. The Water in Hobbiton and a river called Running by the Lonely Mountain, and Shippey (*Road* 96, 101) finds no problems with this convention. Why Goering sees a name like 'running water' as unacceptable to Tolkien is unclear. Perhaps this practice is acceptable within the limits of the prescriptive linguistics which Goering may advocate, though he does not present his position or unpack his assumptions in a way that enables the reader to evaluate Goering's argument. In the field of toponymy (the study of place names), an area of Tolkien's expertise, the evolution of common names to particular names is frequent. The name 'Sindhu' in Sanskrit, or 'Indus' in English, is actually the common noun 'river' in Sanskrit, not a proper noun. This kind of evolution is also true for the River Avon.

Goering further argues that Hooker's use of a lenition of word-initial *k* to *g* is not standard in Welsh (4). By only considering a prescriptive view of language, whose assumptions he does not present, and creating an artificially narrow definition of lenition, Goering renders Hooker's view incorrect. This is a classic debating move. As a result, Goering ignores real life counter examples of common Welsh place names, i.e. a descriptive linguistic view of Welsh, as presented by Hooker (*Tolkienothēca* xxxviii-ix), just as he ignored the disconfirming evidence of Benedikz which has been corroborated by Bowers. Tolkien did not hold a favorable view of the dictates of rule-bound, 'correct' usage form in prescriptive linguistics (*Letters* 183, 300).

In defense of his assertion that Tolkien "does not play linguistic games that Hooker attributes to him," Goering cites Tolkien's irritation with an inquiry about the relation of an Elvish word, 'Sauron' with a Greek root which founders on the then unknown reality of Tolkien's invented languages with their grammars (6). This exchange documents Tolkien's insistence on the primacy of his invented languages (Resnik 38) even when their roots were apparent, e.g. to his former student and philologist, J.S. Ryan (*Letters* 380), not that Tolkien was a stick-in-the-mud. Now the English, French and Latin roots of Nevbosh (*Bio* 36), Latin and Spanish roots of Naffarin (*C&G* 2.631), the Gothic roots of Gautisk, the Finnish influence on Qenya and the contribution of Welsh to Gnomish (*C&G* 2.632) are readily acknowledged. Goering asserts that somehow, invented languages, Tolkien's "secret vice," are immune from Tolkien's well known sense of humor (*Bio* 130, *Letters* 289).

Christopher Tolkien's discussion of his father's punning between invented and real world languages does not agree with Goering's position (*LT1* 282, see also 'incánus' and 'Orthanc' in *Unfinished Tales* 400). Bowers documents Tolkien's appreciation of the pun in Spanish of Cervantes' name 'Rocinante' for Don Quixote's horse, in relation to Chaucer's 'rouncy', a term used for the steed ridden by the Shipman in the "General Prologue" (Bowers 181, see also 131). Furthermore, Tolkien unpacks the vicissitudes of the Gothic *'midu' to 'miruvóre' (QL 61). Again, disconfirming evidence is ignored.

In summary, Goering's claim to comprehensively and compelling refute Hooker's analysis is vitiated and invalidated by logical flaws, e.g. a twenty-first century view of philology instead of the view current in Tolkien's time; turning a blind eye to Benedikz's disconfirming evidence accepted elsewhere (*C&G* 2.965); demanding proof of a level of "expertise" in Sanskrit for Tolkien consistent with the Boden Professor of Sanskrit as opposed to the competence required for the Rawlinson and Bosworth Professor of Anglo-Saxon and his own interests; ignoring many counter examples of Tolkien's playful attitude in general and toward language in particular; and ignoring the evolving nature of Tolkien's cartography.

A&I	*Tolkien, Artist and Illustrator.* Wayne Hammond and Christina Scull. Boston: Houghton Mifflin, 1995.
B&L	*Beren and Lúthien.* J.R.R. Tolkien. Ed. Christopher Tolkien. Boston: Houghton Mifflin. 2017.
Bio	*J.R.R. Tolkien. A Biography.* Humphrey Carpenter. Boston: Houghton Mifflin, 1977.
C&G	*The J.R.R. Tolkien Companion and Guide*, 3 vols. Christina Scull and Wayne G. Hammond. New York: Houghton Mifflin, 2017.
Exeter	*Tolkien at Exeter: How an Oxford Undergraduate Created Middle-earth.* John Garth. Oxford: Exeter College. 2014.
FR	*The Fellowship of the Ring.* J.R.R. Tolkien. Boston: Houghton Mifflin.1954.
GL	Gnomish Lexicon or *"i·Lam na·Ngoldathon. The Grammar and Lexicon of the Gnomish Tongue." Parma Eldalamberon* 11. Ed. Christopher Gilson, Patrick Wynne, Arden R. Smith, and Carl F. Hostetter. 1995.
Great War	*Tolkien and the Great War. The Threshold of Middle-earth.* John Garth. Boston: Houghton Mifflin, 2003.
Letters	*The Letters of J.R.R. Tolkien.* Ed. Humphrey Carpenter with the assistance of Christopher Tolkien. Boston: Houghton Mifflin, 1981.
Lost Road	*The Lost Road and Other Writings.* J.R.R. Tolkien. Ed. Christopher Tolkien. Boston: Houghton Mifflin, 1987.
LT1	*The Book of Lost Tales, Part One.* J.R.R. Tolkien. Ed. Christopher Tolkien. Boston: Houghton Mifflin, 1983.
LT2	*The Book of Lost Tales, Part Two.* J.R.R. Tolkien. Ed. Christopher Tolkien. Boston: Houghton Mifflin, 1984.
OFS	"On Fairy-Stories." *The Monsters and the Critics and Other Essays.* J.R.R. Tolkien. Ed. Christopher Tolkien. Boston: Houghton Mifflin, 1984. 109-161.
PE	*Parma Eldalamberon, The Book of Elven-Tongues.*
Peoples	*The Peoples of Middle-earth.* J.R.R. Tolkien. Ed. Christopher Tolkien. Boston: Houghton Mifflin, 1996.
QL	"Qenya Lexicon" or "Qenyaqetsa, The Qenya Phonology and Lexicon with The Poetic and Mythologic Words of Eldarissa."

	Parma Eldalamberon 12. Ed. Christopher Gilson, Carl F. Hostetter, Patrick Wynne, and Arden R. Smith, 1998.
RK	*The Return of the King*. J.R.R. Tolkien. Boston: Houghton Mifflin, 1955.
S	*The Silmarillion*. J.R.R. Tolkien. Ed. Christopher Tolkien. London: Allen and Unwin, 1977.
S&G	*The Legend of Sigurd and Gúdrun*. J.R.R. Tolkien. Ed. Christopher Tolkien. Boston: Houghton Mifflin, 2009.
TFA	*The Tolkien Family Album*. John and Priscilla Tolkien. Boston: Houghton Mifflin, 1992.
T&S	*Tolkien and Sanskrit, 'The Silmarillion' in the Cradle of Proto-Indo-European*. Mark T. Hooker. Bloomington, IN: Llyfrawr, 2016.
TT	*The Two Towers*. J.R.R. Tolkien. Boston: Houghton Mifflin, 1954.
WJ	*The War of the Jewels*. J.R.R. Tolkien. Ed. Christopher Tolkien. Boston: Houghton Mifflin, 1994.

Bibliography

AFLALO, Frederick George. *A Sketch of the Natural History (Vertebrates) of the British Islands*. Edinburgh & London: William Blackwood and Sons, 1898.

A.L.C. "Correspondence, Theosophy in Western Lands." *The Theosophist* 11. Madras, India: Adyar, 1890.

AMERICAN PSYCHIATRIC ASSOCIATION. *Diagnostic and Statistical Manual of Mental Disorders*. 5th edition. Arlington, VA: American Psychiatric Association, 2013.

AMOS, William. *The Originals. Who's Really Who in Fiction*. London: Macdonald & Co., 1985.

ANDERSON, Douglas. *The Annotated Hobbit. Revised and Expanded Edition*. London: Houghton Mifflin, 2002.

ANONYMOUS. *English Catholic's Vade Mecum*. London: G.J. Palmer, 1883.

ANONYMOUS. "A Dialogue: Discussion by Humphrey Carpenter, Professor George Sayer, and Dr. Clyde S. Kilby recorded September 29, 1979 in Wheaton IL." *Minas Tirith Evening-star*. 9.2 (January 1980), 20-24.

Anonymous. *Field Service Manual, 1914: Infantry battalion (Expeditionary Force)*. London: His Majesty's Stationery Office (Harrison and Sons, printers), 1914.

Anonymous. *Statistics of the Military Effort of the British Empire during the Great War, 1914-1920*. London: The War Office (HMSO), 1922.

ANONYMOUS. *The Public General Statutes: With a List of the Local and Private Acts Passed in the Years [...] of the Reign of King Edward the Seventh Being the [...] Session of the [...] Parliament of the United Kingdom of Great Britain and Ireland*. Volume 48. London: G.E. Eyre and W. Spottiswoode, 1910.

APPLE, Rima D. *Mothers and Medicine: A Social History of Infant Feeding, 1890-1950*. Madison, WI: University of Wisconsin Press, 1987.

ARMSTRONG, Helen. "It Bore Me Away." *Mallorn* 30. September, 1993. 29-32.

ASHER, Michael. *Khartoum: The Ultimate Imperial Adventure*. London: Penguin. 2005.

BADEN-POWELL, R.S.S. *Scouting for Boys: A Handbook for Instruction in Good Citizenship*. London: Horace Cox, 1908.

Bank of England. "Inflation Calculator." URL: www.bankofengland.co.uk/monetary-policy/inflation/inflation-calculator.

Barnard, E.A.B. "The Story of Dresden House, Evesham (1914)." Vale of Evesham Historical Society. http://www.valeofeveshamhistory.org/articles/dresden-house.

Benedikz, B.S. "Some Family Connections with J.R.R. Tolkien." *Amon Hen* 209 (January 2008), 11-13.

Birmingham Oratory. https://www.birminghamoratory.org.uk/tolkien-and-the-oratory/.

Boase, Charles William. *Registrum Collegi Exonionesis*. Oxford: At the Clarendon Press, 1894.

Bowers, John M. *Tolkien's Lost Chaucer*. Oxford: Oxford University Press, 2019.

Bowyer, Richard. *Dictionary of Military Terms*. London: A&C Black, 2002.

Brace, Keith. "Perspective: In the Footsteps of the Hobbits." *The Birmingham Post* May 25, 1968.

Bridoux, Denis. "Book Reviews: *Tolkien: Maker of Middle-earth* by Catherine McIlwaine; *Tolkien Treasures* by Catherine McIlwaine." *Tolkien Studies* 16 (2019), 143-170.

"Letting Images Speak for Themselves: Tolkien's Rebus Letter to Fr. Francis Morgan, August 8, 1904." *Beyond Bree* (October 2020), 1-2.

Brogan, Hugh. "Tolkien's Great War." *Children and Their Books: A Celebration of the Work of Iona and Peter Opie*. Eds. Gillian Avery and Julia Briggs. Oxford: Clarendon Press, 1989, 354-355.

Brown, Andrew and Linda Woodhead. *That Was The Church That Was. How the Church of England Lost the English People*. London: Bloomsbury, 2016.

Bru, J.M. Ferrández. *"Uncle Curro": J.R.R. Tolkien's Spanish Connection*. Edinburgh: Luna Press Publishing, 2017.

Bruce, Alexander M. "The Fall of Gondolin and the Fall of Troy: Tolkien and Book II of *The Aeneid*." *Mythlore* 117/118 (Spring/Summer 2012), 103-115.

Bunting, Nancy. "1904: Tolkien Trauma, and Its Anniversaries." *Mythlore* 34.1/127 (Fall/Winter 2015), 59-81.

"Again Lobelia." *Beyond Bree* (January 2019), 1-5.

"Apologia for Daniel Grotta." *Lembas* 37.180 (October 2017), 149-158.

"Checking the Facts." *Mallorn* 59 (Winter 2018), 52-56.

"Concerning Tolkien's Deadly Spiders. Part I." *Lembas* 38.185 (December 2018), 201-211.

"Concerning Tolkien's Deadly Spiders. Part II." *Lembas* 38.186 (January 2019), 213-224.

"Fairies, Fairy Queens, and the Character of Guinevere in Tolkien's *The Fall of Arthur*." *Lembas* 37.182 (March 2018), 173-180.

"Finding Tolkien in His Stories. *Lembas* 35.174 (May 2016), 73-86.

"Finding Hilary Tolkien in the Works of J.R.R. Tolkien, Part II." *Beyond Bree* (January 2018), 3-7.

"On the *Tolkienothēca*." *Beyond Bree* (April 2020), 6-7.

"*Roverandom*, an Autobiographical Reading. Part 1." *Beyond Bree* (June 2016), 3-6.

"*Roverandom*, an Autobiographical Reading. Part 2." *Beyond Bree* (July 2016), 6-8.

"Tolkien and the Boy Scouts." *Lembas Extra* (2015), 75-87.

"Tolkien in Love: Pictures from the Winter of 1912-1913." *Mythlore* 32.2/124 (Spring/Summer 2014), 5-12.

"Tolkien's *Fantasy Landscape*." *Mallorn* 61, Winter, 2020. 6-15.

and Seamus HAMILL-KEAYS. "Edith Mary, The Other Suffield Aunt, Part 4." *Beyond Bree* (August 2019), 1-7.

BURKE, Janine. *The Sphinx on the Table. Sigmund Freud's Art Collection and the Development of Psychoanalysis*. New York, NY: Walker & Co., 2006.

BURNS, Maggie. "Jane Suffield." http://www.search.connctinghistories.org.uk/engine/resource/exhibition/ sequential.

BURROW, Edward John. *Out and Around in Cheltenham. The Guide for Visitors*. Cheltenham, England: E.J. Burrow, 1921.

CARDEN-COYNE, Anne. *The Politics of Wounds: Military Patients and Medical Power in the First World War*. Oxford: Oxford University Press, 2014.

CARPENTER, Humphrey. *J.R.R. Tolkien. A Biography*. Boston, MA: Houghton Mifflin, 1977.

(in conversation with Lyndall Gordon). "Learning about Ourselves: Biography as Autobiography." *The Art of Literary Biography*. Ed. John Batchelor. Oxford: Clarendon Press, 1995, 267-279.

"Review: *Tolkien and the Great War* by John Garth." *The Sunday Times*, November 23, 2003.

CHAMBERS, William, *Chambers's Etymological Dictionary of the English Language: Pronouncing, Explanatory, Etymological.* Ed. Andrew Findlater. London & Edinburgh: W. & R. Chambers, 1904.

CHINTAMAN, Vinayak Vaidya. *The Mahabharata: A Criticism.* Bombay: A.J. Cambridge & Co., 1905.

CILLI, Oronzo. *Tolkien's Library: An Annotated Checklist.* Edinburgh: Luna Press Publishing, 2019.

CORSINI, Carlo. *The Decline of Infant and Child Mortality. The European Experience 1750-1990.* Leiden: Martinus Nijhoff. 1997.

CRANG, Jeremy A. 2005, "The Abolition of Compulsory Church Parades in the British Army." *The Journal of Ecclesiastical History* 56.1 (2005), 92-106. (DOI:10.1017/S0022046904001459).

CROFT, Janet Brennan and Annika RÖTTINGER (eds.). *"Something Has Gone Crack" New Perspectives on J.R.R.Tolkien in the Great War.* Zurich and Jena: Walking Tree Publishers, 2019.

DRAPER, Karey Lee. *Wartime Huts: The Development, Typology, and Identification of Temporary Military Buildings in Britain 1914-1945.* (Doctoral thesis, 2018). https://doi.org/10.17863/CAM.17581 Apollo. University of Cambridge. https://www.repository.cam.ac.uk/handle/1810/270649.

duPLESSIS, Nicole. "On the Shoulders of Humphrey Carpenter: Reconsidering Biographical Representation and Scholarly Perception of Edith Tolkien." *Mythlore* 37.2 (Spring/Summer 2019), 39-74.

EDWARDS, Raymond. *Tolkien.* London: Robert Hale, 2014.

ELDER, David. *Cheltenham: Unique Images from the Archives of Historic England.* Stroud: Amberley Publishing, 2018.

ELLIS, John. *Eye-Deep in Hell: Trench Warfare in World War I.* Baltimore, MD: Johns Hopkins University Press, 1989.

"Tolkien's Art." *Mallorn* 30 (1993), 21- 28.

FIMI, Dimitra. *Tolkien, Race, and Cultural History: From Fairies to Hobbits.* New York, NY: Palgrave Macmillan, 2009.

FLOWERS, Michael. "Tolkien in East Yorkshire, 1917-1918: A Hemlock Glade, Two Towers, The Houses of Healing, and a Beacon." *"Something Has Gone Crack" New Perspectives on J.R.R.Tolkien in the Great War.* Ed. Janet Brennan Croft and Annika Röttinger. Zurich and Jena: Walking Tree Publishers, 2019, 121-150.

FOREMAN, Amanda. *Georgiana, Duchess of Devonshire.* New York, NY: Modern Library, 2001.

Forest-Hill, Lynn. "Elves on the Avon." *Times Literary Supplement* (*TLS*), 8 July 2005, 12–13.

French, David. *Military Identities: The Regimental System & the British People c.1870-2000*. Oxford: Oxford University Press, 2005.

Furnivall, Frederick James, Edmund Brock, and William Alexander Clouston (eds.). *Originals and Analogues of Some of Chaucer's Canterbury Tales*. London: N. Trübner & Co., for the Chaucer Society, 1872.

Garth, John. "Book Reviews: *Parma Eldalamberon* 21, *Parma Eldalamberon* 12, and *Arda Philology* 3." *Tolkien Studies* 11 (2014), 225-240.

Tolkien and the Great War. The Threshold of Middle-earth. Boston, MA: Houghton Mifflin, 2000.

Tolkien at Exeter: How an Oxford Undergraduate Created Middle-earth. Oxford: Exeter College, 2014.

The Worlds of J.R.R. Tolkien. The Places that Inspired Middle-earth. Princeton, NJ: Princeton University Press, 2020.

Gilliver, Peter M. "At the Wordface: J.R.R. Tolkien's Work on the *Oxford English Dictionary*." *Proceedings of the J.R.R. Tolkien Centenary Conference 1992*. Eds. Patricia Reynolds and Glen H. Goodknight. Altadena, CA: Tolkien Society and Mythopoetic Press, 1995, 173-186.

Goering, Nelson. "[Book Review:] *Tolkien and Sanskrit* (2016) by Mark T. Hooker." *Journal of Tolkien Research* 3, Article 6.

Gorelik, Boris. "'Africa … always moves me deeply': Tolkien in Bloemfontein." *Mallorn* 55 (Autumn 2014), 5-10.

Grafton, Charles Chapman. *The Works of the Rt. Rev. Charles C. Grafton: A Catholic Atlas; or Digest of Catholic Theology*. London: Longmans Green, 1914.

Graves, Robert (von Ranke). *Goodbye to All That. An Autobiography*. London: Penguin Books, 2011.

Grotta-Kurska, Daniel. *J.R.R. Tolkien, Architect of Middle Earth*. Philadelphia, PA: Running Press, 1976.

Haines-Bellamy, Paula. "Everyday Wear from the Past." *Nelson Mail, New Zealand*, June 22, 2013.

Hall, Brian N. "The British Army and Wireless Communication, 1896-1918." *War in History*. Newbury Park, CA: Sage 2012, 290-321.

Hamill-Keays, Seamus. "Tolkien and the Zeppelins." *Journal of Tolkien Research* 11.1 (2020) Article 1. https://scholar.valpo.edu/journaloftolkienresearch/vol11/iss1/1.

HAMILL-KEAYS, Seamus and Nancy BUNTING. The Buckland in 'The brewing of the Tale.'" Lembas 39, # 190. June, 2020. 257-262.

HAMMOND, Wayne and Christina SCULL. *'The Lord of the Rings', A Reader's Companion.* Boston, MA: Houghton Mifflin, 2005.

Tolkien: Artist and Illustrator. Boston, MA: Houghton Mifflin, 1995.

HARRIS, R.G. *50 Years of Yeomanry Uniforms.* London: Frederick Muller, 1972.

HILEY, Margaret. "Stolen Language, Cosmic Models: Myth and Mythology in Tolkien." *MFS Modern Fiction Studies* 50.4 (Winter 2004), 838-860.

HOOKER, Mark T. "In Search of Tolkien's First-World Towers, Part II." *Beyond Bree* (September 2020), 4-7.

"A System of Dots." *Beyond Bree* (April 2020), 5.

Tolkien and Sanskrit. 'The Silmarillion' in the Cradle of Proto-Indo-European. Bloomington, IN: Llyfrawr, 2016.

Tolkien and Welsh. Essays on J.R.R. Tolkien's Use of Welsh in his 'Legendarium'. Bloomington, IN: Llyfrawr, 2012.

Tolkienotēca: Studies in Tolkiennymy; Or, Searching for the Origins of Elvo-Indo-European in Tolkien's Elvish Lexicon; With an Addendum to 'Tolkien and Sanskrit', and a Lexicon of Elvish Month Names. Bloomington, IN: Llyfrawr, 2019.

HORSTMAN, Allen. *Victorian Divorce.* London: Routledge, 1985.

JACKSON, R. (chairman). "Air Defence against the Zeppelin 1915-1917." *Defending Northern Skies 1915-1995.* Ed. A.F.C. Hunter. London: RAF Historical Society, 1996, 15-22. www.rafmuseum.org.uk/documents/research/RAF-Historical-Society-Journals/Journal-16A-Defending-Northern-Skies.pdf.

JACOBS, Alan. *The Narnian. The Life and Imagination of C.S. Lewis.* New York, NY: Harper Collins, 2005.

JAMES, Lt.-Col. Lionel, DSO. *The History of King Edward's Horse (The King's Own Dominions Regiment).* London: Sifton, Praed and Co., 1921.

JEFFERSON, James W. and John R. MARSHALL. *Neuropsychiatric Features of Medical Disorders.* New York, NY: Plenum Medical Book Company, 1981.

JEFFRIES, Sheila. *The Spinster and Her Enemies: Feminism and Sexuality 1880-1930.* London: Pandora Press, 1986.

JENSEN, Anika. "Flowers and Steel: The Necessity of War in Feminist Tolkien Scholarship." *Tolkien Studies* 16 (2019), 59-72.

JONES, Henry Albert. *The War in the Air.* Vol. III. Oxford: Clarendon Press, 1931. https://archive.org/details/warinairbeingst01rale/page/86/mode/2up.

KAPLAN, Harold I. and Benjamin J. SADOCK. *Comprehensive Textbook of Psychiatry.* Baltimore, MD: Williams & Wilkins, 1989.

KEATON, Michael P. "Fairies at War: *The Fall of Gondolin* as the Cornerstone of Middle-earth." *Tolkien Studies* 17 (2020), 25-49.

KENNEDY, Michael. *The Concise Oxford Dictionary of Music.* Oxford: Oxford University Press. 2007.

KILBY, Clyde. *Tolkien and The Silmarillion.* Berkhamstead: Lion Publishing, 1976.

LEE, Stuart E. "'Tolkien in Oxford' (BBC, 1968): A Reconstruction." *Tolkien Studies* 15 (2018), 115-176.

LEGGETT, Bernard John. "Wireless Telegraphy in Warfare." *Wireless Telegraphy: With Special Reference to the Quenched-spark System.* New York, NY: E.P. Dutton, 1921, 332.

LEWIS, Alex and Elizabeth CURRIE. *The Epic Realm of Tolkien. Part One: Beren and Lúthien.* Merton-in-Marsh: ADC Publications, 2009.

The Forsaken Realm of Tolkien: J.R.R. Tolkien and the Medieval Tradition. Oswestry: Medea, 2005.

J.R.R. Tolkien: Codemaker, Spy-master, Hero. An Unauthorised Biography by Elansea. Amazon CreateSpace Indepentent Publishing, 2015.

LEWIS-STEMPEL, John. *Six Weeks: The Short and Gallant Life of the British Officer in the First World War.* London: Weidenfeld and Nicholson, 2010.

LONG, Josh. "Clinamen, Tessera, and the Anxiety of Influence: Swerving from and Completing George MacDonald." *Tolkien Studies* 6 (2009), 127-150.

LONGSTREET, Hilary. "Merry in Focus: On Ring fever, having adventures, being overlooked, and not getting left behind." *Mallorn* 43 (2005), 43-48.

MARTSCH, Nancy. "Tolkien Reading Day and 'Eyes Clear As Glass'." Beyond Bree. April, 2021. 9

MATHISON, Phil. *Tolkien in East Yorkshire 1917-1918. An Illustrated Tour.* Newport: Dead Good Publications, 2012.

McILWAINE, Catherine. *Tolkien: Maker of Middle-earth.* Oxford: Bodleian Library, 2018.

MENN, Lise. "Elvish Loanwords in Indo-European: Cultural Implications." *An Introduction to Elvish.* Ed. Jim Allan. Frome: Bran's Head Books, 1978, 143-151.

MONIER-WILLIAMS, Sir Monier. *A Sanskrit-English Dictionary*. Oxford: Clarendon, 1872.

MORTON, Andrew H. and John HAYES. *Tolkien's Gedling. The Birth of a Legend*. Warwickshire: Brewin Books Ltd., 2008.

NELSON, Thomas H., William E. CLARKE, and F. BOYES. *The Birds of Yorkshire*. London: Brown & Sons, 1907.

ORDWAY, Holly. *Tolkien's Modern Reading. Middle-earth Beyond the Middle Ages*. Park Ridge, IL: Word on Fire, 2021.

PATCH, Harry and Richard VAN EMDERS. *The Last Fighting Tommy*. London: Bloomsbury, 2014.

PIGOTT, B.A.F. *Flowers and Ferns of Cromer and its Neighborhood*. London: Jarrold & Sons, 1885.

PINCHBECK, Ivy and Margaret HEWITT. *Children in English Society. Volume 2: From the Eighteenth Century to the Children Act 1948*. London: Routledge and Kegan Paul, 1973.

PLIMMER, Charlotte and Denis. "The Man Who Understands Hobbits." *The Telegraph*, March 22, 1968.

PLOTZ, Richard. "J.R.R. Tolkien Talks about the Discovery of Middle-earth. The Origins of Elvish." *Seventeen* (January 1967), 92-93, 118.

PRIESTMAN, Judith. *J.R.R. Tolkien, Life and Legend*. Oxford: Bodleian Library, 1992.

PYLE, Howard. *The Garden Behind the Moon, A Real Story of the Moon Angel*. New York: Charles Scribener's Sons, 1895.

QUILLER-COUCH, Arthur. *In Powder and Crinoline*. (Illustrations by Kay Nielsen.) London: Hodder and Stroughton, 1913.

In Powder and Crinoline. Old Fairy Tales, retold by Anne Carter. London: Hodder and Stoughton and Gallery Five, 1979.

RANGANATHANANDA. *Human Being in Depth: A Scientific Approach to Religion*. Albany, NY: SUNY Press, 1991.

RATELIFF, John D. *The History of the Hobbit*. (2 volumes: *Part One: Mr. Baggins* and *Part Two: Return to Bag-End*). New York, NY: Houghton Mifflin, 2007.

RESNIK, Henry. "An Interview with Tolkien." *Niekas* 18 (Spring 1967), 37-47.

RIDGWAY, P. "Trinity House and the Great War." *Flash* 22 (Winter 2014), London: Trinity House. https://www.trinityhouse.co.uk/asset/1319/download?1457365991.

RIEDI, Eliza. "Brains or Polo? Equestrian Sport Army Reform and the Gentlemanly Officer Tradition 1900-1914." *Journal of the Society for Army Historical Research* 84.339 (Autumn 2006), 236-253.

ROBINSON, Douglas H. "The Zeppelin Bomber; High Policy Guided by Wishful Thinking." *Airpower* 8.3 (July 1916), 130-147.

ROBBIE, David and Scott WHITEHOUSE. "Staffordshire Tolkien Trail." https://www.staffordshire.gov.uk/environment/RightsofWay/distancewalks/Staffordshire-Tolkien-Trail.aspx.

ROSE, Lionel. *The Erosion of Childhood, Child Oppression in Britain 1860-1918.* New York, NY: Routledge, 1991.

SAGAN-FENTON, Michael. *Penzance. The Biography.* Stroud: Amberley Publishing, 2015.

SAYER, George. "Recollections of J.R.R. Tolkien." *Tolkien: A Celebration. Collected Writings on a Literary Legacy.* Ed. Joseph Pearce. San Francisco, CA: Ignatius Press, 1999, 1-16.

SCULL, Christina and Wayne G. HAMMOND. *The J.R.R. Tolkien Companion and Guide.* 3 vols. New York, NY: Harper Collins Publishers, 2017.

SELDON, Anthony and Peter SNOWDON. *The Conservative Party.* Stroud: Sutton Publishing, 2004.

SETH, Priya. "Tudor, Elizabethan and Jacobean Connections" PriyaSethTolkienFan, March 14, 2018. https://priyasethtolkienfan.wordpress.com/2018/02/09/tudor-elizabethan-and-jacobean-connections/.

SHIPPEY, Tom A. *J.R.R. Tolkien. Author of the Century.* London: HarperCollins Publishers, 2000.

The Road to Middle-earth. Boston, MA: Houghton Mifflin, 2003.

Roots and Branches: Selected Papers on Tolkien. Zurich and Jena: Walking Tree Publishers, 2007.

SIMKINS, Peter. *Kitchener's Army. The Raising of the New Armies, 1914-1916.* Manchester: Manchester University Press, 1988.

SIMPSON, Eileen. *Orphans, Real and Imaginary.* New York, NY: NAL Penguin, 1987.

SLEMON, J. Morris. *The Prospective Mother, A Handbook for Women During Pregnancy.* Original publication 1912. Reprinted: Whitefish, MT: Kessinger Legacy Reprints, 2010.

SPIERS, E.M. "Reforming the Infantry of the Line 1900-1914." *Journal of the Society for Army Historical Research* 59.238 (Summer 1981), 82-94.

STRATTON, Rebecca J., Ceri J. GREEN, and Marinos ELIA. *Disease-related Malnutrition, An Evidence-based Approach to Treatment*. Boston, MA: CABI, 2003.

SULLOWAY, Frank J. *Freud: Biologist of the Mind. Beyond the Psychoanalytic Legend*. New York, NY: Basic Books, 1979.

TATTERSALL, Robert. *Diabetes. The Biography*. Oxford: Oxford University Press, 2009.

TESTI, Claudio. *Pagan Saints of Middle-earth*. Zurich and Jena: Walking Tree Publishers. 2018.

THOMAS, Clayton L. *Taber's Cyclopedic Medical Dictionary*. 13th edition. Philadelphia, PA: F.A. Davis Company, 1977.

TOLKIEN, Hilary. *Black and White Ogre Country. The Lost Tales of Hilary Tolkien*. Ed. Angela Gardner. Moreton-in-Marsh: ADC Publications, 2009.

TOLKIEN, John and Priscilla. *The Tolkien Family Album*. Boston, MA: Houghton Mifflin, 1992.

TOLKIEN, J.R.R. "The Alphabet of Rúmil and Early Noldorin Fragments." *Parma Eldalamberon* 13 (2001).

"Beowulf: The Monsters and the Critics." *The Monsters and the Critics and Other Essays*. Ed. Christopher Tolkien. Boston, MA: Houghton Mifflin, 1984, 5-48.

Beren and Lúthien. Ed. Christopher Tolkien. Boston, MA: Houghton Mifflin. 2017.

The Book of Lost Tales. Part One. (The History of Middle-earth 1). Ed. Christopher Tolkien. Boston, MA: Houghton Mifflin, 1983.

The Book of Lost Tales. Part Two. (The History of Middle-earth 2). Ed. Christopher Tolkien. Boston, MA: Houghton Mifflin, 1984.

The Fellowship of the Ring. Boston, MA: Houghton Mifflin, 1963.

The Hobbit. Boston, MA: Houghton Mifflin, 1963. adjust date

"*i·Lam na·Ngoldathon*. The Grammar and Lexicon of the Gnomish Tongue." *Parma Eldalamberon* 11 (1995).

Lays of Beleriand. (The History of Middle-earth 3). Ed. Christopher Tolkien. Boston, MA: Houghton Mifflin, 1985.

"Leaf by Niggle." *A Tolkien Miscellany*. Boston: Houghton Mifflin, 2002, 149-162.

The Legend of Sigurd and Gudrún. Ed. Christopher Tolkien. Boston, MA: Houghton Mifflin, 2009.

The Letters of J.R.R. Tolkien. Ed. Humphrey Carpenter, with the assistance of Christopher Tolkien. Boston, MA: Houghton Mifflin, 1981.

The Lord of the Rings. Boston, MA: Houghton Mifflin, 1963.

The Lost Road and Other Writings. (*The History of Middle-earth* 5). Ed. Christopher Tolkien. Boston, MA: Houghton Mifflin, 1987.

(interviewed by Denys Gueroult). *Now Read On.* BBC Radio 4 (recorded November 26, 1964, aired December 16 1970).

"On Fairy-Stories." *The Monsters and the Critics and Other Essays.* Ed. Christopher Tolkien. Boston, MA: Houghton Mifflin, 1984, 109-161.

The Peoples of Middle-earth. (*The History of Middle-earth* 10). Ed. Christopher Tolkien. London: HarperCollinsPublishers, 1996.

"Qenya Lexicon or Qenyaqetsa or The Qenya Phonology and Lexicon with The Poetic and Mythologic Words of Eldarissa." *Parma Eldalamberon* 12 (1998).

The Return of the King. Boston, MA: Houghton Mifflin, 1963.

Roverandom. Eds. Christina Scull and Wayne G. Hammond. Boston, MA: Houghton Mifflin, 1998.

Sauron Defeated. (*The History of Middle-earth* 9). Ed. Christopher Tolkien. New York, NY: Houghton Mifflin, 1992.

"A Secret Vice." *The Monsters and the Critics and Other Essays.* Ed. Christopher Tolkien. Boston, MA: Houghton Mifflin, 1984, 198-223.

The Shaping of Middle-earth. (*The History of Middle-earth* 4). Ed. Christopher Tolkien. New York, NY: Houghton Mifflin, 1986.

The Silmarillion. Ed. Christopher Tolkien. London: George Allen and Unwin, 1977.s

Unfinished Tales of Númernor and Middle-earth. Ed. Christopher Tolkien. Boston: Houghton Mifflin Co. 1980.

"Words, Phrases, and Passages in Various Tongues in *The Lord of the Rings.*" *Parma Eldalamberon* 17 (2007).

TOLKIEN, Priscilla. "J.R.R. Tolkien and Edith Tolkien's Stay in Staffordshire 1916, 1917, and 1918." *Angerthas in English* 3 (1997), 5-7.

TOMASEVEŠKIJ, Boris. "Literature and Biography." *Authorship: From Plato to the Postmodern. A Reader.* Ed. Seán Burke. Edinburgh: Edinburgh University Press, 1995.

TUCKER, Spencer and Priscilla Mary ROBERTS. *World War I Encyclopedia. Vol. 1: Censorship.* Santa Barbara, CA: ABC-CLIO, 2005.

Unwin, Rayner. *George Allen & Unwin: A Remembrancer.* Ludlow: Merlin Unwin Books, 1999.

Walkowitz. Judith R. *Prostitution and Victorian Society.* Cambridge: Cambridge University Press, 1988.

White, Michael. *The Life and Work of J.R.R. Tolkien.* New York, NY: Alpha, 2002.

William, Arthur. *An Etymological Dictionary of Family and Christian Names.* New York, NY: Seldon, Blakeman & Co., 1857.

Windrow, Andrew. *The British Army Regular Mounted Infantry 1880-1913.* Abingdon: Routledge, 2017.

Wright, Elizabeth M. *The Story of Joseph Wright: Man and Scholar.* Oxford: Oxford University Press, 1934.

Wright, Walter Page. *Popular Garden Flowers.* New York, NY: Doubleday Page & Co., 1911.

XE Currency Converter. URL: https://www.xe.com/currencyconverter/.

G

Gandharva marriage, 205, 211, 220

Gateley, Stephen, Edith Bratt's guardian, 29, 32, 45-46, 56-57, 59, 62-63, 64, 80, 89, 93, 102, 221

Gautisk, 71, 76, 168, 234

Gilson, Rob, Ronald Tolkien's friend, 52, 98, 100-01, 140, 159

Gloucester, birthplace of Edith Bratt, 1, 8-10, 15-16, 17-19, 20, 21, 22

Gnomish (Goldogrin) Lexicon, 47, 77, 99, 124, 127, 136, 139, 175, 182

Gollins, Annie, 46, 78

governess, 3-4, 5-6, 29, 220

    Fannie Bratt, 2, 5-6, 29, 110, 220

    Mabel Tolkien, 29, 110

    Victorian, 3-4

    Watt, Alice and Kate, 40

Great Haywood, xii, 94, 123, 136, 148-55, 156, 158, 160, 167-69, 170, 196, 207, 211

The Grey Bridge of Tavrobel, 195-196, 211, 216

Grove, Jennie (Mary Jane), 24, 26-28, 30, 46, 93-94, 96, 115, 123, 143, 153, 156, 160, 162, 168, 172-75, 185, 217

Grownupishness, 81

H

Handsworth, 1, 2, 8, 20, 24-27, 31, 46

Harrogate, 170-71, 172-73, 217

Here, 105-106, 112, 120, 122-23, 212

Hornsea, 174, 177-78, 187, 217

hospital care in World War I, 159-60, 170-72, 186, 188

I

i glin grandin a Dol Erethrin Airi, or *Three Designs Represzenting the Towns of Tavrobel [Great Haywood], Cortirion [Warwick], and Celbaros [Cheltenham]* or *The Fair (walled) Towns of (the) Holy/Sacred Tol Eressëa (the Lonely Isle)*, xvii, 136, 149, 170, 196, 207, 209-16, 217, 223, 228

    Celbaros/Cheltenham 136, 212-216

    Cortirion/Warwick, 136, 207-08, 210

    Tavrobel/Great Haywood, 123, 136, 211

illegitimacy, xvi, 1, 9, 11, 15, 64, 201, 203-04, 206

    neglect of illegitimate children, 15, 18, 20, 21

    stigma, prejudice toward, 24, 29, 31, 67, 144

Incledon, (Ronald Tolkien's) cousins, 58, 70, 78, 98, 103, 131, 145, 160, 192, 219

Incledon, Edith Mary (May), Ronald Tolkien's aunt, 58, 70, 72, 78, 80, 98, 101, 103, 114-15, 117, 131, 145, 160, 162, 191, 219

Incledon, Marjorie, Ronald Tolkien's cousin, 47, 70, 72, 99, 131, 145, 160

W

Endorsements

Nancy Bunting and Seamus Hamill-Keayes's's biography of Edith Bratt Tolkien is by turns diligently documented and daringly speculative. Many hitherto untapped records and sources are deployed in support of this new assessment of Edith's early life and character. In their concluding chapter, Bunting and Hamill-Keays mount a well-reasoned defense for their challenge to, in Dimitra Fimi's phrase, Tolkien's "biographical legend."

Janet Brennan Croft
(editor of *Mythlore*)

An examination and documentation of Edith Bratt's influence and inspirational presence in the life of J.R.R. Tolkien is long overdue and greatly desired. This biography and study fills that large gap in Tolkien studies and research. The detailed chronological, historical, and creative emphasis on Edith Bratt's biographical information in relation to already-known facts related to Tolkien's own biography provides a fuller picture of her contributions to the development and creation of Tolkien's *legendarium*.

Bradford Lee Eden, Ph.D.
(editor of *Journal of Tolkien Research*)

For far too long the examination and evaluation of the life of J.R.R. Tolkien has been limited to a narrow range of his academic work and a few of his male colleagues and friends. In concentrating on this narrow range, the picture of the creator of Middle-earth has so far lacked a more rounded and useful dimension and has therefore been limited in value.

Here in this new book Bunting and Hamill-Keays have brought to the fore the person who would have been closest to Tolkien – his wife Edith. Far from being a bland and unimportant figure in his life as some have suggested, in *The Gallant Edith Bratt* we discover an interesting person in her own right with a key role in Tolkien's creative life. The love affair between the young Tolkien and the love of his life Edith was as passionate and remarkable as some of the love stories Tolkien told about his own created characters such as Aragorn and Arwen, and Beren and Lúthien.

The authors have used much recent material to build a picture of Edith's background, who her parents were, and just how financially independent she was prior to marrying Tolkien. They have persuasively shown how much at the core of his creativity Edith belonged – along with Tolkien's younger brother Hilary. Without her, we would simply not have had the stories as we know them.

We find out more about the things that drove J.R.R. Tolkien to create what he did, and discover in his wife not only a partner in matters physical, but also a wise and gifted counsellor to her husband as well as an important source of inspiration to him during his whole life.

The style of the book is very accessible and it is a pleasure to read and very informative.

Alexander Lewis
(Chairman (1988-1992) and Secretary (2013-2015) of the Tolkien Society)

A fascinating re-examination of the life of Edith Tolkien, née Bratt, that explores interesting themes and ideas in relation to the development of JRR Tolkien's early writing and the evolution of Middle-earth. An enjoyable new perspective that will hopefully stimulate much debate and further research in years to come.

Scott Whitehouse
(librarian & historian: Staffordshire County Council & Tolkien Trail)

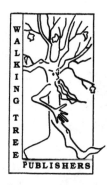

Walking Tree Publishers
Zurich and Jena

Walking Tree Publishers was founded in 1997 as a forum for publication of material related to Tolkien and Middle-earth studies.

www.walking-tree.org

Cormarë Series

The *Cormarë Series* collects papers and studies dedicated exclusively to the exploration of Tolkien's work. It comprises monographs, thematic collections of essays, conference volumes, and reprints of important yet no longer (easily) accessible papers by leading scholars in the field. Manuscripts and project proposals are evaluated by members of an independent board of advisors who support the series editors in their endeavour to provide the readers with qualitatively superior yet accessible studies on Tolkien and his work.

News from the Shire and Beyond. Studies on Tolkien
Peter Buchs & Thomas Honegger (eds.), Zurich and Berne 2004, Reprint, First edition 1997 (Cormarë Series 1), ISBN 978-3-9521424-5-5

Root and Branch. Approaches Towards Understanding Tolkien
Thomas Honegger (ed.), Zurich and Berne 2005, Reprint, First edition 1999 (Cormarë Series 2), ISBN 978-3-905703-01-6

Richard Sturch, *Four Christian Fantasists. A Study of the Fantastic Writings of George MacDonald, Charles Williams, C.S. Lewis and J.R.R. Tolkien*
Zurich and Berne 2007, Reprint, First edition 2001 (Cormarë Series 3), ISBN 978-3-905703-04-7

Tolkien in Translation
Thomas Honegger (ed.), Zurich and Jena 2011, Reprint, First edition 2003 (Cormarë Series 4), ISBN 978-3-905703-15-3

Mark T. Hooker, *Tolkien Through Russian Eyes*
Zurich and Berne 2003 (Cormarë Series 5), ISBN 978-3-9521424-7-9

Translating Tolkien: Text and Film
Thomas Honegger (ed.), Zurich and Jena 2011, Reprint, First edition 2004 (Cormarë Series 6), ISBN 978-3-905703-16-0

Christopher Garbowski, *Recovery and Transcendence for the Contemporary Mythmaker. The Spiritual Dimension in the Works of J.R.R. Tolkien*
Zurich and Berne 2004, Reprint, First Edition by Marie Curie Sklodowska, University Press, Lublin 2000, (Cormarë Series 7), ISBN 978-3-9521424-8-6

Reconsidering Tolkien
Thomas Honegger (ed.), Zurich and Berne 2005 (Cormarë Series 8), ISBN 978-3-905703-00-9

Tolkien and Modernity 1
Frank Weinreich & Thomas Honegger (eds.), Zurich and Berne 2006 (Cormarë Series 9), ISBN 978-3-905703-02-3

Tolkien and Modernity 2
Thomas Honegger & Frank Weinreich (eds.), Zurich and Berne 2006 (Cormarë Series 10), ISBN 978-3-905703-03-0

Tom Shippey, *Roots and Branches. Selected Papers on Tolkien by Tom Shippey*
Zurich and Berne 2007 (Cormarë Series 11), ISBN 978-3-905703-05-4

Ross Smith, *Inside Language. Linguistic and Aesthetic Theory in Tolkien*
Zurich and Jena 2011, Reprint, First edition 2007 (Cormarë Series 12),
ISBN 978-3-905703-20-7

How We Became Middle-earth. A Collection of Essays on The Lord of the Rings
Adam Lam & Nataliya Oryshchuk (eds.), Zurich and Berne 2007 (Cormarë
Series 13), ISBN 978-3-905703-07-8

Myth and Magic. Art According to the Inklings
Eduardo Segura & Thomas Honegger (eds.), Zurich and Berne 2007 (Cormarë
Series 14), ISBN 978-3-905703-08-5

The Silmarillion – Thirty Years On
Allan Turner (ed.), Zurich and Berne 2007 (Cormarë Series 15),
ISBN 978-3-905703-10-8

Martin Simonson, *The Lord of the Rings and the Western Narrative Tradition*
Zurich and Jena 2008 (Cormarë Series 16), ISBN 978-3-905703-09-2

*Tolkien's Shorter Works. Proceedings of the 4th Seminar of the Deutsche Tolkien Gesellschaft
& Walking Tree Publishers Decennial Conference*
Margaret Hiley & Frank Weinreich (eds.), Zurich and Jena 2008 (Cormarë Series
17), ISBN 978-3-905703-11-5

Tolkien's The Lord of the Rings: Sources of Inspiration
Stratford Caldecott & Thomas Honegger (eds.), Zurich and Jena 2008 (Cormarë Series
18), ISBN 978-3-905703-12-2

J.S. Ryan, *Tolkien's View: Windows into his World*
Zurich and Jena 2009 (Cormarë Series 19), ISBN 978-3-905703-13-9

Music in Middle-earth
Heidi Steimel & Friedhelm Schneidewind (eds.), Zurich and Jena 2010 (Cormarë
Series 20), ISBN 978-3-905703-14-6

Liam Campbell, *The Ecological Augury in the Works of JRR Tolkien*
Zurich and Jena 2011 (Cormarë Series 21), ISBN 978-3-905703-18-4

Margaret Hiley, *The Loss and the Silence. Aspects of Modernism in the Works of
C.S. Lewis, J.R.R. Tolkien and Charles Williams*
Zurich and Jena 2011 (Cormarë Series 22), ISBN 978-3-905703-19-1

Rainer Nagel, *Hobbit Place-names. A Linguistic Excursion through the Shire*
Zurich and Jena 2012 (Cormarë Series 23), ISBN 978-3-905703-22-1

Christopher MacLachlan, *Tolkien and Wagner: The Ring and Der Ring*
Zurich and Jena 2012 (Cormarë Series 24), ISBN 978-3-905703-21-4

Renée Vink, *Wagner and Tolkien: Mythmakers*
Zurich and Jena 2012 (Cormarë Series 25), ISBN 978-3-905703-25-2

The Broken Scythe. Death and Immortality in the Works of J.R.R. Tolkien
Roberto Arduini & Claudio Antonio Testi (eds.), Zurich and Jena 2012 (Cormarë
Series 26), ISBN 978-3-905703-26-9

Sub-creating Middle-earth: Constructions of Authorship and the Works of J.R.R. Tolkien
Judith Klinger (ed.), Zurich and Jena 2012 (Cormarë Series 27),
ISBN 978-3-905703-27-6

Tolkien's Poetry
Julian Eilmann & Allan Turner (eds.), Zurich and Jena 2013
(Cormarë Series 28), ISBN 978-3-905703-28-3

O, What a Tangled Web. Tolkien and Medieval Literature. A View from Poland
Barbara Kowalik (ed.), Zurich and Jena 2013 (Cormarë Series 29),
ISBN 978-3-905703-29-0

J.S. Ryan, *In the Nameless Wood*
Zurich and Jena 2013 (Cormarë Series 30), ISBN 978-3-905703-30-6

From Peterborough to Faëry; The Poetics and Mechanics of Secondary Worlds
Thomas Honegger & Dirk Vanderbeke (eds.), Zurich and Jena 2014
(Cormarë Series 31), ISBN 978-3-905703-31-3

Tolkien and Philosophy
Roberto Arduini & Claudio R. Testi (eds.), Zurich and Jena 2014
(Cormarë Series 32), ISBN 978-3-905703-32-0

Patrick Curry, *Deep Roots in a Time of Frost. Essays on Tolkien*
Zurich and Jena 2014 (Cormarë Series 33), ISBN 978-3-905703-33-7

Representations of Nature in Middle-earth
Martin Simonson (ed.), Zurich and Jena 2015, (Cormarë Series 34),
ISBN 978-3-905703-34-4

Laughter in Middle-earth
Thomas Honegger & Maureen F. Mann (eds.), Zurich and Jena 2016
(Cormarë Series 35), ISBN 978-3-905703-35-1

Julian Eilmann, *J.R.R. Tolkien – Romanticist and Poet*
Zurich and Jena 2017 (Cormarë Series 36), ISBN 978-3-905703-36-8

Binding Them All. Interdisciplinary Perspectives on J.R.R. Tolkien and His Works
Monika Kirner-Ludwig, Stephan Köser, Sebastian Streitberger (eds.), Zurich and Jena
2017 (Cormarë Series 37), ISBN 978-3-905703-37-5

Claudio Testi, *Pagan Saints in Middle-earth*
Zurich and Jena 2017 (Cormarë Series 38), ISBN 978-3-905703-38-2

Music in Tolkien's Work and Beyond
Julian Eilmann & Friedhelm Schneidewind (eds.), Zurich and Jena 2019 (Cormarë
Series 39), ISBN 978-3-905703-39-9

Sub-creating Arda: World-building in J.R.R. Tolkien's Works, its Precursors, and Legacies
Dimitra Fimi & Thomas Honegger (eds.), Zurich and Jena 2019 (Cormarë Series 40),
ISBN 978-3-905703-40-5

"Something Has Gone Crack": New Perspectives on J.R.R. Tolkien and the Great War
Janet Brennan Croft and Annika Röttinger (eds.), Zurich and Jena 2019 (Cormarë
Series 41), ISBN 978-3-905703-41-2

Tolkien and the Classics
Roberto Arduini, Giampaolo Canzonieri & Claudio A. Testi (eds.), Zurich and Jena 2019 (Cormarë Series 42), ISBN 978-3-905703-42-9

Middle-earth, or There and Back Again
Łukasz Neubauer (ed.), Zurich and Jena 2020 (Cormarë Series 44), ISBN 978-3-905703-44-3

Tolkien and the Classical World
Hamish Williams (ed.) Zurich and Jena 2021 (Cormarë Series 45), ISBN 978-3-905703-45-0

Beowulf and the Dragon

The original Old English text of the 'Dragon Episode' of Beowulf is set in an authentic font and bound in hardback as a high quality art book. Illustrated by Anke Eissmann and accompanied by John Porter's translation. Introduction by Tom Shippey. Limited first edition of 500 copies. 84 pages. Selected pages can be previewed on: www.walking-tree.org/beowulf

Beowulf and the Dragon
Zurich and Jena 2009 , ISBN 978-3-905703-17-7

Tales of Yore Series

The *Tales of Yore Series* provides a platform for qualitatively superior fiction that will appeal to readers familiar with Tolkien's world:

The Monster Specialist

Sir Severus le Brewse, among the least known of King Arthur's Round Table knights, is preferred by nature, disposition, and training to fight against monsters rather than other knights. After youthful adventures of errantry with dragons, trolls, vampires, and assorted beasts, Severus joins the brilliant sorceress Lilava to face the Chimaera in The Greatest Monster Battle of All Time to free her folk from an age-old curse. But their adventures don't end there; together they meet elves and magicians, friends and foes; they join in the fight to save Camelot and even walk the Grey Paths of the Dead. With a mix of Malory, a touch of Tolkien, and a hint of humor, The Monster Specialist chronicles a tale of courage, tenacity, honor, and love.

The Monster Specialist is illustrated by Anke Eissmann.

Edward S. Louis, *The Monster Specialist*
Zurich and Jena 2014 (Tales of Yore Series No. 3), ISBN 978-3-905703-23-8

Tales of Yore Series (earlier books, presently unavailable)

Ray Woollard, *The Terror of Tatty Walk. A Frightener*
CD and Booklet, Zurich and Berne 2000 (Tales of Yore Series No. 1), ISBN 978-3-9521424-2-4
Ray Woollard, *Wilmot's Very Strange Stone or What came of building "snobbits"*
CD and booklet, Zurich and Berne 2001 (Tales of Yore Series No. 2), ISBN 978-3-9521424-4-8

Information for authors

Authors interested in contributing to our publications can learn more about the services we offer on the "services for authors" section of our web pages.

www.walking-tree.org/authors

Manuscripts and project proposals can be submitted to the board of editors (please include an SAE):

Walking Tree Publishers
CH-3052 Zollikofen
Switzerland

e-mail: info@walking-tree.org

Walking Tree Publishers, Zurich and Jena, 2021

CPSIA information can be obtained
at www.ICGtesting.com
Printed in the USA
LVHW080506280821
696317LV00003B/4

9 783905 703467